亜東経済国際学会研究叢書⑰
東北亜福祉経済共同體フォーラム①

東アジアの社会・観光・企業

原口俊道　監修

朴峰寛・劉水生・盧駿崴　編著

五絃舎

序　文

　これまで日本を初めとして東アジアの国々は長い間輸出依存型経済を志向してきたが，輸出依存型経済には世界経済の変動による影響を受けやすいという難点がある。東アジアの国々は，従来の輸出依存型経済発展から内需主導型経済発展への転換を図るべき時期に来ているといえる。このように，経済の面だけでも東アジアの国々は共通した問題を抱えているが，さらに社会の面では格差問題，失業率の上昇問題，少子高齢化問題などの共通した問題を数多く抱えている。こうした経済や社会の諸問題は，今や各国が単独で問題解決にあたるには限界があり，相互に連携・協力して問題解決にあたることが肝要である。

　亜東経済国際学会は，1989年に東アジアの経済経営の研究者・実務家によって結成された。爾来東アジアの大学・学会と共催して40回の国際学術会議を共同開催し，その研究成果を取り纏めて東アジアの有名出版社から下記の如く16冊の研究叢書を出版し，東アジアの経済経営の研究者・実務家に対して一定程度の影響を及ぼしてきた（詳しくは巻末の「亜東経済国際学会の概要」を参照されたい）。

第1冊　　1992年『企業経営の国際化』（日本・ぎょうせい）
第2冊　　1994年『東亜企業経営（中文）』（中国・復旦大学出版社）
　　　　　1995年『東アジアの企業経営（上）』（中国・上海訳文出版社）
　　　　　1995年『東アジアの企業経営（下）』（中国・上海訳文出版社）

第3冊	1997年『中国三資企業研究（中文）』（中国・復旦大学出版社）	
第4冊	1999年『中国対外開放與中日経済関係（中文）』（中国・上海人民出版社）	
第5冊	2002年『国際化與現代企業（中文）』（中国・立信会計出版社）	
第6冊	2004年『企業国際経営策略（中文）』（中国・復旦大学出版社）	
第7冊	2006年『中日対照　経済全球化與企業戦略』（中国・立信会計出版社）	
第8冊	2008年『亜洲産業発展與企業発展戦略（中文）』（中国・復旦大学出版社）	
第9冊	2010年『東亜経済発展與社会保障問題研究（中文）』（中国・江西人民出版社）	
第10冊	2009年『東亜産業発展與企業管理（中文・繁体字）』（台湾・暉翔興業出版）	
第11冊	2010年『亜洲産業経営管理（中文・繁体字）』（台湾・暉翔興業出版）	
第12冊	2011年　亜東経済国際学会創立20周年記念論文集『アジアの産業発展と企業経営戦略』（日本・五絃舎）	
第13冊	2011年『東亜産業與管理問題研究（中文・日文・英文）』（台湾・暉翔興業出版）	
第14冊	2012年　劉成基博士傘寿記念論文集『東アジアの産業と企業』（日本・五絃舎）	
第15冊	2012年『東亜産業経営管理（中文・英文・日文）』（台湾・暉翔興業出版）	
第16冊	2014年『東亜社会発展與産業経営（中文・日文）』（台湾・暉翔興業出版）	

　亜東経済国際学会はこの数年来東北亜福祉経済共同體フォーラムと連携・協力して数回の国際学術会議を国内外で開催してきた。両者が連携・協力して，2013年12月14日に鹿児島国際大学で第38回「東アジアの社会・産業・企業発展国際学術会議」を，2014年7月18日〜19日に韓国済州ベネキア・マリンホテルで第39回「東亜の福祉ビジネス・産業経営国際学術研討会」を開催した。経済問題と社会問題は意外に重なり合うところが多いので，両者の連携・協力は誠に有益である。今後も両者の連携・協力が長く持続することを念願している。

東北亜福祉経済共同體フォーラムは,「共同體主義」の必要性を早くから認識し, 1952年創立以来, 児童・高齢者・障害者など多様な階層を対象に, 幅広い形態の福祉サービスを提供してきている韓国長善綜合福祉共同體の理念と経営哲学を生かし,「地域主義」と「共同體主義」というこの時代のキーワードを積極的に認識し, またこれを具体的に実践しながら, なおかつこれと関連する従来の論議とのネットワークを強化し, 同一の漢字文化圏域内のいくつかの多国家間の福祉経済交流および開発協力の共同體を達成しようとして2008年に結成された。2014年現在, 韓国・日本・中国・台湾などからの福祉経済分野の各専門家たち約50人程度が毎年定期的に集会や会議を開催しているが, 2010年からは"福祉ビジネスの国際連携会議"を設けて毎年夏には日本の福岡市と韓国の釜山市において交互にこの福祉ビジネスの国際連携会議を開催することになっている。2014年7月には亜東経済国際学会との連携で特別に韓国の済州道で共催したことは誠に光栄で成功であった。

　本書は亜東経済国際学会と東北亜福祉経済共同體フォーラムの連携・協力の記念として出版が企画されたもので, 亜東経済国際学会研究叢書の第十七冊目にあたり, また東北亜福祉経済共同體フォーラム研究叢書の第一冊目にあたる。本書は東アジアの会員諸氏が寄稿した論文に対して, 国内外の大学院博士指導教授クラスの研究者による厳格な査読審査を行い, 最終的に査読審査に合格した論文を収録したものである。本書は2編16章から構成される。

　第1編は「東アジアの社会・観光・企業」に関する日本語論文で, 10篇の日本語論文から構成されている。第1章～第2章までが東アジアの社会問題を, 第3章～第5章までが東アジアの観光産業を, 第7章～第8章までが東アジアの日系企業を, 第9章～第10章までが東アジアの企業問題を取り上げ, 考察している。

　第2編は「東アジアの社会・観光・企業」に関する英語論文で, 6篇の英語論文から構成されている。第11章では東アジアの社会・文化問題を, 第12章～第13章までが東アジアの観光産業・外食産業を, 第14章～第16章までが東アジアの企業問題・消費者問題を取り上げ, 考察している。

　本書を出版するにあたり, 五絃舎代表取締役である長谷雅春氏から数々の貴

重なアドバイスをいただいた。本書は「東アジアの社会・観光・企業」を主に論じた研究書である。本書が広く江湖に受け容れられることを期待する次第である。

監修者　原口俊道

編者　朴峰寛　劉水生　盧駿葳

2015 年 2 月 6 日

目　次

第1編　東アジアの社会・観光・企業

第1章　東北亜福祉経済共同體の構築と実行課題そして展望 ─── 21
1. はじめに　*21*
2. 地域と国境を超えた交流やネットワークを目指して　*22*
   (1) 福祉経済共同體の考え方　*22*
   (2) 東北アジアへの視点と基本的理念　*24*
3. 東北亜幸福共同體の構想と五つの政策提言　*26*
4. 結び　*32*

第2章　台湾におけるゴールデン・エージの健康管理 ─── 35
1. はじめに　*36*
2. 社会福祉と儒教　*37*
   (1) 研究の動機　*37*
   (2) 高齢者関連の先行研究　*38*
3. 台湾における社会福祉のルーツ・儒教　*39*
   (1) 儒教の中心思想「仁」と四書の著者　*39*
   (2) 儒教の古典的価値　*40*
4. 台湾におけるゴールデン・エージの健康管理　*41*
   (1) 高齢者の福祉　*41*
   (2) ゴールデン・エージの健康管理　*42*
5. 結び　*43*

第3章　台湾における観光産業と環境保護──────45
　1．はじめに　*46*
　2．サービス産業の経済化と発展　　*47*
　　（1）サービスが経済発展の動因　　*47*
　　（2）サービス産業の領域と分類　　*48*
　　（3）サービス産業の特徴　　*48*
　3．ホスピタリティ産業（観光産業）の意義と領域　　*49*
　　（1）ホスピタリティ産業（観光産業）　　*49*
　　（2）ホスピタリティ産業の本質と重要性　　*50*
　　（3）日・台のホスピタリティ精神の相違　　*51*
　4．環境保護と観光発展　　*51*
　　（1）環境保護の無視とマイナス経済　　*51*
　　（2）台湾におけるサービス産業の現況と観光発展　　*53*
　5．結び　*54*

第4章　観光消費者行動への影響要因──────57
　─鹿児島県の国内観光客へのアンケート調査を中心として─
　1．はじめに　*57*
　2．観光産業の発展　　*58*
　　（1）戦後復興段階（1945～1962年）　　*59*
　　（2）高度経済成長段階（1963～1989年）　　*60*
　　（3）バブル経済崩壊段階（1990～2002年）　　*61*
　　（4）観光立国の新たな段階（2003～現在）　　*61*
　3．観光マーケティングに関する先行研究の整理　　*62*
　　（1）ピアース（2005）の研究　　*63*
　　（2）大城侑人（2008）の研究　　*63*
　　（3）金戸幸子（2013）の研究　　*64*
　　（4）中井郷之（2012）の研究　　*65*

(5) 先行研究の問題点　　*65*
　4．本研究の分析モデルと仮説　　*66*
　5．仮説の検証結果　　*66*
　　　(1) 仮説1の検証結果　　*69*
　　　(2) 仮説2の検証結果　　*70*
　　　(3) 仮説3の検証結果　　*71*
　6．結び　　*71*

第5章　観光目的地の選択に影響を及ぼす要因―――――*75*
　　　――台湾への日本人観光客を例として――

　1．はじめに　　*75*
　2．観光行動理論に関する文献整理　　*76*
　　　(1) 観光の定義　　*76*
　　　(2) 観光行動論の体系　　*76*
　　　(3) 観光行動理論に関する文献整理　　*77*
　　　(4) 問題点の抽出　　*78*
　3．分析モデルと仮説の構築　　*78*
　　　(1) 分析モデル　　*78*
　　　(2) 仮説の構築　　*79*
　　　(3) 研究対象とアンケート調査の概要　　*79*
　　　(4) アンケートの設計　　*80*
　　　(5) データの分析方法　　*80*
　4．分析結果　　*81*
　　　(1) 日本人観光客の個人属性　　*81*
　　　(2) 因子分析の結果　　*81*
　　　(3) 一元配置分散分析（one-way ANOVA）の結果　　*83*
　　　(4) 重回帰分析の結果　　*84*
　5．仮説の検証結果　　*85*

10

6. 結び　*86*

第6章　中国日系繊維製造企業の競争戦略と競争優位 ——— *89*
―――中国日系電機製造企業との比較―――

1. はじめに　*89*
2. 中国日系企業の競争戦略と競争優位に関連する先行研究　*90*
   (1) 中国日系企業の競争戦略と競争優位に関連する先行研究　*90*
   (2) 中国日系企業の競争戦略と競争優位に関連する先行研究の問題点　*94*
   (3) 筆者の研究方法　*95*
3. 分析課題と調査方法　*95*
   (1) 分析課題　*95*
   (2) 調査方法　*96*
4. 中国日系繊維製造企業の競争戦略と競争優位　*97*
   (1) 対中国直接投資の経営戦略と現地事業戦略　*97*
   (2) 競争戦略　*100*
   (3) 競争優位　*103*
5. 結び　*107*

第7章　日系サービス企業のマーケティング戦略への影響要因 ——— *113*
―――中国と台湾の日系サービス企業の比較分析―――

1. はじめに　*113*
2. 先行研究とその問題点　*114*
3. 分析モデルと研究仮説　*115*
4. アンケート調査の概要　*115*
5. 分析結果　*116*
   (1) 中国日系サービス企業のサンプル分析　*116*
   (2) 台湾日系サービス企業のサンプル分析　*116*

(3) 信頼性分析　　117
        (4) 相関分析　　117
        (5) 影響力分析　　120
        (6) 仮説検証の結果と考察　　124
    6. 結び　　125

第8章　中国日系小売企業の経営現地化の重視度―――――127
―――中国日系自動車部品製造企業との比較―――

    1. はじめに　　127
    2. 中国日系企業の経営現地化に関する先行研究と
       その問題点　　128
        (1) 原口俊道の研究　　128
        (2) 関満博らの研究　　129
        (3) 古田秋太郎の研究　　129
        (4) 喬晋建の研究　　130
        (5) 原口俊道・戦俊の研究　　130
        (6) 5つの先行研究の問題点　　131
    3. 中国日系小売企業の経営現地化の実態　　131
        (1) 調査の方法　　131
        (2) 最も進めている経営現地化の側面　　132
        (3) 社長の現地化　　133
        (4) 経営幹部の現地化　　134
    4. 中国日系小売企業の経営現地化の重視度　　137
    5. 結び　　138

第9章 日本の自動車生産における非常時対応について ―― 141
　　――非常事態への対処にみる生産ネットワークと企業間信頼――
1. はじめに　*141*
2. 平常時の生産とサプライチェーン　*142*
3. ネットワークと企業間信頼　*143*
4. 事故や災害等に伴う生産中止事例　*145*
5. 非常時の支援と生産ネットワーク機能　*148*
6. 結びに代えて　*151*

第10章 警備員の生理的ストレス反応と職務満足 ―― 153
　　――第二報――
1. はじめに　*154*
2. 評価指標　*155*
　(1) 唾液アミラーゼ活性　*155*
　(2) 調査票　*155*
3. 研究目的　*156*
4. 研究方法　*157*
　(1) 研究仮説　*157*
　(2) 対象　*158*
　(3) 研究デザイン　*158*
　(4) 統計解析　*159*
5. 分析結果　*159*
　(1) 回答者（被験者）の基本情報　*159*
　(2) 唾液アミラーゼ活性の結果　*160*
　(3) 調査票の結果　*160*
　(4) 唾液アミラーゼ活性と調査票の関連結果　*162*
　(5)「健康いきいき職場モデル」の検証　*163*
　(6) モデレーター要因の検証　*163*

6. 結果の考察　　*164*
7. 結び　　*165*

第2編　東アジアの社会・観光・企業（英文）

Chapter 11　The Cross-cultural Conflicts at Sino-foreign Enterprises in China —— *171*

1. Introduction　*171*
2. The Conflicts between the Two Sides of Sino-foreign Enterprises　*172*
   (1) Illusions of the Foreign Staffs　*172*
   (2) Illusions of the Chinese Staffs　*173*
   (3) The Illusions of Both Sides　*174*
   (4) Cultural Differences Have Been the Cause of Many Conflicts　*174*
3. The Hidden Causes for the Conflicts　*175*
4. How to Bridge the Gap　*178*
5. Conclusions　*182*

Chapter 12　Competitiveness in the Reception of Mainland Tourists in Taiwan's Travel Industry —— *185*

1. Introduction　*186*
2. Literature Review　*188*
   (1) Definition of Competitiveness　*188*
   (2) Competing Relationship　*189*
3. Research Methods　*192*
4. Results of Research and Analysis　*193*
5. Conclusions　*201*

Chapter 13 Determination and Interpretation of Correlations between Perceived Quality, Relationship Quality and Brand Evaluation among Patrons at Kagoshima Restaurants —————— *205*

1. Research Background and Motives *205*
2. Research Purpose *206*
3. Literature review *207*
   (1) Perceived quality *207*
   (2) Relationship quality *207*
   (3) Brand evaluation *207*
   (4) Summary of questions *207*
4. Research Design *208*
   (1) Research Framework *208*
   (2) Research Hypotheses *208*
   (3) Research Scope and Subjects *209*
   (4) Questionnaire Collection Process *209*
   (5) Questionnaire Design and Measurement *209*
   (6) Data Analysis Methodology *210*
5. Research Results and Analysis *210*
   (1) Analysis of Socioeconomic Backgrounds of Restaurant Patrons *210*
   (2) Analysis of Variable Factors *210*
   (3) Factor Analysis of Perceived Quality, Relationship Quality and Brand Evaluation *211*
6. Correlation Analysis of Patrons' Perceived Quality and Relationship Quality *211*
7. Correlation Analysis of Patrons' Relationship Quality and Brand Evaluation *211*

8. Analysis of Influence of Patrons' Perceived Quality on Relationship Quality *212*
9. Analysis of Influence of Patrons' Relationship Quality on Brand Evaluation *213*
10. Conclusions and Suggestions *214*
    (1) Distribution of Patron Samples *214*
    (2) There is a significant correlation between patrons' perceived quality and relationship quality. *214*
    (3) There is a significant correlation between patrons' relationship quality and brand evaluation. *214*
    (4) Patrons' perceived quality has a significant effect on relationship quality. *214*
    (5) Patrons' relationship quality has a significant effect on brand evaluation. *215*

Chapter 14 Business Strategies of the Taiwanese Audio Equipment Manufacturers ——— *219*

1. Introduction *220*
2. Literature Review *221*
   (1) Five Force Shape Strategy *221*
   (2) Value Chain *223*
   (3) Typology of Alliance *224*
3. Defining Competitive and Cooperative Strategies *225*
4. Research Method *227*
   (1) Model Construction and the Evaluation Framework *228*
   (2) Hypotheses *229*
   (3) Methodology *229*
5. Estimation Results *230*

      (1) Descriptive Statistics   *231*
      (2) Factor Analysis   *233*
      (3) SWOT Analysis   *234*
  6. Conclusions and Findings   *238*
  7. The Limitations and Future Study of This Research   *239*

Chapter 15   Research of the Consumer's Preference Behavior for Japanese Healthy Food —— *243*

  1. Introduction   *244*
  2. Literature Review   *244*
      (1) Definition of Consumer Preferences   *245*
      (2) Consumer Preferences (Personal characteristics)   *246*
  3. Research Methods   *247*
      (1) Secondary Data Method   *247*
      (2) Research Process   *247*
  4. Data Analysis   *248*
  5. Conclusions and Suggestions   *252*

Chapter 16   The Application of Game Theory in the Investment Strategy —— *257*

  1. Introduction   *257*
  2. Theoretic Model of Game Theory   *258*
      (1) The Doctrinal Model of Game Theory   *259*
      (2) The Strategic Model of Game Theory   *260*
      (3) The Application of Theoretical Model in Investment Strategy   *262*
  3. Conclusions   *265*

亜東経済国際学会の概要	267
東北亜福祉経済共同體フォーラムの概要	272
索　引	273
執筆者一覧	277
監修者・編者紹介	278

第 1 編

東アジアの社会・観光・企業

第1章　東北亜福祉経済共同體の構築と実行課題そして展望

【要旨】
　東北亜福祉経済共同體構想は，同じ範疇・地域内の国々が様々な方法に基づいて，相互に協力して国レベルでは解決することが困難な課題を克服するために，関係性による福祉や経済交流を志向する地域主義と共同體主義と呼ばれるこの時代の課題をより積極的に認識し，これを具体的に実践しようと図るものである。これは，"福祉"を媒介にして，東北アジア地域の様々なコミュニティが具体的な交流や経済協力などを成し遂げて，共同の繁栄を達成しようと図るものである。東北アジアの平和秩序を脅かす昨今の北朝鮮の問題や韓半島の平和定着の問題などの当面の問題を包括的に解決して行くことができる最も効率的で合理的な方案を模索しようというのがまさに東北亜福祉経済共同體の考え方である。

【キーワード】：福祉と経済，コミュニティ，東北アジア，公益価値投資ビジネス

1.　はじめに

　今，世界は，一国の福祉と経済のステムを構築しようとした20世紀の国民主義を超えて，同じ範疇・地域の国々が様々な方法に基づいて，相互に協力しながら国レベルでは解決することが困難な課題を克服するために，関係性による福祉や経済交流を目指す"地域主義"と"共同體主義"の時代に突入しているといっても過言ではないだろう。東北亜地域共同體構想とこれに関連する既

存の議論との間には，同じ範疇・地域内の複数の国の間での経済協力，開発協力及び安全保障協力を骨子としている点が共通している。東北亜地域共同體構想は"地域主義"と"共同體主義"という21世紀の大きなトレンドに即応しなければならない。しかし，実際には，各地域（国）の住民（国民）の主体的な参加と努力が反映されずにいる状況である。特に経済面で地域主義が急速に拡張している背景には，EU（欧州連合）の「ブロック化」がある。これは排他的であり，域外差別的な自己完結的な経済体制を追求する傾向が懸念される。米国を中心としたNAFTAに対応し，東アジア地域の成長と中国の市場開放による新成長産業に対応し，経済の成長と発展を図るための戦略として，先を争って市場を共有するのに適切なパートナーを見つけ出す選別的な地域協定が爆発的に増加している。

したがって，東北亜福祉経済共同體構想は地域主義と共同體主義と呼ばれるこの時代の課題をより積極的に認識し，これを具体的に実践しようと図るものである。これは，"福祉"を媒介にして東北アジア地域の様々なコミュニティが具体的な交流や経済協力などを成し遂げて，共同の繁栄を達成しようと図るものである。

併せて，東北アジアの平和秩序を脅かす昨今の北朝鮮の問題や韓半島の平和定着の問題などの当面の問題を包括的に解決して行くことができる最も効率的で合理的な方案を模索しようというのがまさに東北亜福祉経済共同體の考え方である。

2. 地域と国境を超えた交流やネットワークを目指して

(1) 福祉経済共同體の考え方

ほとんどの地域協力の場合，民間部門の機能的協力が先行され，制度的な協力が後に続く形となる。韓国の場合も，最初のパートナーとして選択したチリは同時多発的FTA戦略を推進するための学習過程としての例外であると言うなら，今後の地域協定は民間部門の実質的な交流が盛んな地域との協定になる。

地域協定の成果はしきい値を下げれば，商品やサービスはもちろん，資本や技術，さらに進んだ場合，労働者や制度に至るまでの流れを拡張することで得られるものである。

すなわち，国は，交流をより容易にするための役割を担っており，国家間の地域協定の締結は制度的補完としてネットワークや高速道路と同様に，制度面のインフラであると思う。地域主義のこのような背景の下で，東北アジア地域でも，経済共同體の必要性とこれに対する研究・推進の方法は無数に提起されたが，東北アジア地域の歴史的，政治的，経済的，安全保障的状況の性質上，多くの限界を見せて漂流している。

したがって，これらの制約要因を克服しながら，またこれまで見過ごされてきた"市民"が主体となって"共同體"の論理に立脚した福祉経済共同體を構築する必要があるという趣旨は実に大きな意味があるだけでなく，東北アジア地域の問題に関心の高い人たちにも非常に説得力があると思われる。さらに，福祉は他の部門とは異なり，国民の保健に関連する管理監督が必要である。つまり制度的側面が重要な部門である。一方では増大する福祉需要に比べて質的にも量的にも不十分なレベルに留まっている福祉サービス供給の問題を解決するために，福祉サービスの産業化やビジネス化は必要である。

しかし，社会福祉部門を企業資本に任せることは困難である。生活保障と生活の質の改善において，韓国，日本，台湾，シンガポールなどの東アジアの国々の市場への依存度はいわゆる自由主義的福祉国家よりも高くなっており，東アジアの福祉サービスの拡張を市場に依存させる方向に行くのかの問題は，綿密な検討が必要である。

最近，韓国内の「福祉論争」では幸いなことに，表面的には誰も福祉政策を拡張しなければならないという考えに異論をはさまない。ただ論争者達は今は福祉政策を拡張する条件を備えているか，適切な時点であるかをめぐり熾烈に争っており，これらの多様な主張の共通点は人間ではなく，効率のロジックである。しかし，今，私たちは，地球グローバル化の流れの中で人類中心の，つまり人本中心の福祉に注目しなければならない。また，互恵平等の機会主義に

立脚した福祉の展開を通じて，国内の福祉だけを重視する偏狭な考え方から抜け出さなければならない。

人の叡智を根幹とする儒教と漢字文化圏を共通の背景とした東北アジア諸国の共同體構想は既に随分前から広く知られてきており，その実現可能性についても非常に高い期待が持たれてきたが，第2次大戦後には東北アジア諸国は世界的な列強の角逐の場へと変貌し，特に朝鮮半島をめぐる平和と秩序の危機は現在進行中であり，関連諸国（韓国，北朝鮮，中国，台湾，日本など）は今では世界で最も個性が強い国によって影響を受けているために，これらの共同體の構想はあまりにも実現不可能な課題であると受け取られてきた。

それにもかかわらず，我々は，東北アジア共同體への期待と希望を決して見捨てることができない。その理由は，何よりも＜世界の平和と人類福祉＞を念願するからであり，この望みを守り維持していくためには，まさにこの東北アジア地域の平和は絶対に維持されなければならない。

同時にこの東北アジア地域の平和を担保するための絶対値が朝鮮半島の平和定着から始まることは言うまでもない。最終的に我々は，東北亜福祉経済共同體構想という課題に誠心誠意を尽くして直面せざるを得ないのである。

(2) 東北アジアへの視点と基本的理念

東北亜福祉経済共同體構想は同じ範疇・地域の国々が様々な方法に基づき，相互に協力して国レベルで解決することが困難な課題を克服しようと，関係性による福祉や経済交流を志向する地域主義と共同體主義と呼ばれるこの時代の課題をより積極的に認識し，これを具体的に実践しようと図るものである。これは，"福祉"を媒介にして東北アジア地域の様々なコミュニティが具体的な交流や経済協力などを成し遂げて，共同の繁栄を達成しようと図るものである。

併せて，東北アジアの平和秩序を脅かす昨今の北朝鮮の問題や韓半島の平和定着の問題などの当面の問題を包括的に解決して行くことができる最も効率的で合理的な方案を模索しようというのがまさに東北亜福祉経済共同體の考え方である。この東北亜福祉経済共同體の考え方は最終的には東北アジアの国民の

幸福を目標とするものであるので，東北亜福祉経済共同體は東北亜幸福共同體と言い換えることができる。

筆者はすでに数年前に東北亜幸福共同體の実現のための総合的な理念を次の5つの領域に分けて具体化し，領域別の実施方法を整理した。

* 倫　理　蘇　生 >>>> 国民福祉・生涯教育の定着
* 地域共同體蘇生 >>>> Community Total Care System の構築
* 経　済　蘇　生 >>>> 広義の福祉産業の育成に注力して公益価値
　　　　　　　　　　　　の投資ビジネスを振興させる経済政策
* 新福祉文化の暢達 >>>> ニューボランタリズムの土着化
　　　　　　　　　　>>>> 3公（公正, 公平, 公益）と3共（共同, 共生, 共栄）
　　　　　　　　　　　　の精神の具現
* 地域共同體の自治を促進する政治（行政）文化の具現
　　　　　　　　　　　>>> コーディネート行政と民生本位のサービスの政治
　　　　　　　　　　　　　文化
　　　　　　　　　　　>>> 真の住民自治・住民主体を後ろ盾に政治・行政の
　　　　　　　　　　　　　体質改善

図表1-1　東北亜幸福共同體

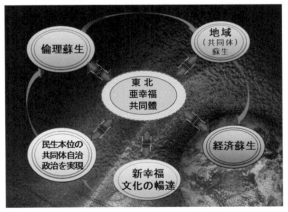

（出所）筆者作成。

3. 東北亜幸福共同體の構想と五つの政策提言

このような基本構想の上に，筆者は次のような内容の具体的な政策提言を表明したい。

第1に，私たちは"東北アジア"という観点から福祉を注視する必要があり，そのような福祉においてはまさしく"普遍的福祉を通じた福祉社会"への方向性は拒否できない流れになっているという事実を直視しなければならない。

普遍的福祉とは，一生涯にわたる普遍的な収入の保護とライフ・サイクルごとの社会的サービスの保障を意味し，主な分野として，労働，教育，様々な社会福祉プログラムなどが含まれる広義の概念である。特に，普遍的福祉社会において福祉と経済は二分法的な対立関係や分離された概念ではなく，有機的統合体の関係である。

新自由主義の両極化体制の下では，福祉と経済が有機的に統合された普遍的福祉社会へとパラダイムを転換するためには，草の根のような市民の政治的覚醒と市民運動が必要である。また，国家レベルの経済協力の下で，地域・市民レベルの福祉交流を通じた地域経済共同體を構築しょうとする努力を拡張するためには，東北アジアの国・地域の交流を通じ，"国家"ではなく"国民（住民）"が主体となる人間中心の福祉社会を実現するための"草の根の人々の協力"に準拠した真の地域共同體の実現に向けて最善の努力を傾注する必要がある。

新自由主義の国の下では市場競争で勝利した者だけが所有者になったが，普遍的福祉社会では市民権に基づいて国民の皆が社会の主人公となる。したがって，所有者になろうとする国民は皆"権利と責任"が同時に重要になる。人間の尊厳，社会的連帯，正義の価値などを具現しようとするのが普遍的福祉社会である。最終的には，先に述べたパラダイムの転換が必要であり，草の根の市民の福祉社会の実現に向けた熱望が溢れ出てくるような草の根の市民が社会変革の能動的主体となるように，"起きている市民"を組織しようとする草の根の市民政治運動の拡張のために東北亜福祉経済共同體はその先駆けとなるであ

ろう。

　それだけでなく，今後，東北亜福祉経済共同體フォーラムの活動を通じて，東北アジア福祉経済の専門家が先進的な外国の事例をもとに，大きな画像の福祉社会を新たにデザインして，保育，教育，医療などの不安を解消すれば，そして雇用対策，住宅対策，老後保証対策などを講じれば，ここに経済と福祉が有機的統合体となる。このような論理に立脚して，経済の適切なプログラムを包括する具体的な青写真を提示するであろう。

　経済の両極化が深刻化して市場から脱落する人々の数が増えれば，その分福祉のための税金負担が増えるべきであるのに，福祉の税金負担者と受益者が分離されていて，中産階級以上の国民は福祉のための税金負担を好まず，むしろ減税を要求する。それゆえに，最終的には選別的福祉は時間が経つにつれて小さくなり，福祉サービスの質が低下するしかない。一方，普遍的福祉は市場から脱落した人でも成功した人でも誰でも福祉の主体となる。福祉の受益者と負担者が一致することになる。そのために，中産階級以上の国民が税金負担を喜んでしようとする。このような社会では税金を納めることが社会的責務であり，福祉を権利として受けることが当然のことと思われる。社会連帯を強調している東北亜福祉経済共同體は一つの社会規範を立てるのに先駆けとなるであろう。

　そのためは，"普遍的福祉社会を基盤として徐々に選別的福祉へと注意を拡充"するという方向を模索することが重要であり，また普遍的福祉社会のために国民の価値観の再構築を図ることが重要であり，さらに草の根，すなわち地域社会の住民が中心となるようにパラダイムを転換させるという時勢に合った課題を遂行することが重要である。

　第2に，東北亜福祉経済共同體は"国民福祉教育"に責任をもち，"地域住民の参加を通じた福祉教育共同體"を実現しなければならない。

　生涯教育体制を通じた国民の福祉教育が定着して拡張されなければならない。国民の福祉教育は，現在私たちの社会で盛んな生涯学習などを加えて定義づけがされたとき，国民各位のボランティア活動への参加や寄付行為を誘発す

る文化の形成と繋がる。長期的に見ると，最終的には地域社会のコミュニティのために本人が死ぬまで一生参加が保障される社会が実現されるだろう。その結果として，"福祉コミュニティ"と呼ばれる非常に理想的な実体を，我々が具体的な成果として作り上げることができるが，それは徐々に次世代に譲ることができる持続可能な大きな精神文化遺産になると考える。教育は個人が自己実現を図り，健全な社会生活を営むことを基本にしなければならない。それだけでなく，国民の生活の質を向上させ，国民の統合を図ることができる手段となるべきである。福祉の教育と実践を常設化するためには，全国の各小中高大学に国民福祉教育支援センターを設置し，関連専門人材を配置して展開する方法が有効である。全国民の福祉意識を涵養し，地域教育コミュニティへの参加と"ノブレスオブリス"の実践に力を入れて，個人が自己実現を図り，健全な社会生活を営むための基礎を提供する手段として，また国民の生活の質を向上させ，国民の統合を図ることができる手段として，国民福祉教育に最善の努力が傾注されるべきである。したがって，国民福祉教育を通じた住民の参加と自治を中心とした福祉教育共同體の実現によって，幼い頃から日常生活で福祉の重要性を認識させることができ，地域住民が協力して様々な生涯教育機関と地域社会に散在している社会福祉機関を通じて福祉教育を運営することを実質的に可能にするものである。東北亜福祉経済共同體は希望を生み出して幸せを提供する福祉教育の力を確信する。

　第3に，衰退している地域共同體意識を回復させるものである。すなわち，私たちが住んでいる地域社会を再発見し再構築するためには，地域の回復が必要であると主張したい。地域に居住している私たち住民や市民の三安時代，すなわち安心，安定，安全を確保するためには，福祉コミュニティが必要である。ここで「安心」というのは心を楽にするということで，「安全」は住民が身の危険を受けないようにすることで，「安定」は最も基本的な生計が維持されることを保証することをいう。ここでは，コミュニティの地域性と共同性ということを考えており，特に共同性というのは，住民の精神文化の体系や交流の体系にますます重要なものである。住民が共有できる共感性を発見して提示し，

誰もが参加していくような雰囲気を創出しなければならない。

　地域の回復を通して様々な市民社会団体の活発な社会参加が行われ，市民社会団体が既存の制度内の保健福祉機関に刺激や課題を与え，市民社会団体と制度内の民間社会福祉とのダイナミックな相互作用が実りをもたらすことができるよう，相互の協力と調和が要求されている。

　もう少し具体的に言えば，地域において従来の福祉分野，医療分野及び保健分野を統合したモデルを作っておくべきであろう。また，それが地域共同體の中で協力の締結を維持していく方法である。それはさらには，「コミュニティ・トータル・ケアシステム（community total care system）」という非常に理想的な目標を構築していくことにもつながる。一方では，現行の社会福祉事業法の改正を通じて，全国の市郡区ごとの地域社会福祉計画の策定から，「コミュニティ・トータル・ケアシステムの構築」という概念に基づいて，市町村中心の地域福祉総合計画の策定，その傘下の同ユニットの実行計画の策定及び広域市ごとの対応計画の策定へと変更する政策を制度化することが望ましい。

　第4に，経済分野に関しては言えば，従来もっぱら認識されてきた経済の概念を完全に変えて，公益価値の拡張のための経済蘇生を目指して行かなければならない。

　これは昔から言い伝えられている経世済民，経国済世の意味を生き返らせて，元の経済という用語がなぜ出て来たかを考えて，その本来の姿を私たちが見つけなければならないということである。これは国をよく治め，民を救済するというような次元の内容であり，この本来の趣旨で経済政策を推進しなければならない。そのためには，今は歪曲された経済の中で強調されてきた成長志向や開発志向の考え方を思い切って捨てて，新しい福祉のパラダイムを作って行かなければならないということである。そのような観点から見れば，既に広く知られ，以前から重要視されてきた環境，省エネ，再生，分かち合い，バランスなどを考慮した経済が今注目を集めている。現在大きな課題として浮上している雇用問題に関しては，広義の福祉分野から雇用の創出を期待して計画しなければならない。最近急増している脱北者，多文化家族などの人々にも積極的に

雇用を提供し，一般の人々が忌避する業種に計画的に就業させることも意味がある。「東北アジア」という共同體的な観点から見れば，柔軟な構想を立てることができる。

同時に，福祉財源確保のための対策を考える必要があることは言うまでもない。様々な意見があるが，筆者は「税収の拡張を通じた国民負担の増加」は避けられないと考える。しかし，そのような政策の実施のためには国民の理解と合意を得ることができるかが，重大な課題であるといえる。

一方，経済蘇生と関連して，地域社会の「エコマネー」制度を提案したい。コミュニティや地域の共同によって福祉貨幣を開発して通用し，それが最終的には寄付やボランティアの参加を振興させることができるようにしたい。最終的には，利用者とボランティアに参加する人々はその対価を得て，地域社会の中で使用するようにして，地域社会のドナーもその貨幣を使用できるようにするなど，すべての地域住民が連携して，積極的に導入する案を自治体に検討を促したい。さらに，福祉産業に関連したユニバーサル・デザインの視点を徐々に拡張させることで，健全な経済基盤の形成に寄与するようにする案も有効であると考えられる。

第5に，社会的企業の育成や企業資本の福祉サービス業への参加という社会政策的な対応が必要である。最近，地域の様々な福祉需要に対処し，地域経済を活性化させる有効なモデルとして社会的企業が注目されている。社会的価値を実現する企業・団体や，成長の可能性が高い企業・団体と連携して，地域の特性が反映された社会的企業を育成する必要があると思う。

しかし，これと類似した従来の事業者（社会的企業，コミュニティ・ビジネス，ソーシャル・ベンチャー等）は，ますます大きな限界にぶつかっており，これらは最終的には国（自治体）のサポートがなければほとんど自立や自活が不可能である。これらは最も重要な根本的な理念の不明確さ，事業の零細性・脆弱性（補助金依存性）などにより，現在強力な批判と再評価に直面している。

このような状況の下で，従来の自活事業や社会的企業を促進するためには，基本的な立場を転換することが求められている。つまり，既存の期間限定の人

件費支援型の案は最終的には形式的かつ限定的であり，一時的な雇用効果で終わるというポリシーの限界が既に検出されている。MB政府に入って拡張されているバウチャー関連事業者も同様の結果が予想される。したがって，筆者は全く新しい感覚の公益価値投資ビジネスを構想するようになった。これがまさにCVNB (Community Volunteer Network Business) である。このコミュニティ・ボランティア・ネットワーク・ビジネスの観点から見ると，政府や自治体もより積極的な参加（投資）の意志を発揮することが望ましい。例えば，第5セクターの形式でビジネス（経営と雇用）の主体に出て様々な形態で公共投資を行うだけの価値のあるビジネスを展開する形が望ましい。もちろん，世界的には既にアスペン研究所や第4セクターのネットワークなどのような国際的な団体がフォーラムなどを組織化して社会的ベンチャー・キャピタルの活性化のための関連研究と議論が進められている。これを参考にして，より具体的には現行の関連法規（ボランティア活動基本法など）や制度などを整備補強して仮の市郡区単位のCVNBコーディバンクをインストール（既存のボランティアセンターなどの活用も可能）するようにするのである。

そして，この事業展開のためにCVNBコーディバンクにコーディネーター（センター）の役割機能を付与し，行政と制度金融会社からは積極的な財政投資と直接参加を誘導し，一定のビジネス環境とノウハウを確保した企業，団体，個人などに接続して第5セクター型の自律的なビジネス（経営と雇用）が発展するように，また公共価値のある物への投資が行われるように，産業基盤を形成するようにするのである。この場合，もちろんCVNBコーディバンクは投資家や事業開発との接続，経営コンサルティング，教育研修，情報提供，ネットワーキング，事業評価などのコーディネートの役割機能を充実し，各種のCVNB事業所は自分で自己責任の下で雇用と経営に努力を傾注し，また価値と黒字の創出に努力を傾注していくべきである。

同時に，このCVNBセンターは今後，再議論が予想される基礎自治体単位の保健福祉事務所の設置の問題と関連して一つの解決策を提示することができる。公共福祉の分野では，2004年から試験的に実施されたが，問題が導出さ

れて中断された市町村社会福祉事務所の設置の課題については，福祉分野，医療分野及び保健分野を統合して，保健福祉事務所の形態をモデルにしていかなければならないだろう。保健福祉事務所の設置は，実際の保健医療部門と社会福祉部門の統合された地域社会福祉計画の策定と実施を通じて，公共部門の保健福祉行政の効率的な執行を行い，また地域社会に対するサービスの拡張・質の向上を図ることで地域単位の保健福祉行政体系としての性格を強化する意義を持っている。併せて地域社会の人々は一生涯にわたるライフ・サイクルごとの社会サービスの保障を使ってカスタマイズされた保健医療福祉サービスを受けることになる。

図表 1-2　展開構図

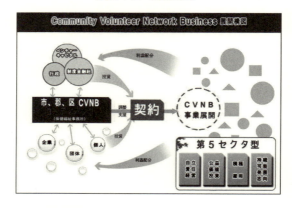

（出所）筆者作成。

4. 結び

最後に，グローバル化の流れは国の境界を越えて多国籍企業が主導する経済貿易分野に限定されず，社会の各分野の開放に波及している。これまで継続的に行われている地方化は各地域社会の共同體が中央部から脱却し，地方の自主性を回復・増大させていく過程や結果を意味する。われわれは Glocalization の

趣旨を積極的に浮上させて，東北アジアの国々が自発的な地域協力に参加し，これをサポートしてすべてがWin-Winのできる条件を用意しなければならない。参加国や各地域の立場と時期に差があるので多くの難関が予想されるが，"最も地域的なものが最も世界的なもの"という認識を共有し，世界の平和と人類の福祉のために相互扶助に基づく利他的文化を志向することが東北亜福祉経済共同體の構築の推進力となるので，これに対する具体的なアプローチを模索する必要がある。その実行策としては何よりも人中心の人的交流や文化交流が優先順位に含まれる。人的交流や文化交流の分野では，歴史的，政治的，経済的，地域安保的状況など，いくつかの制約要因を超えた交流と協力が可能である。東北アジア地域の人々の生活の質の向上のためにも，各地域の文化を国際的に交流し，理解して享有する必要がある。

(朴峰寛)

第2章　台湾におけるゴールデン・エージの健康管理

【要旨】

　高齢者を日本で「シルバー」と称し，欧米では「ゴールデン・エージ（Golden age）」と称している。台湾では「楽齢」と称しているが，これは「快楽学習，忘記年齢」と言う意味であるという。高齢者の問題は多々ある。生産（経済的）能力の低下による「貧」，身体的衰弱から病気・介護を必要とする「介護病人」，生活を家族に頼る「自活不能」などの社会問題が累積している。このような社会問題の大部分が「貧困」によって引き起こされ，「社会福祉」に関することが重視されるようになった。そして，多くの場合慈善事業としてキリスト教や仏教などの宗教団体が係わっている。

　しかし，高齢化社会における社会問題は，慈善事業による解決策のみでは不十分であり，産官学の制度と高齢者自身の経済的基礎・健康管理が重要である。金子光一の『社会福祉のあゆみ』を拝読して，欧米の研究だけでなく東洋思想である「儒教」の研究も必要であることを知った。儒教といえば台湾は「敬老」と「親孝行」の社会であり，社会福祉思想の源流は儒教の「老吾老以及人之老。幼吾幼以及人之幼〔わが老（としより）を老（とうと）びてよそ人の老（としより）に及ぼし，わが幼（さなご）を幼（いつく）しんでよそ人の幼（おさなご）に及ぼす〕」という「ホスピタリティ」社会思想である。台湾の政府には「衛生福利部国民健康署」があり，その所轄に各市の「衛生局」があって，「楽齢」者のために健康中心（センター）という機構が健康を管理し，大学でも「老人福利学科」などが設置されている。

　しかし，高齢者は「より美しく老いること」を自覚することが重要である。高齢者自ずから自立・参画・ケア・自己実現・尊厳の五原則に立脚し，余生で

はなく第三の人生，あるいは第四の人生として考えるべきである。「健康管理」は外部からの提供のみでは効果が薄く，「自己管理」が重要な意味をもつ。幻の詩人サムエル・ウルマンの『青春の詩』によれば，「青春とは人生のある期間ではなく，心の持ちかたをいう。年を重ねただけで人は老いない。理想を失うとき初めて老いる。人から神から美・喜悦・勇気・力の霊感を受ける限り君は若い」[1] というが，「心の持ちかた」が重要である。

【キーワード】：楽齢，心情的幸福，経済的余裕，健康，老吾老以及人之老

1. はじめに

台湾は，1993年末ごろから国連が定義している「高齢化社会」に入った。65歳以上の人口が7%を超えたら「高齢化社会」と称し，高齢化率が14%を超えたら「高齢社会」と呼称する。高齢化の原因は，生活水準，医療水準，公共衛生水準の向上などにより，平均寿命が高くなったためである。このため実際には，定年後も80%以上の元気な高齢者が「元気」でいきいきと暮らしている。そして新しいライフ・スタイルとして，人間は「よりよい歳をとる」「うまく老いる」「恵まれた老後を過ごす」「よりよく老いる」「より美しく老いる」などが求められている[2]。

しかし，今日では少子高齢化がすすみ，世界全体の人がいらいらと焦燥を感じ，人間関係は相互不信の危機にある。国連のアナン事務総長は，1999年の「国際高齢者年とその後の10年」のはじめに，22世紀のはじめには地球上の人口の3分の1が60歳を越えることを予測した。この状況に対して「すべての年代がともに生きる社会」を創り出す必要があり，このためには，高齢者自らが下記の五原則[3]に立脚することが必要であると提起している。

①自　　立：日常生活身辺の自立，経済的自立。老年学によると，75歳までの高齢者の7割は，50歳代の体力を維持。

②参　　加：ボランティアとしての社会参加と政策決定段階への参加。
③ケ　　ア：高齢になるにしたがいケアが必要である。自立をめざしてのケア，介護保険の保障。
④自己実現：ケアの最終目的は自己実現である。自己実現こそ生き甲斐につながる。やりたい仕事・学習・趣味活動（趣味は２つ以上もつこと）。
⑤尊　　厳：終末から旅立ちに至るまでのケアのあり方・ホスピス（hospice）の問題。

すなわち，高齢者は如何に「健康」に，そして「楽しく」余生を過ごしたらよいのか。それは新しい価値を見出し，相互に高め合いながら，積極的に生きることであり，第三・第四の人生であり，自己実現に向かって生きる新たなステージであり，健康管理が必要である。

本論の一部は既に発表済であるが，理解を深めるために修正加筆した。本論の構成は，1.はじめに，2.社会福祉と儒教──（1）研究の動機，（2）高齢者関連の先行研究──，3.台湾における社会福祉のルーツ・儒教──（1）儒教の中心思想「仁」と四書の著者,(2)儒教の古典的価値──，4.台湾におけるゴールデン・エージの健康管理──（1）高齢者の福祉，（2）ゴールデン・エージの健康管理──，5.むすび，という構成である。

2.　社会福祉と儒教

(1) 研究の動機

辞書に「社会福祉」について，「社会の人々全体，特に，〔恵まれない人びと〕の幸福」という解釈があった。そして，少子高齢化の中で「子育て不安，児童や高齢者の虐待，認知症や寝たきりの老人の増加などが社会問題化して」，社会福祉の研究が必要になった。

また，「理論研究」と「歴史研究」は，相互に依存しているという[4]。これは，歴史的事実を抜きにして理論を構築することは不可能であるということで

ある。

「福祉」の広義の意味は「幸福」であり，狭義の，そして厳密な意味は「日常生活要求（Needs）の充足努力」という。それは「心情的な幸福」，すなわち"Happy"よりも快適な人生"Well-being"に近い用語だという。その起点となる日常生活要求（ニーズ）は下記の三つのレベルでとらえられるという[5]。

①基礎的生活要求（Basic Needs）：衣，食，住，保健衛生など。

②社会的生活要求（Social Needs）：家族，隣人，友人，仲間，職業など。

③文化的生活要求（Cultural Needs）：遊び，レクリエーション，趣味，学習など。

そしてこの世から，「老い」をなくすみちは，欲望を最大限に満たすのでなく，人間的能力を最大限に開発することであり，真の教養こそが人間を「老い」から救うものである。理想を失うとき初めて老いる。

台湾の大学では「楽齢大学」の講座を設置し，保健所では高齢者のために運動や健康な飲食などの講座を開設している。多方面の趣味をもつ高齢者に積極的に参加するように働きかけている。

(2) 高齢者関連の先行研究

筆者は，「高齢化社会」の一員として「健康」に「楽しく」余生を如何に過ごすか，どの様な高齢者問題があるのか，という問題意識から何冊かの文献に目を通した。

高齢者問題に関連する大熊信行著『生命再生産の理論』のなかに，「高齢者と経済」，「生活経営学」，「人間生命の再生産」などが取り上げられていることがわかった。また，その副題は「人間中心の思想」と記されており，その内容は二つある。一つは「資源配分の理論」，二つは経済学上の「再生産」である[6]。そして，「この世から〔老い〕をなくすみち（下，第五章）」という項があった。「欲望を最大限に満たすのでなく，人間的能力を最大限に開発すること」こそが真の教養であり，人間を「老い」から救うものであるという。「老年期の〔性〕を美しく」するための項（下，第六章）もある[7]。

一番ケ瀬康子・河畠修編『高齢者と福祉文化』のなかに，「それぞれの年代．

世代が共生である社会」において，高齢者自ずから自立・参画・ケア・自己実現・尊厳の五原則に立脚し，余生ではなく第三の人生，あるいは第四の人生として考えるべきであることが記されている。

社会福祉と言えば，キリスト教と仏教を連想するが，孔子は「四海之内，皆兄弟也」[8]と主張しているように，儒教の中心思想「仁」の哲学（福祉国家）も無視せずに探究することが望まれる。

3. 台湾における社会福祉のルーツ・儒教

(1) 儒教の中心思想「仁」と四書の著者

儒教は漢民族の伝統的信仰であり，同時に哲学信念でもある。中国史の常識として，唐以前の儒教は「五経」が中心で，宋以後の儒教は「四書」が中心である[9]。四書とは「論語・孟子・大学・中庸」であり，五経とは「易経・書経・詩経・礼記・春秋」である。

『論語』は，孔子（名は丘，字は仲尼，紀元前551～前479年）と弟子の応答した記録書である[10]。孔子は春秋時代の後期に活躍した中国史上著名な思想家・教育家で，儒学派の創始者である。当時の極度な混乱状態にあった社会秩序の再構築を"仁義"を以って再構築し，「礼」を文化的基礎として，社会資源の有限性と人間欲望の無限性の矛盾を解決しようとした。また，生涯に『詩・書・礼・楽』を著作し，『春秋』を編修した[11]。

『孟子』の著者孟子は孔子以後約100余年（周朝の烈王4年，紀元前372年から赧王26年，紀元前289年）の戦国時代に活躍した思想家である[12]。

『大学と中庸』は元来『礼記』の中の一篇であり，「中庸」は孔子の孫，子思の著作とされ，「大学」は孔子の弟子曽子の著作とされているが，必ずしも正確ではない[13]。

次に，儒教の中心哲学は「仁」である。四書のなかで論じているのは政治思想に関することで，「仁」一字を以ってすべての儒教の思想をあらわしている。

日本の儒学者吉川幸次郎は，『論語』のなかで最も現われるTopicは「仁」

であり，全492章のうち58章に105度この「仁」の字が現われていることによっても分かるという[14]。

"樊遲問仁，子曰，愛人（樊遅，仁を問う。子曰く，人を愛す）"[15]。これが儒教の中心哲学の起点であり「人類愛」である。そして「わが老（としより）を老（とうと）びてよそ人の老（としより）に及ぼし，わが幼（さなご）を幼（いつく）しんでよそ人の幼（おさなご）に及ぼす」という「ホスピタリティ」社会の実現を期待している。

(2) 儒教の古典的価値

『儒教の独逸政治思想に及ぼせる影響』（日本の儒学者五來欣造の著書）の総論に，「三千年の古に於いて，世界に此理性の太陽を以て，其周囲の蛮民を照した国民が二つある。一つは西洋に於ける希臘で，一つは東洋に於ける支那（China）。後者は秩序の"合理主義"で周辺の民族を感化し，四書五経を教書とし，仁義道徳と倫理を中心とした教義」である。このように，孔子によって創設された儒教文化の思想は，長期的に潜移黙化させ，中国周辺の国家に影響を及ぼしたのみならず，遠くは西洋の国家などにも人類の観念，行為，習俗，信仰，思維方式，情感の状態などの面で影響を及ぼした。

また，徳川時代の最も有名な儒学者伊藤仁斉（1627～1705）も，「論語は最上至極，宇宙第一の書」と絶賛した[16]。そして『論語』あるいは『孟子』などの内容が，人類の文化遺産として，または今日の教養として価値のないものであるなら，すでに消え去ったであろうと称賛している。『孟子』の古典としての優秀さは，孟軻（子）の人格の崇高さにあり，孟子の主張には多くの新しい現代的な意味があり，その文章が立派である[17]。このように，二千数百年前，孔子やその弟子達および孟子によって記録された儒学論著の古典的価値に対する古今の国内外の学者や専門家による評価と称賛は非常に高い。

ただし「儒教」を宗教と称することはできない[18]，中国には特に「宗教」を表示した言葉はない。宗教は仏教用語であり，英語のReligionの訳語である。Max Weberの著書，『Konfuzianismus und Taoismus（儒教と道教）』の中で，「孔子

教の正式な中国名は〈読書人の教義〉と表示され，ただ〈教〉と〈礼〉のみ」としている[19]。

また，儒教は「関係性」を強調し，仏教は「空無性」を説明し，道教は「生命哲学」の教義を論ずるものである。しかし，仏教と道教の両教義は儒教の影響を受け「三教帰儒」と称し，「大衆儒教文化」的事象が形成され，明朝以降の中国で盛んになった[20]。

4. 台湾におけるゴールデン・エージの健康管理

(1) 高齢者の福祉

　社会問題の大部分が「貧困」によって引き起こされ，「社会福祉」に関することが重視されるようになったのは最近40年来のことであり，高度経済成長はすべての人類の日常生活要求に満足を与えることができなかった。また，台湾は1993年末に「高齢化社会」に入った。2000年の台湾の平均寿命は，76.08歳であり，2015年には男は77.29歳，女は84.05歳に成るだろうと予測されている（台湾行政院経済建設委員会，2006〜2051）。

　台湾の「老人福祉」として，この「貧困」に「些かの助け」になる現金支給がある。高齢者に対して，基本保証年金の支給額（補助金額）として毎月3,500台湾元（約115米ドル）が支給される。その申請資格は，満65歳以上で，国内に籍があって，最近3年間毎年183日間以上台湾に居住し，政府の全額補助を受けていない者，軍人，公務員，政務人員，社会福祉の補助を受けていない者，最近の1年間の総合所得が50万台湾元（約167万米ドル）以下の者，個人の土地や住宅の価値が500万台湾元以下の者などが支給対象者である（富者の排除）。

　次に，「重陽節敬老礼金（敬老の日）（台北市在住者）」は，年齢によって異なる。65〜79歳＝1,500台湾元，80〜89歳＝2,000台湾元，90〜98歳＝5,000台湾元，99歳以上＝10,000台湾元である。

　第三は，公的交通の優待である。まず市内バスは，満65歳以上の市民に毎月60回分無料で，その他の市町村や外国人は半額である。長距離バス，高速

鉄道（新幹線），地下鉄，国内航空なども満65歳以上は半額である。徹底した「敬老」哲学であり，これは〔わが老（としより）を老（とうと）びてよそ人の老（としより）に及ぼし〕のホスピタリティ社会実現の一端といえないだろうか。

(2) ゴールデン・エージの健康管理

　台湾の高齢者，ゴールデン・エージは定年後も80％以上は「元気」でいきいきと暮らしている。そして新しいライフ・スタイルとして，ゴールデン・エージは老後を子孫に頼らず，「よりよい歳をとる」「うまく老いる」「恵まれた老後を過ごす」「よりよく老いる」「より美しく老いる」などを求めている。

　そして，政府も「衛生福利部（日本の省相当）国民健康署」と担当部署を格上げし，各市町村に慢性病のケアのための予算を計上している。「台北市糖尿病共同照護網」「台北市政府衛生局」などの部署に「健康服務中心（センター）」を設置し，60歳以上の慢性糖尿病者のケアに当たっている。それで，健康服務中心が主催して飲食の管理，運動の管理などのケア活動をしている。しかし，これについては筆者の体験報告で，アンケートによる実態調査ではないので，正確な実態はいまだ不明である。

　台湾では，「没有健康，没有人生（健康がなければ，人生ない）」という。また，筆者が参加している日本の団体の特別講演では，「健康」と「病気」の間に「未病」が存在し，「未病を治す」医療産業のことに触れ，「医食同源」や「東西医療の融合」という発想から食事のバランスの重要性を強調していた。健康服務中心は無料で，ライフ・スタイルの見直し，健康寿命の創出などの講座以外にも運動を取り入れている。運動は一週間に2時間程度，3ヵ月が一期である。参加者は女性が多く，男性は4分の1程度と少ない。講師は栄養士，専門の医者，老人向けの体操講師などである。

5. 結び

　孔子と孟子の「仁」の実は，父母に対して「孝」を実践し，孔孟の「義」の実は兄弟に対して「悌」を実践することという。今日儒教文化圏の社会福祉を研究する研究者が増えてきた。儒教国家は，正確にいうと儒家文化色彩の濃い国家であるというのが適切であろう。政治家や学者先賢は「社会福祉問題」を重要であると感じているが，社会福祉の哲学・思想の研究は1970年代以降のことであり，「社会福祉」の歴史研究の独自性は，社会的側面と生活的側面を「歴史性」において，総合的に追求する点にあるという[21]。そして，宗教・慈善団体の「貧困の救済」を除き，為政者は制度的側面からこの問題を考えるべきであろう。

　一方，高齢者は日常生活において「時間」を自由に支配できる。高齢者は仕事から離れ，「時間的余裕」を享受することができる。しかし，高齢者は「なまけ」の慢性に陥り易い。食事習慣による民族病であるのか，あるいは富裕になって「なまけ」の結果であるのか，糖尿病の罹病率は高い。この病気の併発は無視できない。台湾では公的健康管理制度があるが，ゴールデン・エージは自己管理の重要性を自覚し，健康増進活動に積極的に参加し，そしてこれを継続して実行することが大事である。

【引用文献】
(1) 宇野収・作山宗久共著（1988），『「青春」という名の詩：幻の詩人サムエル・ウルマン』産業能率大学出版部。
(2) 林雅文（2009），「シルバービジネスの発展に関する日台比較研究」鹿児島国際大学大学院経済学研究科博士学位請求論文。
(3) 一番ケ瀬康子・河畠修編（2006），『高齢者と福祉文化』有斐閣，pp.9～12。
(4) 金子光一（2009），『社会福祉思想のあゆみ』有斐閣。
(5) 一番ケ瀬康子等編（2006），『福祉文化論』有斐閣，pp.1～2.
(6) 大熊信行（1975），『生命再生産の理論』上，東洋経済新報社，序。
(7) 大熊信行（1975），前掲書，下，pp.391～412。
(8) 一番ケ瀬康子等編（2006），前掲書，pp.201～202。

(9) 島田虔次（1972），『大学・中庸』朝日新聞社，p.1。
(10) 『前漢書』巻三十芸文志，p.9。
(11) 司馬遷（1977），『史記』一〜五，大申書局（台湾），（三）孔子世家，pp.1905-1945。
(12) 金谷治（1972），『孟子』朝日新聞社，pp.8〜9。
(13) 島田虔次（1972），前掲書，解説，p.4。
(14) 吉川幸次郎（1972），『論語』上，朝日新聞社。
(15) 吉川幸次郎（1972），『論語』下，顔淵第十二，朝日新聞社，p.99。
(16) 吉田賢抗（1965），『論語の言葉』黎明書房，p.1。
(17) 金谷治（1972），前掲書，pp.1〜2。
(18) 「宗」と「教」は本来みんな「佛教」用語である。一般に「宗教」は信仰する「神」があり，同時に「聖書」と「信徒」がある。この点，儒教は孔子を祖とする古代中国が発展させた教学である。しかし，孔子は「神」でない。ゆえに儒教は宗教でない。
(19) Max Weber，木全徳雄譯（1971），『儒教と道教』創文社，p.244。
(20) 野口哲郎編（2000），『道教の生命観と身体論』雄山閣出版，p.5。
(21) 金子光一（2009），前掲書，pp.1〜3。

【参考文献】
[1] 吉川幸次郎（1972），『論語』上，下，朝日新聞社。
[2] 金谷 治（1972），『孟子』朝日新聞社。
[3] 島田虔次（1972），『大学・中庸』朝日新聞社。
[4] 田中謙二（1973），『史記』春秋戦国編，朝日新聞社。
[5] 武者小路実篤（1968），『論語私感』芳賀書店。
[6] 吉田賢抗（1965），『論語の言葉』黎明書房。
[7] 島田虔次（1974），『朱子学と陽明学』岩波書局。
[8] 野村茂夫（2008），『老子・荘子』角川文庫。
[9] Max Weber, Konfuzianismus und Taoismus (Gesammelte Aufsatze zur Religionssoziologie 1., Vierte, Photomechanish gedruckte Auflage, Tubingen, Verlag von J.C.B.Mohr, 1947)，全徳雄譯（1971），「儒教と道教」創文社。
[10] 金子光一（2009），『社会福祉思想のあゆみ(Progress of Social Welfare)』有斐閣。
[11] 一番ケ瀬康子・河畠修編（2001），『高齢者と福祉文化』明石書店。
[12] 一番ケ瀬康子・河畠修・小林博・薗田碩哉編（2006），『福祉文化論』有斐閣。
[13] 硯川眞旬編（2005），『社会福祉の課題と研究動向』中央法規。
[14] 司馬遷（1977），『史記』一〜五，大申書局（台湾）。
[15] 劉偉民（1977），『司馬遷研究』国立編譯舘（台湾）。
[17] 孔健（1990），『孔子的経営哲学』門出版社（台湾）。
[18] 大熊信行（1975），『生命再生産の理論』上，下，東洋経済新報社。

（劉成基）

第3章 台湾における観光産業と環境保護

【要旨】

　20世紀は経済発展が優先したために，環境を破壊し，企業倫理を無視した結果，不祥事や公害問題が多発した。21紀は環境保護の時代であり，同時に倫理道徳のルネサンスの時代である。経済と環境保護および倫理道徳は共生できるので，同時に循環型経済社会の実現の時代でもある。そして，とくにサービス産業は環境保護を重視すべきである。

　21世紀は心の時代であり，エコロジーの時代ともいわれている。それは，20世紀がモノづくり中心であり，モノの豊かさに反比例しヒトの心が見失われた。モノはサービスの心がなければ売れなくなった。日本は1970年代，台湾は1990年代にサービス産業の生産額が全体経済の50％を超えた。また，経済においてはサービス経済化が進み，高度なサービスは人件費を含め無料ではなく，その対価が支払われなければならなくなった[1]。台湾は1990年代にサービス産業の生産額が全体経済の50％を超え，「サービス社会」に入った。そして，21世紀にはサービス産業の生産額が73.16％になった。

　また，サービス産業の中で，観光は世界でも大きな産業の一つとなっている。世界観光機構は21世紀に観光が成長産業であると予測し，2010年には旅行者が10億人を超え，観光産業が世界GDPの12.5％を占めると予測した。台湾政府も観光産業を重視し，重点的に強化を決定し，挙国で促進発展に着手し始めた。台湾政府は「観光の島」，あるいは「ホスピタリティに富む台湾」など観光産業の発展を重視した。観光産業は地域経済の活性化にも寄与する。観光産業で最も重要な事は「接客術」であり，ホスピタリティ・マインドはサービスの本質であり，原点・基本でもある。また，環境保護はホスピタリティ・マインドによって達成できる。

【キーワード】：グリーン産業，経済成長，マイナス経済，循環型経済社会，環境保護

1. はじめに

20世紀は経済を優先させ発展させた結果，日本を先頭に，続いてアジアの4小竜（韓国・台湾・香港・シンガポール），続いて東南アジアの5虎（タイ・インドネシア・マレーシア・ベトナム・ラオス）が高度経済成長を達成した時代であった。経済優先で企業倫理が無視された結果，日本をはじめアジアの多くの国では環境が破壊され，公害問題が多発し，京都議定書を策定することが必要になるほど大きな企業不祥事が多発した。

21世紀はエコロジーの時代であり，モラロジーのルネサンス時代である。経済，環境保護及び倫理道徳は同時に共生し，循環型経済社会を実現させるべき時代である。今日ではサービス産業は多様な産業群から構成され，サービス供給を除き，共通の基準では定義づけや説明ができない。そして，今日ではサービス社会からさらにホスピタリティ社会へ進化しなければならない[2]ともいわれている。

そして，台湾におけるサービス産業はすでに経済の73.16％を占め，政府も観光産業を重点的に強化することを決定している。これは，「ホスピタリティに富む台湾」をスローガンとしていることからもわかる。しかし，観光重視のために，過度な観光地開発によって災害を引き起こす可能性のある農地がでて問題化した。レジャー農場の宿泊施設が，不法に建築され社会問題となっている。しかし，筆者は，観光地開発も環境保護もホスピタリティ・マインドによって達成できると考えている。

本論の構成は，まず2.サービス産業の経済化と発展――（1）サービスが経済発展の動因，（2）サービス産業の領域と分類，（3）サービス産業の特徴――を述べ，次に3.ホスピタリティ産業（観光産業）の意義と領域――（1）ホス

ピタリティ産業（観光産業），(2) ホスピタリティ産業の本質と重要性，(3) 日・台のホスピタリティ精神の相違——を説明する。そして，第三番目に4. 環境保護と観光発展——(1) 環境保護の無視とマイナス経済，(2) 台湾におけるサービス産業の現況と観光発展——について略述する。

2. サービス産業の経済化と発展

本節と次節の内容は，筆者の別の論文で発表済みであるが，理解を強める意味で加筆したものである。

(1) サービスが経済発展の動因

約2000年前の漢の時代，司馬遷の『史記』の中に富の追求は，「農不如工，工不如商（農は工に如かず，工は商に如かず）」[3]という記述がある。ここで台湾の『国内外の経済統計指標』によると，「農業」・「工業」・「サービス（服務）業」と分類されているので，「商」は「サービス業」と言い換えてもよいと考える。

社会が成熟するに伴って，第一次産業から第二次産業へ，そして第三次産業へと発展してゆく状況は日本や台湾など成熟した国々に当てはまる[4]。

これを，17世紀のウィリアム・ペティは「農業よりも製造業，製造業よりも商業によるほうが利得が多い」と述べた。さらにコーリン・クラークは，経済の進歩に伴い第一次産業から第二次産業へ，第二次産業から第三次産業へと資本，労働力および所得が移動して産業構造の相対的比重が高まるという歴史的法則を指摘し，これを各国の諸統計をもって最初に実証した。サイモン・クズネッツは，この産業構造の趨勢をさらに体系的に実証し，ノーベル経済科学賞を受賞した[5]。これを，「ペティの法則」，あるいは「ペティ＝クラーク＝クズネッツの法則」とも称している。そして一国の経済の「サービス経済化」が進行し，製造業でもサービス経済化が進み，逆にサービス産業では工業技術の導入が盛んになったことを論じている[6]。

サービス経済発展の動因は多岐にわたっているが，モータリゼーション，余

暇時間の増加，教育産業の発展，女性の社会参加，高齢化や福祉サービスの産業化などにより，「サービスがサービスを生み出すこと」を指摘している[7]。これがサービス産業の経済化であり，サービスが経済発展の動因である。

(2) サービス産業の領域と分類

　サービス産業の代表的なものに輸送産業，保険・金融産業，教育産業，修理サービス，観光，宿泊，飲食，余暇関連産業などがある。このように，産業の分類は複雑である。

　簡潔に整理すると，第一次産業は，自然に働きかけて価値を生産する産業である。そして，第二次産業がこれらの一次資源を加工して，商品生産を行う。第三次産業は，上記の産業にサービスを提供して付加価値を増幅させる労働を指す。

　そしてサービス産業は，技能不要のサービスと熟練を必要とするサービスとに分けられる。また，産業向けのサービスと大衆向けのサービスとに分けることもできる。さらに，先端技術産業向けのサービスもある。

　このように，今日ではサービス産業が「工業化」し，製造業は逆に「サービス化」して，産業間の区別は必ずしもはっきりしなくなってきている。サービスと工業生産は相互依存の関係になったといえる[8]。

(3) サービス産業の特徴

　観光産業や外食産業などのサービス産業に共通する特徴には下記に述べる事項がある[9]。
　①選択性が高い：競合企業が多く，提供されるサービス商品の品質には差があまりない。ホテルやレストランは気軽に選択できる。
　②代替性が高い：気候やその他なんらかの理由で，容易にサービス商品を変更する。例えば，映画はビデオやテレビで代替する。
　③必需性が低い：絶対にそのサービス商品を消費するというものではない。取り止めても別にかまわない。

④緊急性が低い：例えば海外旅行やその他のレジャーなど，今すぐやる必要もなく，来月でも，来年でもかまわない。
⑤感覚の影響が大きい：提供されるサービス商品の感じが悪ければ，止める。

それから，サービスの提供は，接客担当者と顧客との人間的接触と協働，人的・物的環境要素との相互作用などによって顧客の欲求を満足させるプロセスである。

そして，サービスは一方的に提供されるものではなく，サービス商品には①在庫不能である，②品質には接客担当者と顧客との協力が必要である，③無形性，④変動性，⑤消滅性などの特性がある[10]。

さらに，サービス産業は人を中心としたビジネスである。これに対して，ホスピタリティ産業はサービス産業の内で観光，宿泊，飲食，余暇関連産業及びその他で上述の5項目の特徴を有する産業を指す。ちなみに，米国では観光産業，健康産業，教育産業などが明確に区別されている[11]。

3. ホスピタリティ産業（観光産業）の意義と領域

(1) ホスピタリティ産業（観光産業）

「観光産業」という分類はない。観光産業は，旅行関連が大部分を占めレジャー産業とも称する。レジャー（Leisure）とは，活動の観点からいうと自由時間の活動の総称であり，レクリエーション（recreation＝再創造）あるいは再活性の意味があり，観光という概念も含まれている。レクリエーションは，①休み，②リラックス，③自己啓発などの三機能を有する。そして観光はレジャーの三機能を満足させる産業である。また，観光産業は旅行業，旅館業，輸送業，飲食業，土産品業などからなるが，実際には旅行業が中心の産業である。また，過去の「見る」目的の観光行為から，「食べる」「ショッピング」「体験」「国際交流」などが観光要素として比較的に重要になった。

この成熟社会に臨み，観光者や旅行者のニーズは「知的好奇心」「国際相互理解」「異文化に接触する欲望」「快適さや癒しを追求する」などを重視するよ

うになり，観光者・旅行者のスタイルには短時間旅行と安心・安全傾向を重視するという大きな変化がみられる。また，成熟社会の生活経験者はホスピタリティ・マインド（Hospitality mind）に敏感に反応する。しかし，従来の経済学ではある程度サービスの研究はあったが，ホスピタリティについては無視されてきた[12]。

(2) ホスピタリティ産業の本質と重要性

ホスピタリティ産業という言葉は，「好ましいもてなし」を主な商品内容とする産業分野において，具体的には宿泊産業と外食産業の総称として用いられることが多く，また一般化している[13]。しかし，ホスピタリティの広義の意味では観光，医療，教育，公務，学術研究などが挙げられているが，最広義では人間生命の尊厳，人類と自然との共生や思いやり精神も含むとされている。また，ホスピタリティの語源はラテン語の「ホスピタリア（hospitalia）」で，主人がお客さまをもてなす場所ということである。ホスピタリティの派生語としてホスピタル，ホテル，ホスト，ホステスなどがあるが，いずれも「思いやり，心遣い，心・気持ちを込める，親切心，心からのおもてなし，お客さまの立場に立ち，親切心をもって接待・歓待する[14]」などの意味がある。

中国では「己所不欲，勿施於人（己れの欲せざる所，人に施す無かれ）[15]」という諺がある。自分がやって欲しくないことは，他人も同様に嫌がるだろうという思いやりや心遣いの現れである。しかし，ホスピタリティは双方の以心伝心，対等関係・共創関係であるという。東京ディズニー・リゾートは来園者をゲスト，従業員をキャスト（配役）と称しているが，従業員は大部分が契約社員やアルバイトでホスピタリティ・マインドを備えた人材である。彼らは人をもてなすことに喜びを感じる素養をもつ人達であるという[16]。彼らはゲストとキャストがともに対等関係・共創関係にあると意識し，共に楽しむ。

ホスピタリティは物事を心や気持ちで受け止め，心から，気持ちから行動することである。人を中心とするサービス産業でホスピタリティはもっとも大切なことである。思いやりや心遣いが顧客にはっきり伝わる。東京ディズニーラ

ンドはホスピタリティを確立し，十何回も来園する顧客がこのことを物語っている。施設やアトラクション，ゲストへの対応や清潔さも働く人たちを中心にホスピタリティの環境が整備されている。同じ態度，動作，表情，しぐさでもそこに心や気持ちがこもると全然違うものになる。ホスピタリティがあるサービスがまことのサービスである。今後，ホスピタリティにあふれるサービスを商品として確立した企業が生き残れるという[17]。

(3) 日・台のホスピタリティ精神の相違

　台湾のホスピタリティ精神のレベルは，日本のような高いレベルにあるとは思えない。ただし，日・台の教育や環境が似ていることから，サービス精神やホスピタリティ精神の表現などは受け入れられ易いと考えられる。

　日・台間のホスピタリティ精神の違いを挙げれば，台湾は機能的な品質要素を重視した形而下的機能を重視するために，サービスはご馳走やグルメに重点をおき，日本のような情緒的な品質要素を重視した形而上的機能を重視していない。台湾では日本の料亭や娯楽施設などのようにサービス提供場所の雰囲気や環境を重視する姿勢や，丁寧な対人的な接客行為はあまり見受けられない。

　大学の観光学科では理論が優先し，実践が不足している。台湾の大きな課題は，ホスピタリティ精神のレベルアップを図ることであろう。

4. 環境保護と観光発展

(1) 環境保護の無視とマイナス経済

　企業経営の経験から経済発展と環境保護とのバランスの重要性を理解し，法制以外に道徳，宗教，習俗などの規律も必要であることを知った。特に企業の社会的責任の重要性は，法の規制より優先しなければならない。企業の社会的責任として特に重要なのが公害問題である。

　公害問題は戦前から発生し，警告があったにもかかわらず，戦後の経済発展の重視によって，大きな代価を払ったといえる。現在では，国家レベルや国際

レベルの問題になっている。新聞に「西日本で風に乗って飛んでくる越境大気汚染」という見出しがあった。西日本を中心に大気環境が悪化している。春先から梅雨にかけ，都市部以外でも空が霞む現象が発生している。夏に多いはずの光化学スモッグが春や冬でも頻発するようになってきたという。専門家は中国から越境してきた大気汚染物質の流入が原因と指摘している。

10年ほど前から確認され，発生源がほとんどない離島でも観測されるなど，影響が目立ち始めた。九大応用力学研究所の竹村俊彦准教授は「石炭など化石燃料が燃えるときに発生する硫酸塩やすすなど，直径5マイクロ（マイクロは100分の1）メートル以下の細かい粒子」だという。カドミウムや鉛など重金属も多いと指摘している。このような国際問題は，一国の力では対応できないであろう。

過去の20世紀は経済発展を過度に重視し，環境保護を無視した結果，生態系は著しく破壊され，結果的に多くの公害病を発生させた。21世紀は円経済圏と華人経済圏の競合時代であるという。同時に緑の革命・心の革新時代でもある。そして経済は系列経済から徐々に関係経済へ移行しつつある。だから，世界の各国は環境保護（緑の革命）のことを理解し，モラル・ルネサンス（心の革新）の重要性を知らなければならない。アジア諸国の人々は本来人間関係を重視し，人と人との間は礼，仁，徳を以て秩序を維持しなければならないと強調しているのに，経済発展一点張りで先のこと，あるいは他人のことを忘れがちであった。

過去20世紀は，低コスト操業戦略であったために，生産拠点を発展途上国へ移転していった。そのため経済関係は系列経済であり，相手国に少しの財富を与え，環境を破壊した。今後はこのような状況は，許されなくなってきている。関係経済（協力関係）の方向へ前進しなければならない。これはモラル・ルネサンス（心の革新）によって初めてこの境地に到達できる。古くから「共生理念」は環境と人間との間の共生を意味していた。資本主義はただ資本家の利益だけを考えるのではなく，労働者・従業員の生活や環境保護などの問題も配慮しなければならないだろう。

20世紀の経済主役は，製造業や工業であったために，廃棄物の集積による公害が多発した。社会とは，共同生活を営む人間の集団である。企業はその生活を営む上で必要な物質的・精神的な商品の生産やサービスの提供を目的として活動している経済単位であり，営利を目的とし価値の増殖を図り，資本の増殖を得て企業の活動を継続的に発展させている。しかし，企業経営は営利を目的としているが，倫理と社会的な規範も必要であり，重視されなければならない。今日のように生産性が増大し，工業化が進めば，マイナスの価値の生産もあることを銘記すべきであり，自然環境の破壊や人間・生物に対する害などが付随して起こるゆえに，企業は社会的責任を果たさなければならない。

(2) 台湾におけるサービス産業の現況と観光発展

台湾は日本と同様にサービス産業が増加した原因として，消費者サービスの需要が増加したこと，教育水準の向上，老齢化社会の来臨，グリーン産業意識の台頭，製造業の海外移転（とくに中国大陸への進出）などが挙げられている。その他にも賃金の高騰や環境破壊・環境汚染などの要因もある。

台湾の全生産額に占める各産業の割合は，農林水産業が1.71%，工業が25.13%，サービス業が73.16%である。そして，とくに観光産業の発展が顕著である。台湾政府は2008年～2009年を観光年とし，訪台客400万人を目標に掲げた。そして，「ホスピタリティに富む台湾」というスローガンのもとに，交通部（日本の運輸省に当たる）傘下の観光局は，日本や韓国などの主な都市にキャンペンを展開している。ここでは特に，台湾におけるレジャー農場について説明する。これは環境汚染に関連するからである。

台湾のレジャー農場は生活，生産，生態，生命の『4生』を訴求している。その中で，観光機能をとくに重視し，品質向上とブランド化の確立に取り組んでいる。台湾のレジャー農場は，日本の観光農園と異なる。日本の観光農園は研究開発と生産に主眼をおいているが，台湾のレジャー農場は観光面を重視している。台湾のレジャー農場は快適な宿泊施設や地産地消の健康飲食を提供し，農村文化に関わるイベント，環境教育的意義が高いDIY体験，環境生態学習

などを企画している。台湾レジャー農業発展協会によれば，台湾のレジャー農場は家族旅行や修学旅行に最適であるという[18]。

5. 結び

「はじめに」の項で，サービス社会からさらにホスピタリティ社会へ進化しなければならないことを述べた。一方『ホスピタリティ産業論』という著書には，観光・サービス産業からホスピタリティ産業へ転換しなければならないと，類似した記述がある。

日本のホスピタリティ精神のレベルは高く，伝統と文化が融合している。日本のホスピタリティ精神は，「気配り，目配り，心配り」で客を心からもてなす。そして，ホスピタリティ精神の深化は茶道文化にみられるという。茶道文化は，ホストとゲストが相互に呼応しあう双方の以心伝心や対等関係・共創関係で，その上清潔さと洗練性を重視するもてなしかたである[19]。

このホスピタリティ精神は，観光地を開発する際にも重視されなければならない。過度の観光地開発は，災害をもたらすだろう。1960年に，日本の内閣が国民所得倍増計画を発表し，わずか七年間で達成したが，その反面恐るべき公害が全国的に広がった。日本は公害先進国と言われた。台湾はこの教訓から学ばなければならないであろう。

【引用文献】
(1) 酒井光雄（2005），『プロフェッショナル・サービス』日本能率協会マネジメント・センター，p.3。
(2) 山上徹（2008），『ホスピタリティ精神の深化』法律文化社，p.14。
(3) 司馬遷（1977），『史記』（五）「貨殖列伝」大申書局，p.3273。
(4) 鶴田俊正編（1985），『成熟社会のサービス産業』有斐閣，p.5。
(5) 鶴田俊正編（1985），前掲書，pp.2〜4。
(6) 鶴田俊正編（1985），前掲書，はしがき。
(7) 鶴田俊正編（1985），前掲書，pp. i 〜iii。
(8) 福永昭・鈴木豊編著（1986），『ホスピタリティ産業論』中央経済社，p.3。
(9) 鶴田俊正編（1985），前掲書，pp.6〜8。

(10) 長谷正宏編著（2006），『観光学辞典』同文舘，p.186。
(11) 持本志行（1993），『顧客満足学』産能大学出版部刊，pp.122〜126。
(12) 福永昭・鈴木豊編著（1986），前掲書，p.24。
(13) 長谷正宏編著（2006），前掲書，p.131。
(14) 力石寛夫（2003），『ホスピタリティ』K.K. 商業界，p.199。
(15) 吉川幸吉郎（1972），『論語下』朝日新聞社，p. 68。
(16) 酒井光雄（2005），『プロフェッショナル・サービス』日本能率協会マネジメント・センター，pp.118〜120。
(17) 力石寛夫（2003），前掲書，pp.50〜58。
(18) 台湾観光協会（2012），『台湾』観光月刊。
(19) 力石寛夫（2003），前掲書，pp.179〜196。

【参考文献】
［1］鶴田俊正編（1985），『成熟社会のサービス産業』K.K. 有斐閣選書。
［2］力石寛夫（2003），『ホスピタリティ』K.K. 商業界。
［3］飯盛信男（1998），『規制緩和とサービス産業』新日本出版社。
［4］持本志行（1993），『顧客満足学』産能大学出版部。
［5］山上徹（2008），『ホスピタリティ精神の深化』法律文化社。
［6］酒井光雄（2005），『プロフェッショナル・サービス』日本能率協会マネジメント・センター。
［7］長谷正宏編著（2006），『観光学辞典』同文舘。
［8］福永昭・鈴木豊編著（1986），『ホスピタリティ産業論』中央経済社。

（劉水生）

第4章　観光消費者行動への影響要因
―鹿児島県の国内観光客へのアンケート調査を中心として―

【要旨】

　本研究では，鹿児島県の国内観光客を対象として観光消費者行動に影響を及ぼす要因についてアンケート調査を行った。計1,000部のアンケートを配布し，765部の有効回答を得た（有効回答率は76.5％）。統計分析の結果によれば，これまで観光消費者行動に影響を及ぼす要因として観光消費者の個人属性，観光消費者の旅行への認識などが挙げられてきたが，個人属性の中でも年齢によって観光消費者の旅行への認識に差異があること及び性別によって観光消費者の旅行行動に差異があることが判明した。さらに，観光消費者の旅行への認識と観光消費者の旅行行動との間に部分的に正の相関があることが分かった。

【キーワード】：観光産業，観光マーケティング，観光消費者行動

1.　はじめに

　21世紀に入り，観光産業とその織りなす経済効果が日に日に増加しており，日本を含む各国政府は，観光産業が経済発展のひとつの方策であり，主要な収入源であると認識しはじめている。日本では自然風景，文化，歴史などの観光資源が多く，外国人観光客だけではなく，日本人も足を運ぶ要因となり，また観光客へのサービスの質とおもてなしの姿勢はよく知られている。日本では2007年から観光立国の推進計画が始まり，日本は今までの研究開発・技術立国に加えて，観光産業発展への道を歩み始めている。観光産業発展のためには，

旅行会社が観光マーケティング活動を効果的に行うことが重要である。

これまで観光マーケティングに関する研究は数多くなされてきたが，観光消費者行動と観光マーケティングとを有機的に結びつけた研究は非常に少なかった。しかし，旅行会社が観光マーケティング活動を効果的に行うためには観光消費者行動を解明することが不可欠の前提条件になる。

このような認識に基づいて，まず本論文では観光消費者行動を解明することにしたい。観光消費者行動の特性を踏まえた観光マーケティング戦略の策定についての考察は次の機会に譲ることにしたい。

本論文では，観光消費者行動への影響要因として，①観光消費者の属性，②観光消費者の旅行への認識，という2つの要因を選び，分析モデルと仮説をつくり，アンケート調査によって得られたデータを統計分析し，3つの仮説の検証を行う。

2．観光産業の発展

観光産業を研究するにあたって，観光産業発展の推移を理解する必要がある。しかし，その段階の分け方については，研究者のなかで認識と意見が微妙に異なっているのが現状である。観光産業の発展に関連する代表的な研究は次のとおりである。

1) 王琰（2005）の三段階説[1]
    ①斡旋業時代（戦前期・戦後復興期）
    ②企画商品の造成による商品化市場（高度成長期からバブル期まで）
    ③細分化した旅行市場（1990年代から）
2) 石森秀三（2009）の三段階説[2]
    ①マス・ツーリズムの時代：高度経済成長期
    ②ニューツーリズムの時代：バブル経済からその崩壊へ
    ③次世代ツーリズムの萌芽：情報インフラの台頭と「観光創造型アプローチ」

3) 田代洋一（2006）の四段階説 [3]
   ① 戦後復興期（1945～54年）
   ② 高度経済成長期（1955～74年）
   ③ 高度成長破綻・低成長（新自由主義の政策）期（1975～84年）
   ④ 経済のグローバリゼーション期（1985年～）
4) 溝尾良隆（1995）の六段階説 [4]
   ① 産業復興期（1945～54年）
   ② 高度成長・前期（1955～64年）
   ③ 高度成長・後期（1965～74年）
   ④ 低成長期（1975～84年）
   ⑤ バブル経済・バブル破綻期（1985～94年）
   ⑥ インターネットによる経済のグローバリゼーション展開期（1995年～）
5) 深川三郎（2010）の九段階説 [5]
   ① 鎖国開放
   ② 外国人観光客の受け入れの黎明期
   ③ 外国人観光客を誘致する体制づくり
   ④ 国民旅行のはじまり
   ⑤ 戦後復興
   ⑥ 国際観光時代の幕開け
   ⑦ 経済成長下・大旅行時代
   ⑧ バブル崩壊
   ⑨ 21世紀を迎えて新たな時代へ

以上の諸説を踏まえつつ，観光産業発展を四段階に分け，その歩みを概観する。

(1) 戦後復興段階（1945～1962年）

戦後，日本の国際観光振興は，外貨獲得に重点を置いた外国人観光客の誘致から始まった。国際交流や国際親善を増進することを強調する宣伝が海外事務

所を通じて行われるようになった。先進諸国の経済水準の向上により，訪日外国人観光客数は米国を中心に順調に増加した。

　国内観光が1950年以降活発になった。それまでの国内観光は，帰省，大手会社の社員旅行及び修学旅行などで，多くの国民にとって観光はまだまだ贅沢なものであった。

　この時期，一般の日本人は，国内観光ですら簡単に行けなかった。ましてや海外観光は叶わない夢のようなものであった。国は，国内旅行を少しずつ拡大させながら，訪日外国人観光客の誘致を重要政策として積極的に推進した。

(2) 高度経済成長段階（1963～1989年）

　1963年に観光基本法が制定された。観光基本法では，国際収支の改善及び外国との経済・文化の交流を目的とした外国人観光客の来訪の促進が第一の政策目標に掲げられた。観光基本法に基づいて，具体的には，海外における宣伝活動の充実強化，国際交通機関の整備，出入国に関する措置の改善，接遇の向上，国際観光地・国際観光ルートの形成などに必要な施策が講じられた。

　そして1964年に戦後外貨不足を理由に禁止されていた日本人の海外観光旅行は解禁され，海外旅行が自由化されたのである。同年，東京オリンピックも開催され，その後も日本人の海外旅行は経済成長とともに急速な伸びを続け，欧米以外では最大の観光客を送り出す市場にまで成長した。

　1965年以降，高度経済成長期を経て，観光需要の急速な増大とともに観光産業が急激な発展を遂げた。その発展が新たな観光行動を誘発する時期でもあった。国内では，東海道新幹線開通やジャンボジェット機就航，交通や港湾インフラや宿泊施設などの整備及び接遇の向上が意欲的に推進され，観光客を受け入れるための基礎的なインフラが整備された。高度経済成長期において観光客数は，年率7.7%と大きな伸び率を示したが，オイルショック時代は年率2.4%と伸び率が鈍化した。その後，観光客数の伸びが安定し，年率2.3%と安定的に増加している。

　プラザ合意後，海外旅行は著しい成長を遂げた。海外観光マーケットの急成

長は，当然ながら観光産業の急成長も実現させることになった。1986年から海外旅行者数は毎年平均10％増加したのに対して，国内旅行者数は毎年平均2.3％増と海外旅行者数に比べて低い成長率にとどまっている。

(3) バブル経済崩壊段階（1990〜2002年）

1990年は海外出国の延べ人数が1,000万人の大台を突破した年である。プラザ合意を契機に観光産業はここまで劇的な成長を遂げた。しかし，その後バブル経済が崩壊し，企業が人件費などの経費抑制の姿勢を強め，同時に家計収支も右肩下がりの状態へと転じることとなった。その結果，観光客数が最盛期から見ると大きく落ち込んだ。

バブル崩壊が少し経過したころから，国民の観光に対する価値観が多様化し始め，また観光そのものも多角化し，特定の観光商品が以前のような大きなブームになることはなくなりつつある。特に海外旅行では，若者層は明らかな減少傾向にある。

バブル経済崩壊による不況は観光業界全体に激震を起こした。全国の観光関連会社や観光施設はその影響を受けた。老舗を含むホテルの廃業，企業等の保養所の撤退が相次いだ。ある観光地では景観までもが大きく変化してしまったと言われている。

マーケット規模が縮小へと向かう中で，シェアの奪い合いのための低価格競争が激化の一途をたどるという，非常に厳しい事態を迎えることになった。その一方，観光産業は高度成長期が過ぎてから，他業界からの新規参入があり，更に競争が激化している。1990年代中頃から，インターネット販売が始まり，他業界からの参入企業が業界の勢力図を大きく塗り替えた。

(4) 観光立国の新たな段階（2003〜現在）

2003年1月に小泉首相（当時）は第156通常国会の施政方針演説において，観光振興に国を挙げて取り組み，年間500万人にとどまっている訪日外国人旅行者数を2010年までに1,000万人にすることを目標とすることを発表し

た。観光立国の目標は，短期的には観光を基軸にした「地域再生の実現」であり，中長期的には「暮らしといのちが輝く国づくり」である。

さらに 2007 年 1 月に政府は「観光立国推進基本法」を施行し，2008 年 10 月には観光庁を設立した。観光を国の重要な政策に掲げ，訪日外国人旅行客の誘致に本格的に取り組み始めた。

観光産業は地方において経済を支え発展させる重要な産業である。政府だけではなく，各自治体も観光客増加のために努力をしているが，観光地の衰退は全国的に見られるために，地方自治体や観光施設運営者は地域づくり，まちおこしなどさまざまな手法で観光客の誘致に知恵を絞っている。しかし，国内観光需要が海外旅行需要に食われて空洞化する中で，多様化する国内観光需要を掴み取り，誘客に結びつけることは容易ではない。その一方，国内の観光地の中には，ターゲット客を国内観光客から外国人観光客に切り替え，その需要獲得に成功している地域や施設がある。

観光立国推進基本法により，観光は 21 世紀における日本の重要な政策の柱として初めて明確に位置づけられた。観光立国推進基本法の趣旨はただ日本観光産業の増収を図ることだけではない。それには，観光分野における国際相互交流を促進すること，国際競争力ある観光地を形成すること，日本の伝統・文化などを海外にアピールし，「日本」という国の魅力を世界に発信すること，なども含まれる。

3. 観光マーケティングに関する先行研究の整理

観光マーケティングに関する既存の研究を概観すると，インバウンド観光に関する論文は数多くあるものの，国内観光客に関する論文は極めて少ないことが分かる。国内観光客に関するテーマは，重要な研究テーマであるにもかかわらず，訪日観光客数の予測，インバウンド，国内での観光行動の実態，訪日観光市場などに関する研究しか行われていないのが現状である。

フィリップ・コトラー（2001）は，「市場を細分化する唯一の方法は存在し

ない。マーケターは，市場構造を解明する最善の方法を見つけ出すために，さまざまな細分化変数を単独あるいは組み合わせによって試してみるべきである。」[6] と指摘している。

　現在，消費財市場の細分化で用いられる基準変数として試行されているものには，地理的変数（地方，市・都，人口密度，気象など），人口動態変数（年齢，性別，家族の人数，家族構成，所得，職業，教育，宗教，人種，国籍など），サイコグラフィック変数（社会階級，ライフスタイル，パーソナリティなど），行動変数（態度，求めるベネフィット，ロイヤルティの状態，使用率など）などがある。

(1) ピアース（2005）の研究

　ピアースは，旅行先の認識と選択にかかわるシステムの類型化に関し，次の6つのシステムを提示している[7]。①諸活動，②自然環境，③設備・施設，④サービス，⑤ホスト，⑥経営（同表の Emphasis の項では①-③は物的な現象，④～⑥は社会的な現象だと説明されている）。ピアースは，①から⑥までのシステムを検討した結果，マーケティングと経営の側面から研究がなされるべきであると最終的に結論づけている。

　旅行先（観光地）がどのような影響を観光客に与えるかは，観光地のプロモーションにかかっている。ピアースは，市民のプライドと経済的効果（利益）の2つの側面から将来の観光を見つめながら，うまくそれらを結合していかなければならないと述べている。

(2) 大城侑人（2008）の研究

　大城の研究では沖縄旅行を終えた観光客を対象に那覇空港において直接面談方式でアンケート調査を，2007年10月から2008年2月にかけて計6回12日間実施した。回収した総サンプル数は293部で，有効サンプル数は175部であった[8]。

　アンケート調査票の主な項目は次のとおりである。
1) 個人属性（年齢・性別・職業・住所・結婚・子どもの有無）

2) 旅行全般に関する質問（旅行頻度・海外旅行経験・旅行先決定要因・旅行先に求めるもの）

3) 今回の沖縄旅行に関する質問（沖縄旅行経験・沖縄に来た理由・グループ構成・再度来訪希望・将来の沖縄への居住希望）

4) 観光行動調査（来訪場所・移動手段）

　この研究は観光客の行動特性等のツーリズムに関する理解を深めるものである。具体的にはアンケートの集計結果をもとに行動特性に影響を及ぼす要因として旅行先決定要因を設定し分析を行った。データマイニングの代表的手法であるアソシエーション分析を用いて，観光客が多く訪れる観光地の相関ルールの抽出を行い，観光客の行動特性についての考察を行っている。この分析では観光客が訪れた場所と施設との間の繋がりについて相関ルールの抽出を行った。ここで，主要観光地に基づき沖縄を 10 のエリアに分類した。その結果，特定のエリアでは旅行の重点項目に関わらず多くの観光客が訪れ，その他のエリアでは観光目的を満たすエリアを訪れることが明らかとなった。

(3) 金戸幸子（2013）の研究

　金戸は，2012 年 9 月下旬より 2013 年 2 月中旬までの間，北海道さっぽろ観光案内所を中心に，道内の観光協会や札幌市内のホテルを含め合計 6 カ所に四言語（英語版，中国語繁体字版，中国語簡体字版，韓国語版）による調査票を配布した。その結果，約三十の国・地域の観光客から合計 492 部を回収した[9]。

　金戸が明らかにした点は次のとおりである。第一に，旅行の目的，回数，滞在日数，情報入手手段などから，「リピーター化」や「個人化」の傾向が再確認されたことである。インターネットをはじめ，友人・知人のネットワークの存在もこうした傾向をさらに促していることがうかがえる結果となった。

　第二に，「リピーター化」や「個人化」の傾向と関連するが，北海道を訪れる目的をはじめ，観光消費行動が想像以上に多様化していることである。また，北海道の好きな場所やスポットとして，国・地域ごとで一定程度の傾向は見受けられたものの，「新婚旅行」（香港，台湾），「日本語の勉強」（香港），「異国情

緒の体験」(香港),「労組の文化体験」(韓国),「業務関連で先進地域見学」(韓国),「軍の友人を訪ねる」(アメリカ) といった目的で北海道を訪れている者も決して少なくなく,同じ国・地域のなかでも,動機や目的が多様化しつつある姿も浮き彫りになった。

　第三に,北海道訪問後もインターネットを駆使して情報収集する傾向が見られたが,北海道さっぽろ観光案内所のような公的機関の観光案内所の果たす役割が決して小さくはないことが確認されたことである。

(4) 中井郷之 (2012) の研究

　中井は,客層の特徴や商品購買の特性について言及し,具体的な事例をもとに中心市街地において独自の観光マーケティングを展開した[10]。中井によれば,従来のように地域商業を活性化するために地元の消費者との結びつきを第一に考えるのではなく,あえて遠方からの来街者なども主要なターゲットとして集客し,売上を向上させることが必要であるという。そこで,中井は客層を分類し,観光客という新たな客層を集客する際,観光客がどのような物品を欲しているかについて分析を行った。

(5) 先行研究の問題点

　観光マーケティングに関する先行研究の整理から判明した主な問題点は下記の2点である。

　①観光マーケティングに関する既存の研究には,インバンド観光に関する論文は数多くあるものの,国内観光客に関する論文は極めて少ないこと。
　②これまで観光マーケティングに関する研究は数多くなされてきたが,観光消費者行動と観光マーケティングとを有機的に結びつけた研究は非常に少なかった。しかし,旅行会社が観光マーケティング活動を効果的に行うためには観光消費者行動を解明することが不可欠の前提条件になる。
　そこで,本論文ではまず観光消費者行動を解明することにしたい。

4. 本研究の分析モデルと仮説

本研究では，鹿児島への観光客（日本人を主に）を対象として，観光消費者の個人属性（年齢，性別，職業，住所，結婚，子どもの有無など），観光消費者の旅行への認識及び観光消費者の旅行行動を調査する。本研究の分析モデルは図表4-1のとおりである。

図表 4-1　分析モデル

```
                          ┌─────────────────────────┐
              ┌─── H1 ───→│ 観光消費者の旅行への認識 │
┌──────────┐  │           └─────────────────────────┘
│観光消費者│  │                       ↕ H3
│  の属性  │──┤           ┌─────────────────────────┐
└──────────┘  └─── H2 ───→│   観光消費者の旅行行動  │
                          └─────────────────────────┘
```

（出所）筆者作成。

本研究の仮説は次の3つである。

仮説1（H1）：観光消費者の属性により，観光消費者の旅行への認識に差異がある。

仮説2（H2）：観光消費者の属性により，観光消費者の旅行行動に差異がある。

仮説3（H3）：観光消費者の旅行への認識と観光消費者の旅行行動との間に「正」の相関がある。

5. 仮説の検証結果

2013年3月1日から3月31日にかけて，鹿児島県内の各観光地で観光客（観光消費者）を対象にアンケート調査を実施した。アンケート調査票1000部

を配布し，811部を回収し，記入漏れ及び無効回答を除いた有効回答票は765部であった。その有効回収率は76.5％であった。

図表4-2は765部の記述統計分析の結果である。

図表4-2 観光消費者の基本資料

基本資料		人数	パーセント (%)
年齢	60代以上	60	7.84
	50代	36	4.71
	40代	120	15.69
	30代	198	25.88
	20代	180	23.53
	20歳未満	171	22.35
性別	男性	312	40.78
	女性	453	59.22
婚姻情況	未婚	504	65.88
	既婚	261	34.12
子供の有無	有	189	24.71
	無	576	75.29
職業	公務員	36	4.71
	会社員	186	24.31
	退職	24	3.14
	フリーター	30	3.92
	自営業	246	32.16
	学生	45	5.88
	主婦あるいは主夫	168	21.96
	無職	30	3.92
	その他	0	0.00
普段の旅行期間	お正月	90	11.76
	ゴールデンウィーク	135	17.65
	お盆	81	10.59
	その他	459	60.00
旅行の交通手段番目（3つ以内回答）	飛行機を1番目 (267) +2 (39) +3番目 (36)	342	44.70
	船を1番目 (219) +2番目 (48) +3番目 (51)	318	41.56
	バスを1番目 (128) +2番目 (96) +3番目 (183)	407	53.20
	新幹線を1番目 (72) +2番目 (36) +3番目 (96)	204	26.67
	JRを1番目 (54) +2番目 (210) +3番目 (258)	522	68.23

	自動車を1番目（25）+2番目（336）+3番目（141）	502	65.62
旅行会社に対して重視するもの（3つ以内回答）	価格を1番目（185）+2番目（92）+3番目（177）	454	59.35
	サービスを1番目（132）+2番目（283）+3番目（144）	559	73.07
	コースの内容を1番目（163）+2番目（177）+3番目（145）	485	63.40
	口コミを1番目（91）+2番目（98）+3番目（178）	367	47.97
	コースの時間を1番目（93）+2番目（73）+3番目（68）	234	30.59
	安全性を1番目（101）+2番目（42）+3番目（53）	196	25.62
旅行会社のコースを選ぶ際に重視するもの（3つ以内回答）	ショッピングを1番目（46）+2番目（86）+3番目（388）	520	67.97
	歴史を1番目（133）+2番目（134）+3番目（102）	369	48.24
	自然風景を1番目（193）+2番目（368）+3番目（94）	655	85.62
	宗教活動を1番目（104）+2番目（165）+3番目（89）	358	46.80
	総合を1番目（289）+2番目（12）+3番目（92）	393	51.37

（出所）筆者作成。

　図表4-2から見ると，観光消費者の旅行手段は，「JR」での旅行が一番多く，次に「自動車」である。これは，国内旅行では「JR」と「自動車」がより便利ということであろう。また，この数字から，日本人は自分自身が旅行計画を立て「自動車」で旅行する者が多いことが推測される。旅行会社に対して重視するものでは，「サービス」を重視する観光消費者が559名で，最も多い。旅行会社のコースを選ぶ際に重視するものでは，「自然風景」を選んだ観光消費者が655名で，最も多い。

第4章 観光消費者行動への影響要因　69

図表4-3　観光消費者の旅行への認識と旅行行動についての結果（平均値）

項目	平均値	標準差
観光消費者の旅行への認識		
1. 海外旅行が政策上でしやすくなったら，私の海外旅行の意欲が引き出される。	3.32	1.035
2. 私は旅行社が同じような品質と内容のツアーとサービスを提供すると思っている。	3.22	0.954
3. 私は旅行社が設定した価格が自分の予算より高いといつも思っている。	3.16	0.886
4. 旅行社の旅行活動は一人の旅行より保障がある。	3.45	0.837
5. 私は旅行社が責任も持って，お客さんの問題を解決すると思っている。	3.35	0.874
観光消費者の旅行行動		
1. 私は国内旅行より海外旅行のほうが好き。	2.61	1.130
2. 私は県内旅行より県外旅行のほうが好き。	3.81	1.000
3. 私は居住地近くの旅行が好き（日帰り旅行）。	3.02	0.896
4. 私は旅行の時に積極的に買い物（記念品を含む）し，親友に送る。	3.07	1.016
5. 私は旅行時のサービス品質を重視する。	3.47	0.913

（出所）筆者作成。

　図表4-3によると，「旅行社の旅行活動は一人の旅行より保障がある（平均値3.45）」と考える観光消費者が相対的に多いことがわかる。観光活動に参加するとき，当然，安全のことを第一に考慮するのは当然であろう。また，「国内旅行より海外旅行のほうが好き（平均値2.61）」という観光消費者は少なく，「県内旅行より県外旅行のほうが好き（平均値3.81）」という観光消費者が相対的に多い。

（1）仮説1の検証結果

　図表4-4は，「仮説1（H1）：観光消費者の属性により，観光消費者の旅行への認識に差異がある」の検証結果である。年齢，性別，職業，結婚，子どもの有無などで分析した結果，有意差が見られたのは年齢だけであった。図表4-4では，60代以上を1，50代を2，40代を3，30代を4，20代を5，20歳未満を6として表記した。

図表 4-4 仮説 1 の検証結果（年齢）

項目	F 検定	顕著性 p 値	Scheffe
1. 海外旅行が政策上で開放されると，私の海外旅行の意欲が引き出される。	3.808	0.002*	5>2>1>3>4>6
2. 私は旅行社が同じ様な品質と内容のツアーとサービスを提供すると思っている。	2.904	0.013*	5>6>1>4>2>3
3. 私は旅行社が設定した価格が自分の予算より高いといつも思っている。	5.946	0.000*	1>6>5>4>2>3
4. 旅行社の旅行活動は一人の旅行より保障がある。	4.924	0.000*	6>4>3>2>5>1
5. 私は旅行社が責任も持って，お客さんの問題を解決すると思っている。	3.030	0.010*	6>2>4>5>1>3

注 1：* は p<0.05 である。
（出所）筆者作成。

図表 4-4 から見ると，若者は年配者よりも，旅行社が同じ様な品質と内容のツアーとサービスを提供すると思っており，また旅行社が責任ももって，観光客（観光消費者）の問題を解決してくれると思っている。そして，年配者は若者よりも，旅行社が設定した価格が自分の予算より高いといつも思っている。したがって，仮説 1 は部分的に成立した。

(2) 仮説 2 の検証結果

図表 4-5 は，「仮説 2（H2）：観光消費者の属性により，観光消費者の旅行行動に差異がある」を検証した結果である。年齢，性別，婚姻情況，子供の有無，職業などで分析したが，有意差が見られたのは性別だけであった。

図表 4-5 によれば，日本の観光消費者はあまり海外旅行を好まない。特に女性は男性よりも海外旅行を好まない。また，女性は男性よりも県外旅行を好む。男性は女性より，旅行時のサービス品質を重視する。したがって，仮説 2 は部分的に成立した。

図表 4-5　仮説 2 の検証結果（性別）

項目		平均値	T検定	顕著性 p値
1. 私は国内旅行より海外旅行のほうが好き	男性	2.74	24.435	0.000*
	女性	2.57		
2. 私は県内旅行より県外旅行のほうが好き	男性	3.70	9.174	0.003*
	女性	3.84		
3. 私は居住地近くの旅行が好き（日帰り旅行）	男性	2.98	12.330	0.000*
	女性	3.03		
4. 私は旅行の時に積極的に買い物（記念品を含む）し、親友に送る	男性	3.28	0.185	0.667
	女性	2.99		
5. 私は旅行時のサービス品質を重視する	男性	3.49	26.448	0.000*
	女性	3.47		

注1：* は p<0.05 である。
（出所）筆者作成。

(3) 仮説 3 の検証結果

「仮説3(H3)：観光消費者の旅行への認識と観光消費者の旅行行動との間に「正」の相関がある」を相関分析によって検証した。その結果，「海外旅行が政策上でしやすくなったら，私の海外旅行の意欲が引き出される」と「私は旅行時のサービス品質を重視する」との間に「正」の相関があり，その係数は 0.350 (p<0.000*) である。また，「旅行社の旅行活動は一人の旅行より保障がある」と「私は居住地近くの旅行が好き（日帰り旅行）」との間に「正」の相関があり，係数は 0.224 (p<0.000*) である。したがって，仮説3は部分的に成立した。

6．結び

これまで観光マーケティングに関する研究は数多くなされてきたが，観光消費者行動と観光マーケティングとを有機的に結びつけた研究は非常に少なかった。しかし，旅行会社が観光マーケティング活動を効果的に行うためには観光消費者行動を解明することが不可欠の前提条件になる。

そこで，まず本論文では観光消費者行動を解明することにした。本論文では，観光消費者行動への影響要因として，①観光消費者の属性，②観光消費者の旅

行への認識,という2つの要因を選び,分析モデルと仮説をつくり,アンケート調査によって得られたデータを統計分析し,3つの仮説の検証を行った。

まず,「観光消費者の属性により,観光消費者の旅行への認識に差異がある」という仮説1の検証結果によれば,仮説1は部分的に支持された。即ち年齢によって観光消費者の旅行への認識に差異があることがわかった。

つぎに,「観光消費者の属性により,観光消費者の旅行行動に差異がある」という仮説2の検証結果によれば,仮説2は部分的に支持された。即ち性別によって観光消費者の旅行行動に差異があることがわかった。

最後に,「観光消費者の旅行への認識と観光消費者の旅行行動との間に「正」の相関がある」という仮説3の検証結果によれば,仮説3は部分的に支持された。即ち「海外旅行が政策上でしやすくなったら,私の海外旅行の意欲が引き出される」と「私は旅行時のサービス品質を重視する」との間に「正」の相関があり,その係数は0.350 ($p<0.000^*$) である。また,「旅行社の旅行活動は一人の旅行より保障がある」と「私は居住地近くの旅行が好き(日帰り旅行)」との間に「正」の相関があり,係数は0.224 ($p<0.000^*$) である。したがって,仮説3は部分的に成立した。

本論文では観光消費者行動を分析した。以上の観光消費者行動の特性を踏まえた観光マーケティング戦略の策定についての考察は次の機会に譲ることにしたい。

【引用文献】
(1) 王琰(2005),「戦後日本の旅行市場と旅行業の展開過程」『現代社会文化研究』No.32, pp.69〜85。
(2) 石森秀三・山村高淑(2009),「情報社会における観光革命:文明史的に見た観光のグローバルトレンド」『JACIC情報』Vol.94, pp.5〜17。
(3) 田代洋一他編(2006),『現代の経済政策(第3版)』有斐閣。
(4) 溝尾良隆(1995),『観光学——基本と実践』古今書院, p.134。
(5) 深川三郎(2010),「訪日旅行市場を創造するDMCとしてのマーケティング戦略」『JTBグローバルマーケティング&トラベル』, pp.2〜3。
(6) フィリップ・コトラー,ゲイリー・アームストロング著,和田充夫・青井倫一訳(2001),『新版マーケティング原理』(第11版),ダイヤモンド社。

(7) Pearce, P. L.(2005), *Tourist Behaviour Channel*, View Publications, p. 87
(8) 大城侑人・神谷大介・羽藤英二（2008），『土木計画学研究・講演集（CD-ROM）』「沖縄観光の行動特性に関する分析」巻：p.37：ROMBUNNO.5。
(9) 金戸幸子（2013），「アジア地域からの北海道観光客の観光消費行動に関する比較研究」『一般財団法人北海道開発協会開発調査総合研究所』, p.43～77。
(10) 中井郷之（2012），「商業・観光政策の変遷と中心市街地の観光マーケティングに関する一考察」『社会システム研究』第 24 号。

（祖恩厚）

第5章　観光目的地の選択に影響を及ぼす要因
——台湾への日本人観光客を例として——

【要旨】

　本研究では，台湾への日本人観光客を対象として観光目的地の選択に影響を及ぼす要因についてアンケート調査を行った。計300部アンケートを配布し，222部の有効回答を得た（有効回答率は73％）。統計分析の結果によれば，これまで観光目的地の選択に影響を及ぼす要因として観光イメージ，観光行動欲求および観光重視程度が挙げられてきたが，これら以外にも為替レートや物価などの経済情況が観光目的地の選択に影響を及ぼす要因であることが判明した。さらに，観光イメージが観光行動欲求に対して，また観光行動欲求が観光重視程度に対して顕著な影響を及ぼすことが分かった。

【キーワード】：観光イメージ，観光行動欲求，観光重視程度，観光目的地選択

1. はじめに

　観光行動論は消費者行動論の枠組みの中の新たな学問領域として認識することができる。これまで観光行動を解明するために，観光客の消費者行動論を基礎として観光イメージ，観光行動欲求，観光重視程度および観光目的地選択が個別的に研究されてきたが，観光目的地の選択に影響を及ぼす要因に関する体系的で定量的な研究が非常に少なかった。そのために，観光目的地の選択に影響を及ぼす要因は完全に解明されているとは言えない。

　本研究の課題は観光目的地の選択に影響を及ぼす要因が何であるかを解明することである。本稿では，まず観光行動理論に関する文献整理を行い，その問

題点を明らかにし，つぎに分析モデルと仮説を構築し，台湾への日本人観光客を対象としたアンケート調査の結果に基づいて仮説の検証を行い，最後に研究課題に対する解答を述べる。

2. 観光行動理論に関する文献整理

(1) 観光の定義

世界観光機構（UMWTO）によると，観光は「1年を超えない期間で余暇やビジネス等を目的として，居住地以外の場所を訪れ滞在すること」[1]と定義されている。また，槻本邦夫（2006）は，観光を「観光欲望の充足を目的とした日常空間の一時的・自発的転換行動」[2]と定義している。さらに，今村元義（2007）によると，観光とは「人間の『生活』過程における多様な活動の1つ——個人または家族が可能ならば実現したいと願う非日常的経験・体験のことである」[3]という。

観光は，総合的な多元化産業であり，影響を及ぼす関連産業はかなり広い。観光客が消費活動をする際に，食，衣，住，交通，教育，娯楽などがすべて包括されている[4]。

(2) 観光行動論の体系

観光行動論を消費者行動論の枠組みの中の新たな学問領域と認識し，その分析の枠組みを考える際に，観光行動の歴史（観光行動史），観光行動の理論（観光行動理論）および観光行動の政策（観光行動政策）の3分野に体系化することができる[5]。

観光行動論は，観光学研究の主要な分野であると同時に消費者行動論に包括され，観光客の消費者行動論を基礎として，観光行動に影響を与える諸要因を解明する観光行動理論が観光行動論の中心である[6]。

観光行動理論は，観光行動を惹起させる人間の欲望とその構造の解明，またそれらの欲望がどのような形態をとって観光消費という現象に結びつくのか，

換言すれば「観光行動における消費と欲望の構造を明確にするための様々な事象」を研究する領域である[7]。

(3) 観光行動理論に関する文献整理

これまでの観光行動理論の研究では、観光イメージ、観光行動欲求、観光重視程度および観光目的地選択が個別的にとりあげられてきた。以下、これらについて文献整理をする。

①観光イメージ

一般的に観光は楽しみを求めての旅（traveling for pleasure）である。李昌訓（2002）は、観光イメージを「人々が観光目的地に対して持つ、個人的な選好（individual preference）に基づいた認知である」[8]と定義している。前田勇（1986）は、観光行動が成立するメカニズムの中で、観光イメージは行動の対象となる様々なものに対する漠然とした期待として捉えられると主張した[9]。観光イメージが形成されると、観光行動欲求を喚起し、実際の観光地選択行動へと発展することが考えられる。

②観光行動欲求

一般に人間の行動は、それが意識下にあるか否かを問わず「欲望」がその動機になっていると考えられている[10]。石井淳蔵（1992）によると、商品やサービスを求める消費者行動も、同様に人間の欲望がその根拠にあるという[11]。

井川愛弓・川野兵馬ら（2011）によると、観光行動欲求は美的充足感を求めるなど、「人間的な行為の実現」という意味を含んでいるという[12]。また、観光客の観光行動は「脱日常性欲求」によって引き起こされるという[13]。井川愛弓・川野兵馬ら（2011）によると、「旅に出たい」という新奇性欲求を表す「発動要因」と観光地の持っている風景的魅力やイメージによって観光行動を引き起こす「誘引要因」があり、この2つの要因は相互に作用し、人を観光行動へと動かしていくという[14]。

③観光重視程度

観光重視程度とは、観光に出かける前に収入、制度、交通、時間、安全など

の要因を重視する程度のことである。換言すると，観光客の収入，交通の利便性，宿泊・トイレの設備，旅行に要する時間の長さ，旅行の安全性などを観光客が観光に出かける前に重視する程度のことである。

④観光目的地選択

観光目的地選択とは，複数の観光目的地の中から観光目的地を選択する行為のことである。観光目的地の選択に影響を及ぼす要因として，個人属性，観光イメージ，観光行動欲求，観光重視程度，経済情況など多くの要因を挙げることができる。

(4) 問題点の抽出

観光行動理論に関する文献整理から，下記の2つの問題点を挙げることができる。

①これまで観光客の行動を解明するために，観光イメージ，観光行動欲求，観光重視程度および観光目的地選択が個別的に研究されてきたが，観光目的地の選択に影響を及ぼす要因についての体系的で定量的な研究が非常に少ない。

②これまでの観光客の行動の研究には，為替レートや物価などの経済情況が観光目的地の選択に及ぼす影響についての研究が不足している。

3. 分析モデルと仮説の構築

(1) 分析モデル

本研究では国内外の文献をもとに考察を行い，主にGracea & O'Cass (2004)，Wong & Sohal (2006)，薛昭義・薛榮棠 (2007)，蔡長清ら (2009) などの研究を参考として，図表5-1の分析モデルを構築した。

第 5 章　観光目的地の選択に影響を及ぼす要因　79

図表 5-1　分析モデル

```
    経済情況 ──────────────────────┐
                                        │
                 観光イメージ ──H6──┐  H9
                   ↑    │              │  ↓
                  H1    H4             ↓
    個人属性 ──H2──→ 観光行動欲求 ──H7──→ 観光目的地選択
                   ↓    │              ↑
                  H3    H5             │
                   ↓    ↓              │
                  観光重視程度 ──H8────┘
```

（出所）筆者作成。

（2）仮説の構築

本研究では，この分析モデルに基づいて，下記の 9 つの仮説を構築した。

H1：個人属性と観光イメージには明らかな差異がある。
H2：個人属性と観光行動欲求には明らかな差異がある。
H3：個人属性と観光重視程度には明らかな差異がある。
H4：観光イメージが観光行動欲求に顕著な影響を与える。
H5：観光行動欲求が観光重視程度に顕著な影響を与える。
H6：観光イメージが観光目的地選択に顕著な影響を与える。
H7：観光行動欲求が観光目的地選択に顕著な影響を与える。
H8：観光重視程度が観光目的地選択に顕著な影響を与える。
H9：経済情況が観光目的地選択に顕著な影響を与える。

（3）研究対象とアンケート調査の概要

本研究では研究対象を台湾への日本人観光客とした。本研究ではアンケートを二段階に分けて実施した。第一段階として 2013 年の 9 月にかけて（調査場所：日本の東京）のプレアンケートで各項目の信頼度をチェックし，続いて 2013 年 10 月から 11 月にかけて（調査場所：日本の東京，関東地方）正式なアンケート調査を行った。計 300 部のアンケートを配布し，回答未記入や無効分を除いた有効回答数は 222 部（有効回収率は 73％）であった。

(4) アンケートの設計

本研究では文献整理に基づいて，調査項目を観光客の「個人属性」「観光イメージ」「観光行動欲求」「観光重視程度」「観光目的地選択」および「経済情況」の5つとした。個人属性が名義尺度である以外は，5点リカート尺度を採用して測定を行った（1：全くそう思わない，2：そう思わない，3：どちらともいえない，4：そう思う，5：全くそう思う）。

図表 5-2 アンケートの設計

項目	問題数	参考文献
①観光客の個人属性	10	Gracea & O'Cass (2004), Lages (2005), 蔡長清ら (2009), 呉佳華 (2010) など。
②観光イメージ	21	Grace & O'Cass (2004), 薛昭義・薛榮棠 (2007), 方健頤 (2010), Assael (1984), 李昌訓 (2002), 前田 勇 (1986) など。
③観光行動欲求	11	Lages (2005), Cheng et al. (2007), 井川愛弓・川野兵馬ら (2011), 今村元義 (2007) など。
④観光重視程度	9	蔡長清ら (2009), Sweeney & Swait (2008), Lee et al. (2008), 社団法人日本シーリズム産業団体連合会 (2005) など。
⑤観光目的地選択	4	Grace & O'Cass (2004), 王暁峰 (2008), 王塙泉 (2007) など。
⑥経済情況	4	Wong & Merrilees (2008), Swarbrooke & Horner (1999), 呉明隆 (2008) など。

（出所）筆者作成。

(5) データの分析方法

データの分析方法は記述統計，因子分析，一元配置分散分析（one-way ANOVA）および回帰分析であり，統計ソフトはSPSS12.0を使用した。

4. 分析結果

(1) 日本人観光客の個人属性

　アンケートを回収した日本人観光客で最も多かったのは「女性」(56.8%),「既婚」(67.1%) であり，年齢は「60歳以上」(41.4%) で，次点の「30〜39歳」を加えると6割近くなる。教育レベルは「大学」(43.2%) が最も多く，職業は「自営業業」(23.4%) と「家庭主婦」(23%) を加えると5割近くになる。月収は最も多かったのは「15万円未満」(32%) で，次点の「15万〜25万円」も23%を超えている。滞在日数は最も多かったのは「3日〜4日」，旅行の同伴者は「友達」(41%) が最も多く，次点の「家族」(36.5%) を加えると8割近くになる。旅行費用は「10万円未満」，訪日回数は「第一回」が最も多かった。

(2) 因子分析の結果

①観光イメージに関する因子分析の結果

　観光イメージに関する因子分析の結果によると，主因子法で21項目を抽出しカイザーのルールに基づいて固有値が1を超える共通因子を残し，直交回転によって比較的はっきりした因子負荷の要素を生じさせる (Kaiser 1974，呉明隆 2008)。まずKMO値は0.927で，サンプル抽出が適切であったことを示している。それ以外にバートネットの球面性検定のカイ二乗値は3093.714*** (p < .001) で，因子分析に適した数値が出ている (Kaiser 1974，呉明隆 2008)。軸回転の後3つの因子項目にしぼり，信頼度分析を行ったところ，それぞれの信頼度が規定範囲の中にあった（クロンバックα値は0.944）。累積寄与率は63.30%に達した。したがって，本研究はGrace & O'Cass(2004)の観光イメージに関する研究を参考として，3つの因子項目をそれぞれ「観光地の資源」「観光地の環境」「観光地の雰囲気」と命名した。

図表 5-3　観光イメージに関する因子分析の結果

項目		因子1 観光地の資源	因子2 観光地の環境	因子3 観光地の雰囲気
B12	快適な旅行環境	.852	.119	.168
B13	安全な旅行環境	.785	.049	.246
B11	清潔な旅行環境	.779	.100	.234
B20	家族旅行	.692	.370	.229
B19	リラックス	.685	.309	.166
B21	旅行への評価	.636	.319	.263
B18	情熱的友好	.632	.368	.191
B15	都市化	.614	.074	.471
B14	知名度	.561	.176	.452
B16	空気の品質	.530	.219	.148
B2	歴史文化資源	.226	.837	.199
B1	天然景観資源	.176	.820	.098
B3	人工景観資源	.151	.670	.328
B17	生活の歩調	.475	.647	-.136
B6	特殊景観資源	.193	.627	.404
B5	文化教育資源	.216	.605	.528
B8	旅行情報	.352	.180	.708
B10	交通運輸施設	.474	.176	.673
B9	地方公共サービス	.525	.190	.656
B7	お祭り	.188	.433	.568
B4	宗教景観資源	.077	.530	.539
固有値		5.753	4.147	3.392
分散寄与率 %		27.394	19.756	16.153
累積寄与率 %		27.394	47.150	63.303

Cronbach's α =.944
KMO 値 =.927
Bartlett's 球面性検定 χ^2 値= 3093.714***

注：***p＜.001
（出所）筆者作成。

②観光行動欲求に関する因子分析の結果

　観光行動欲求に関する因子分析の結果によると，主因子法で11項目を抽出しカイザーのルールに基づいて固有値が1を超える共通因子を残し，直交回転によって比較的はっきりした因子負荷の要素を生じさせる（Kaiser 1974，呉明隆 2008）。まず KMO 値は 0.897 で，サンプル抽出が適切であったことを示し

ている。それ以外にバートネットの球面性検定のカイ二乗値は 1869.241***（p ＜ .001）と因子分析に適した数値が出ている（Kaiser 1974, 呉明隆 2008）。軸回転の後 2 つの因子項目にしぼり，信頼度分析を用いてそれぞれの信頼度が規定範囲の中にあった（クロンバックα値は 0.933）。累積寄与率は 70.66％に達した。したがって，本研究は Lages（2005）および Crosby et al.（2008）の観光行動欲求に関する研究を参考として，それぞれ「個人の収益」「良いサービス」と命名する。

図表 5-4 観光行動欲求に関する因子分析の結果

		因子 1 個人の収益	因子 2 良いサービス
C30	施設の享受	.817	.265
C29	サービスへの満足	.800	.313
C28	生態保護	.793	.157
C31	娯楽への満足	.758	.380
C32	解説サービス	.743	.401
C27	文字解説	.560	.560
C23	ストレスの緩和	.186	.894
C24	健康に有益	.239	.866
C22	欲求満足	.331	.766
C25	人間関係の促進	.416	.676
C26	影像解説	.496	.612
固有値		3.997	3.776
分散寄与率 %		36.333	34.324
Cronbach's α =.933			
KMO 値 =.897			
Bartlett's 球面性検定 χ 2 値= 1869.241***			

注：***p＜.001
（出所）筆者作成。

（3）一元配置分散分析（one - way ANOVA）の結果

一元配置分散分析の結果（図表 5-5）から，観光イメージ（資源, 環境, 雰囲気）では，「教育程度」「旅行日数」「旅行費用」「旅行回数」の四項目において差異があり，また観光行動欲求（個人の収益, 良いサービス）では，「旅行回数」の項目においてのみ差異があり，そして観光重視程度では，「旅行同伴」の項目においてのみ差異があることが分かった。

図表 5-5　日本人観光客についての差異検定の結果

	BF1	BF2	BF3	CF1	CF2	D	E	F
1. 性別								
2. 年齢								
3. 職業								
4. 教育程度		○						○
5. 婚姻状況								
6. 平均月収（日本円）								○
7. 旅行日数		○	○					○
8. 旅行同伴						○	○	
9. 旅行費用（日本円）		○	○					
10. 旅行回数	○	○	○		○		○	○

注1：BF1（観光イメージの資源），BF2（観光イメージの環境），BF3（観光イメージの雰囲気），CF1（観光行動欲求の個人の収益），CF2（観光行動欲求の良いサービス），D（観光重視程度グループ），E（観光目的地選択グループ），F（経済状況グループ）。
注2：○（差異がある），空白（差異がなし）。
（出所）筆者作成。

(4) 重回帰分析の結果

重回帰分析の結果（図表5-6）から，観光イメージ，観光行動欲求，観光重視程度および経済情況の4つは観光目的地選択に顕著な影響を与えていることが判明した。さらに，観光イメージが観光行動欲求に対して，また観光行動欲求が観光重視程度に対して顕著な影響を与えていることが分かった。

図表 5-6　各項目の影響力分析―各観察変数と影響力分析

予測変数	B 予測値	標準誤差	回帰係数（β）	t 値	F 値	R2
観光イメージ→観光行動欲求　（H4）						
（常数）	.195	.206		.984	116.960	.619
資源	.587	.072	.512	8.191		
環境	.087	.064	.081	1.362		
雰囲気	.271	.069	.267	3.917		
観光行動欲求→観光重視程度　（H5）						
（常数）	1.306	.151		8.654	139.694	.561
個人の収益	.503	.056	.604	9.050		
良いサービス	.146	.054	.182	2.721		

観光イメージ→観光目的地選択（H6）						
（常数）	.150	.250		.599	80.903	.529
資源	.851	.087	.678	9.761		
環境	.083	.077	.071	1.068		
雰囲気	.005	.084	.004	.057		
観光行動欲求→観光目的地選択（H7）						
（常数）	.879	.230		3.819	87.173	.443
個人の収益	.448	.085	.379	5.290		
良いサービス	.344	.082	.315	4.196		
観光重視程度→観光目的地選択（H8）						
（常数）	.627	.265		2.368	153.620	.411
重視程度総合	.868	.070	.641	12.394		
経済状況→観光目的地選択（H9）						
（常数）	2.399	.190		12.609	63.390	.224
経済状況総合	.408	.051	.473	7.962		

注：*$p < .05$ **$p < .01$ ***$p < .001$
（出所）筆者作成。

5．仮説の検証結果

　台湾への日本人観光客についての一元配置分散分析の結果（図表5-5）から，観光イメージ（資源，環境，雰囲気）では,「教育程度」「旅行日数」「旅行費用」「旅行回数」の四項目において差異があり，したがって，仮説1（H1）は部分成立（△）することになる。観光行動欲求（個人の収益，良いサービス）では，「旅行回数」の項目においてのみ差異があり，したがって，仮説2（H2）は部分成立（△）することになる。そして，観光重視程度では，「旅行同伴」の項目においてのみ差異がある。したがって，仮説3（H3）は部分成立（△）することになる。

　次に，重回帰分析の結果（図表5-6）から，仮説4（H4）～仮説9（H9）は支持された。さらに，観光イメージ，観光行動欲求，観光重視程度および経済情況の4つは観光目的地選択に顕著な影響を与えていることが判明した。さらに，観光イメージが観光行動欲求に対して，また観光行動欲求が観光重視程度に対して顕著な影響を与えていることが分かった。したがって，仮説4（H4）～仮説9（H9）は成立する（○）ことになる。図表5-7は仮説の検証結果を示す。

本研究結果と先行研究の結果とを比較すると，観光イメージ，観光行動欲求および観光重視程度が観光目的地の選択に影響を及ぼす要因である点は共通している。特に本研究結果で注目すべき点は，為替レートや物価などの経済情況が観光目的地の選択に影響を及ぼす要因であることや，観光イメージが観光行動欲求に対して，また観光行動欲求が観光重視程度に対して顕著な影響を及ぼすこと，などが明確になった点である。

図表 5-7　仮説の検証結果

研究仮説	検証結果
H1：個人属性と観光イメージには明らかな差異がある。	△
H2：個人属性と観光行動欲求には明らかな差異がある。	△
H3：個人属性と観光重視程度には明らかな差異がある。	△
H4：観光イメージが観光行動欲求に顕著な影響を与える。	○
H5：観光行動欲求が観光重視程度に顕著な影響を与える。	○
H6：観光イメージが観光目的地選択に顕著な影響を与える。	○
H7：観光行動欲求が観光目的地選択に顕著な影響を与える。	○
H8：観光重視程度が観光目的地選択に顕著な影響を与える。	○
H9：経済情況が観光目的地選択に顕著な影響を与える。	○

（出所）筆者作成。

6. 結び

本研究から判明した主要な点はつぎの3点である。

まず，これまで観光目的地の選択に影響を及ぼす要因として観光イメージ，観光行動欲求および観光重視程度が挙げられてきた。本研究結果でも，観光イメージ，観光行動欲求および観光重視程度は観光目的地の選択に顕著な影響を及ぼす要因であることが判明した。

つぎに，これまで観光目的地の選択に影響を及ぼす要因として為替レートや物価などの経済情況を挙げる研究は非常に少なかった。しかし，本研究結果によって，為替レートや物価などの経済情況は観光目的地の選択に顕著な影響を及ぼす要因であることが判明した。

さらに，これまで観光イメージ，観光行動欲求，観光重視程度の３者間の関係は必ずしも明確ではなかった。しかし，本研究の結果，観光イメージが観光行動欲求に対して，また観光行動欲求が観光重視程度に対して顕著な影響を及ぼすことが分かった。

　本研究の課題は観光目的地の選択に影響を及ぼす要因は何であるかを解明することである。本研究の結果から研究課題に対する解答を要約すると，つぎのようになる。

　「これまで観光目的地の選択に影響を及ぼす要因として観光イメージ，観光行動欲求および観光重視程度が挙げられてきたが，これら以外にも為替レートや物価などの経済情況が観光目的地の選択に影響を及ぼす要因である。さらに，観光イメージが観光行動欲求に対して，また観光行動欲求が観光重視程度に対して顕著な影響を及ぼす。」

　本研究では観光目的地の選択に影響を及ぼす要因として観光イメージ，観光行動欲求，観光重視程度および経済情況を挙げているが，観光客のライフ・スタイルがこれらの要因に重要な影響を及ぼす可能性がある。今後，ライフ・スタイルを含めた新しい分析モデルと仮説を構築し，仮説検証を行うことを計画している。

【引用文献】

(1) 山下晋司（2011），『観光学キーワード』有斐閣双書，p.6。
(2) 槻本邦夫（2006），「観光行動における消費と欲望の構造――観光行動論序説（1）――」『大阪明浄大学紀要』第6号，pp.43～44。
(3) 今村元義（2007），「戦後のわが国における観光政策に関する一試論――地域・経済政策との関連で――」『群馬大学社会情報学部研究論集』第14巻，pp.321～336。
(4) 馬豫芳（2008），「發展台灣觀光之策略研究」『政府與公共政策碩士在職班論文計畫書』，pp.22～23。
(5) 槻本邦夫（2006），「観光行動における消費と欲望の構造――観光行動論序説（1）――」『大阪明浄大学紀要』第6号，pp.43～44。
(6) 槻本邦夫（2006），前掲書，pp.43～44。
(7) 槻本邦夫（2006），前掲書，pp.43～44。
(8) 李昌訓（2002），『長崎国際大学論叢』第2巻，pp.19～25。
(9) 前田勇（1986），「観光における知識とイメージに関する研究」『応用社会学研究』第27号。
(10) 槻本邦夫（2006），「観光行動における消費と欲望の構造――観光行動論序説（1）

——」『大阪明浄大学紀要』第 6 号,pp.43 〜 44。
(11) 石井淳蔵(1992),『マーケティングの神話』日本経済新聞社,pp.36 〜 37。
(12) 井川愛弓・川野兵馬ら(2011),「旅と風景ツーリズムと風景美:ヨーロッパと日本の比較」『地域文化調査成果報告書』。
(13) 井川愛弓・川野兵馬ら(2011),前掲書。
(14) 井川愛弓・川野兵馬ら(2011),前掲書。

【参考文献】
[1] 石井昭夫(2001),「第 12 章観光政策」岡本伸之編『観光学入門』有斐閣。
[2] 大橋昭一・渡辺朗(2001),『サービスと観光の経営学』同文舘出版。
[3] 王塬泉(2007),「観光サービス・マーケティング戦略論研究に関する予備的考察——観光フレームワークの提案——」『明治大学大学院商学研究論集』第 27 号。
[4] 王暁峰(2008),「鳥取県への中国人観光客誘致についての調査研究」,とっとり政策総合研究センター(中国・吉林大学東北亜研究院派遣)日本政府(JNTO:19)。
[5] 長谷政弘(1997),『観光学辞典』同文舘出版。
[6] 室谷正裕(1998),『新時代の国内観光——魅力度評価の試み』運輸政策研究機構。
[7] 山下晋司(2011),『観光学キーワード』有斐閣双書。
[8] 吳佳華(2011),「夜市觀光意象,體驗滿意度與體驗後行為關聯性研究—以六合觀光夜市遊客為例」『商業現代化学刊第六巻第二期』高雄応用科学大学観光暨餐飲管理系出版,pp.59 〜 74。
[9] 吳明隆(2008),『SPS S 操作與應用問卷統計分析実務』台北,五南。
[10] 蔡長清,曾鈞麟,劉鐘珠,侯佩瑜(2009),「遊客參與動機,體驗與體驗後行為相關研究—以高雄食品展為例」『2009 第十屆管理學域國際學術研討會論文集』,pp.159 〜 174。
[11] 薛昭義,薛榮棠(2007),「服務行動對關係品質影響之研究——以臺灣地區觀光飯店為」『2007 年健康與管理學術研討會』,新竹:元培科技大學。
[12] 方健頤(2010),「婚紗旅遊之決策影響因素,服務行動,價值及行為意圖之相關研究—以高雄市為例」『高雄市政府研究發展考核委員會』,高雄。
[13] Assael, H. (1984), *Consumer Behavior and Marketing Action*. Boston: Kent Publishing Co..
[14] Cheng, C. F., & Tsai, D. C. (2007),"How destination image and evaluative factors affect behavioral intentions?", *Tourism Management*, 28, pp.1,115 〜 1,122.
[15] Grace, D. & O'Cass, A.(2004),"Examining service experiences and post-consumption evaluation", *Journal of Services Marketing*, 18, pp.450 〜 461.
[16] Wong, A., & Sohal, A. (2006)," Understanding the quality of relationships in consumer services", *The International Journal of quality & relationships Management*, 1(23), pp. 244 〜 264.

(原田倫妙・原口俊道)

〈原著論文翻訳〉

第6章　中国日系繊維製造企業の競争戦略と競争優位※
――中国日系電機製造企業との比較――

【要旨】

　日本の対中国直接投資の累計件数に占める繊維製造企業のウエイトは極めて大きい。中国日系繊維製造企業の対中国直接投資の基本戦略は「グローバル市場志向戦略」であるために,「品質」や「納期」が重要な競争優位の内容となっている。M.E. ポーターのあげる5つの競争要因のうちで最も重要な要因は「業者間の敵対関係」である。競争優位の水準はそれほど高くなく, 人件費の高騰のために中国における事業意欲が薄らいできている。

【キーワード】：M.E. ポーター，中国日系繊維製造企業，競争戦略，競争優位

1. はじめに

　1980年にM.E. ポーターが『競争の戦略』という著書の中で競争戦略を論じて以来, 経営戦略論の分野では競争戦略が中心的な位置を占めてきた[1]。この競争戦略は, 競合他社よりも競争上優位な立場, すなわち競争優位を獲得するために展開されるものである。言うまでもなく, 競争戦略は国内で活動する企業においてだけでなく, 海外で活動する多国籍企業や日系企業においても極めて重要な戦略である。

　周知の如く, 1990年代前半から日本の対外直接投資に占める対中国直接投資の割合が大きくなったこともあり, これまで日本においては中国日系企業の経営に関する研究は比較的多くなされてきた[2]。しかし, 残念なことに中国日系企業の競争戦略と競争優位の実態に関する研究はまだ緒に就いたばかりで, 筆者の知る限りでは関連する本格的な先行研究は岡本康雄らの研究と筆者

の研究の2つぐらいしかない[3]。したがって,中国日系企業の競争戦略と競争優位の実態はまだ十分に解明されているとは言えない。

中国日系企業の競争戦略と競争優位の実態を分析することの意義は,ポーターの競争戦略に関する主張の一部を検証することができることにあり,また競争環境に直面し,競争戦略の策定や見直しを迫られている中国日系企業に対しても実践的な示唆を与えることができることにある。

日本財務省の『財政金融統計月報』によれば,日本の対中国直接投資の業種別累計金額が最も多いのは電機製造企業であるが,その業種別累計件数が最も多いのは繊維製造企業である[4]。筆者は既に中国日系電機製造企業の競争戦略と競争優位の実態を分析し,その特質を考察したので,本稿では中国日系繊維製造企業の競争戦略と競争優位の実態を分析し,その特質を考察してみたい[5]。もとより筆者は非製造企業の重要性を否定するものではない。しかし,筆者があえて製造企業を分析対象とするのは,岡本康雄らの考えと同じように,製造企業の方が活動内容が多岐に及んでいるので,また日本的経営が実施される程度が高いので,競争戦略と競争優位について包括的に解明することができると考えるからである[6]。

以下では,まず中国日系企業の競争戦略と競争優位に関連する先行研究を考察し,その問題点を明らかにし,つぎに筆者の分析課題と調査方法を述べ,そして中国日系繊維製造企業の競争戦略と競争優位の実態を分析し,最後に結論として分析課題に対する解答と今後の展望を述べる。

2. 中国日系企業の競争戦略と競争優位に関連する先行研究

(1) 中国日系企業の競争戦略と競争優位に関連する先行研究

中国日系企業の競争戦略と競争優位に関連する先行研究として,以下の2つの研究をあげることができる。

① 岡本康雄らの研究(1998年)[7]

岡本康雄らは1998年出版の『日系企業 in 東アジア』において,東アジア

7ヵ国に所在する日系企業58社を対象としたインタビュー調査に基づいて，東アジア日系企業の特質を分析している。岡本らは製造企業のなかでも直接投資金額が相対的に大きい電機（家電・電子を中心とする），自動車・自動車関連，広義の化学の3業種を調査対象業種とした。東アジア地域の調査は1995年～1996年にかけて行われ，タイ所在の13社，マレーシア所在の11社，シンガポール所在の8社，インドネシア所在の5社，中国所在の9社，台湾所在の6社，韓国所在の6社，合計58社（生産子会社53社,地域統括会社5社）をインタビュー調査した。

　岡本らはインタビュー調査を実施するに当たっては，各国における調査の統一性を維持するために事前にインタビュー・ガイドを作成し，このインタビュー・ガイドに基づいてインタビュー調査を行った。岡本らが作成したインタビュー・ガイドは，①子会社の基本戦略と業績，②組織管理，③人事労務，④生産，⑤部品資財調達（関係）の5つの分野からなり，合計60の調査項目から構成された[8]。

　岡本らは，得られた58社のデータを集計するに当たっては，国別集計の方法をとらずに，東アジアとして一括集計する方法をとっている。また，一括集計したデータを重要と思われる項目に基づいてクロス分析する方法をとっている。本稿と直接関係があるのは，前記のインタビュー・ガイドの①子会社の基本戦略と業績の分野の内で，基本戦略と競争優位に関する調査結果である。以下，基本戦略と競争優位に関する岡本らの調査結果を要約紹介する。

　図表6-1は，東アジア日系企業の経営戦略（基本戦略）に関する調査結果を示している。生産子会社53社の内で，「グローバル市場志向戦略」をとる企業が21社で最も多く，「現地市場プラス海外市場志向戦略」をとる企業が17社，「現地市場志向戦略」が15社である。経営戦略のタイプと所有比率とのクロス分析から，「グローバル市場志向戦略」をとる企業は100％所有が多く，「現地市場プラス海外市場志向戦略」をとる企業は多数所有が多く，「現地市場志向戦略」をとる企業は少数所有が多いということが判明した[9]。

図表 6-1　経営戦略（基本戦略）の類型

(単位：社)

	生産会社	地域統括会社
Ⅰ　グローバル市場志向戦略	21	4
Ⅱ　現地市場プラス海外市場志向戦略	17	0
Ⅲ　現地市場志向戦略	15	
無回答	0	1
合　計	53	5

(出所) 岡本康雄編 (1998),『日系企業 in 東アジア』有斐閣, p.16。

図表6-2は，東アジア日系企業の競争優位に関する調査結果を示している。東アジア日系企業が重視する競争優位の内容は「品質」が最も多く，第2位は「生産技術（技術導入を含む）」，第3位は「製品」，第4位は「コスト」である。経営戦略のタイプと競争優位の内容とのクロス分析から，①「グローバル市場志向戦略」をとる企業の場合，競争優位の内容として「製品」，「品質」，「生産技術」，「コスト」などが重視されていること，②「現地市場プラス海外市場志向戦略」をとる企業の場合，競争優位の内容として「製品」と「価格」が重視されていること，③「現地市場志向戦略」をとる企業の場合，競争優位の内容として「品質」が重視されていること，などが判明した[10]。

東アジア日系企業の競争優位の水準は，筆者の計算によれば，5段階評価の平均値が3.5で，中間評価（平均値が3.0）よりも若干高い水準であった[11]。経営戦略のタイプと競争優位の水準とのクロス分析から，①「グローバル市場志向戦略」をとる企業の場合，競争優位の水準（平均値）は3.9で，高いこと，②「現地市場プラス海外市場志向戦略」をとる企業の場合，競争優位の水準が3.5で，中間評価よりも若干高いこと，③「現地市場志向戦略」をとる企業の場合，競争優位の水準が2.9で，中間評価並みであること，などが判明した。また，所有比率と競争優位の水準とのクロス分析から，①100％所有の企業の場合，競争優位の水準が3.9で，高いこと，②多数所有の企業の場合，競争優位の水準が3.5で，中間評価よりも若干高いこと，③少数所有の企業の場合，競争優位の水準が3.1で，中間評価並みであること，などが判明した[12]。

以上のように，岡本らの調査結果は調査した東アジア日系企業を一括集計し

たものであり，国別に日系企業の調査結果を示したものではない。しかし，調査した58社の東アジア日系企業のなかに中国日系企業が9社含まれているので，中国日系企業の競争戦略と競争優位に関連する先行研究の一つに含めることができる。

図表6-2　競争優位（主なもの5つ）

（単位：社）

品質	17	価格	4
製品	12	製品技術（設計含む）	4
生産技術（技術導入含む）	14	現地技術者能力	3
コスト	11	労務管理技術	2
ブランド（イメージ）	6	耐久性	2
先発者利益	6	技術者養成	1
納期	5	（短い）リードタイム	1

（出所）岡本康雄編（1998），『日系企業 in 東アジア』有斐閣，p.24。

②筆者の研究（2007年）[13]

筆者は2007年出版の『アジアの経営戦略と日系企業』において，中国とタイの日系電機製造企業を対象として実施したアンケート調査の結果を比較考察した[14]。アンケート調査は2004年8月に行われ，中国日系電機製造企業142社にアンケートを送り，42社からこれを回収した（回収率は29.6％）。また，同時にタイ日系電機製造企業150社にアンケートを送り，40社からこれを回収した（回収率は26.7％）。主な調査項目は，①意思決定，②日本的経営，③競争戦略と競争優位，④生産管理，⑤人事・労務管理などであった。ここでは③の競争戦略と競争優位に関する中国日系電機製造企業の調査結果を要約紹介する。

中国日系電機製造企業は経営戦略（基本戦略）として「現地市場＋海外市場志向戦略」をとる企業が66.7％を占め最も多く，「グローバル市場志向戦略」をとる企業が26.2％，「現地市場志向戦略」をとる企業が7.1％であった。中国日系電機製造企業が現地事業戦略を策定するに当たって重視している項目は，「利益確保」が第1位，「顧客の満足」と「グローバル戦略の一環」が同比率で第2位，「高品質の実現」が第4位であった。

中国日系電機製造企業の競争状況に対する認識は，5段階評価の平均値が3.9

であり，厳しい認識であることが判明した。中国日系電機製造企業の主要な競争相手は，「日系企業」が50.0％，「現地系企業（すなわち中国企業）」が23.8％，「アジア企業（日本企業以外）」が21.4％を占めた。中国日系電機製造企業の収益率を規定する5つの競争要因についての結果によれば，「産業内の同業者間での競争の激しさ」という回答が圧倒的に多く第1位を占め，第2位は「買い手の交渉力」であった。つまり，ポーターは5つの競争要因をあげているが，中国日系電機製造企業の場合，「産業内の同業者間での競争の激しさ」が最も重要な競争要因であることが判明した。

中国日系電機製造企業の競争優位の内容は，第1位が「品質」，第2位が「コスト」，第3位が「製品企画・設計力」，第4位が「生産技術」であった。マザー工場や現地系企業と対比した場合の中国日系電機製造企業の競争優位の水準はそれぞれ平均値が3.4で，中間評価よりも若干高い水準であった。

以上の中国日系電機製造企業の調査結果は，経営戦略が異なると現地事業戦略が異なるだけでなく，競争戦略（競争状況の認識，主要な競争相手，収益率を規定する5つの競争要因など）も異なり，競争優位（競争優位の内容，競争優位の水準など）も異なることを示唆している[15]。

競争戦略と競争優位は中国日系企業にとって極めて重要であるにもかかわらず，中国日系企業の競争戦略と競争優位に関する研究はまだ緒に就いたばかりである。上述した筆者の研究は，日本の対中国直接投資の累計金額が最も多い電機製造企業（42社）から得られたデータを分析したものであるので，中国日系企業の競争戦略と競争優位に関連する先行研究の一つとして位置づけることができる。

(2) 中国日系企業の競争戦略と競争優位に関連する先行研究の問題点

以上，中国日系企業の競争戦略と競争優位に関連する2つの先行研究を要約紹介した。これらの2つの研究を整理してみて，競争戦略や競争優位を個別的に分析・研究するだけでは不十分であること，①経営戦略，②現地事業戦略，③競争戦略，④競争優位の4者を一体的にとらえて分析・研究する必要

があること，などが判明した⁽¹⁶⁾。

また，問題点は2つあることが判明した。第一に，競争戦略と競争優位が中国日系企業にとって極めて重要であるにもかかわらず，筆者の知る限りでは先行研究の事例が僅かに2つしかなく，研究事例が極めて乏しいということである。したがって，今後もっと研究事例を積み重ねていくことが必要である。第二に，日本の対中国直接投資の業種別累計件数は繊維製造企業が最も多いにもかかわらず，これまで中国日系繊維製造企業の競争戦略と競争優位の実態はほとんど研究されていないので，中国に進出した日系繊維製造企業と日系電機製造企業との間には競争戦略と競争優位の点でどのような差異があるのかが解明されていないことである。

(3) 筆者の研究方法

筆者はこれらの問題点を究明するために，2007年8月に中国日系繊維製造企業を対象としてアンケート調査と訪問調査を行うことにした。また，筆者は2004年8月に中国日系電機製造企業からアンケートを回収しているので，競争戦略と競争優位について中国日系繊維製造企業と中国日系電機製造企業とを比較考察することにした。

3. 分析課題と調査方法

(1) 分析課題

日本の対中国直接投資に占める繊維製造企業のウエイトは大きい。そのため，これまで中国日系繊維製造企業の経営についての研究は比較的多かった。しかし，中国日系繊維製造企業の競争戦略と競争優位の実態を本格的に分析した研究はほとんど見当たらない。本稿は，2007年8月に中国日系繊維製造企業を対象としたアンケート調査に基づいて，中国日系繊維製造企業の競争戦略と競争優位の実態を分析しようとするものである。分析を進めるに当たって，つぎのような5つの課題をもって取り組んだ。

第一の課題は，中国日系繊維製造企業の対中国直接投資の経営戦略（基本戦略）と現地事業戦略の実態を明らかにすることである。

　第二の課題は，中国日系繊維製造企業が競争状況をどのように認識しているか，中国日系繊維製造企業の主要な競争相手は誰であるか，ポーターがあげる5つの競争要因のうちで，どの要因が中国日系繊維製造企業の場合に決定要因であるのか，などを明らかにすることである。

　第三の課題は，中国日系繊維製造企業がどのようなものを競争優位の内容と考えているか，中国日系繊維製造企業はマザー工場や現地系企業と対比した場合の競争優位の水準をどのように考えているか，などを明らかにすることである。

　第四の課題は，進出形態（合弁や独資）とこれらの経営戦略，現地事業戦略，競争戦略，競争優位とのクロス分析から，合弁と独資による結果の差異を明らかにすることである。

　第五の課題は，2004年8月に中国日系電機製造企業にもアンケート調査を実施しているので，中国日系繊維製造企業と中国日系電機製造企業の調査結果を比較し，中国日系繊維製造企業の特徴を浮き彫りにすることである。

(2) 調査方法

　筆者は中国日系繊維製造企業を対象としてアンケート調査を実施した。主な調査項目は，①意思決定，②日本的経営，③現地生産と現地化，④競争戦略と競争優位，⑤環境経営などであったが，筆者の主たる関心は④の競争戦略と競争優位にあった。2007年8月日本人派遣社員のいる中国日系繊維製造企業175社にエアメールを使ってアンケートを郵送し，34社からこれを回収した（回収率は19.4%）。アンケートを回収した34社の進出形態別内訳は独資（日本側100%出資）が23社，合弁が11社であった。図表6-3はアンケートの回収状況を示している。図表6-3の下段は2004年8月中国日系電機製造企業を対象として実施したアンケート調査の回収状況を示している。

第6章　中国日系繊維製造企業の競争戦略と競争優位　97

図表 6-3　アンケートの回収状況

(単位：企業数・％)

中国日系製造企業	調査時期	配布数	回収数	回収率
繊維	2007 年 8 月	175	34	19.4
電機	2004 年 8 月	142	42	29.6

(注) アンケートの配布先は，日本人派遣社員のいる中国日系製造企業である。

4. 中国日系繊維製造企業の競争戦略と競争優位

(1) 対中国直接投資の経営戦略と現地事業戦略

①経営戦略（基本戦略）

　従来から北米に進出した日系製造企業は「現地市場志向戦略」をとり，アジアに進出した日系製造企業は「グローバル市場志向戦略」をとる傾向があることが指摘されてきた[17]。中国日系繊維製造企業の対中国直接投資の経営戦略（基本戦略）はどのようになっているのであろうか。これについて中国日系繊維製造企業の回答を整理したものが図表 6-4 である。図表 6-4 に示されているように，「グローバル市場志向戦略」をとる企業が 70.6％を占め，圧倒的に多い。「現地市場志向戦略」をとる企業は 17.6％しかない。昨今中国の市場規模は大きくなってきているが，企業競争も熾烈になってきているので，急激に「現地市場志向戦略」へと転換する中国日系繊維製造企業は少ないように思われる。今後も当分の間大部分の中国日系繊維製造企業は「グローバル市場志向戦略」をとり続けるであろうと予測される。

　従来からアジアに進出した日系独資は「グローバル市場志向戦略」をとる企業が多く，日系合弁は「現地市場＋海外市場志向戦略」をとる企業が多いと指摘されてきた。また，中国の日系合弁は日系独資よりも「原材料・部品の現地調達比率」が高く，「販売に占める地場市場比率」が高いことが明らかにされてきた。

　しかし，図表 6-4 によれば，中国日系繊維製造企業の場合には合弁は独資と同様に「グローバル市場志向戦略」をとる企業が最も多い。図表 6-5 によれば，

合弁は「原材料・部品の現地調達比率」が47.4％で，異常に低く，「販売に占める地場市場比率」が31.3％で，異常に低いことが分かる。つまり，中国日系繊維製造企業の場合には合弁は独資と同じように輸出への依存度が高いという特異な状況がみられる。これは，①中国の繊維製造企業の場合には現地系企業の数が多いために，現地市場での競争が熾烈であること，②日系合弁繊維製造企業の生産コストが現地系企業よりも相対的に高いために，日系合弁繊維製造企業の製品は中国内において価格競争力が弱く，輸出への依存度を高めざるをえない状況になっていること，などに起因していると考えられる。

対中国直接投資の経営戦略について中国日系繊維製造企業と中国日系電機製造企業の調査結果を比較すると，図表6-4に示されているように，中国日系繊維製造企業の場合には「グローバル市場志向戦略」が70.6％を占め，中国日系電機製造企業の場合には「現地市場＋海外市場志向戦略」が66.7％を占めている。

図表6-4 経営戦略（基本戦略）

(単位：％)

	繊　維			電　機
	合弁	独資	合計	合計
	n＝11	n＝23	n＝34	n＝42
グローバル市場志向戦略	54.5	78.3	70.6	26.2
現地市場＋海外市場志向戦略	18.2	8.7	11.8	66.7
現地市場志向戦略	27.3	13.0	17.6	7.1
合　計	100.0	100.0	100.0	100.0

（出所）筆者作成。

図表6-5 原材料・部品の現地調達と販売に占める地場市場比率・輸出比率

(単位：％・平均値・％)

	繊　維			電　機
	合弁	独資	合計	合計
	n＝11	n＝23	n＝34	n＝42
原材料・部品の現地調達比率	47.4	54.5	52.2	52.5
原材料・部品の現地調達への満足の程度（平均値）	1.8	3.6	3.2	2.5
販売に占める地場市場比率	31.3	21.3	24.5	38.1
販売に占める輸出比率	68.7	78.7	75.5	61.9

（出所）筆者作成。

このように両者の結果には大きな差異があり，このことが以下の現地事業戦略，競争戦略，競争優位などに大きな差異を生じさせる原因となっている。

②現地事業戦略

経営戦略に基づいて現地事業戦略は策定される。従来から北米に進出した日系製造企業は市場競争が熾烈なために，現地事業戦略として「売上高」「市場確保」「市場占有率」などの市場関連指標を重視する傾向があることが指摘されてきた[18]。中国日系繊維製造企業が現地事業戦略を策定するに当たって重視している項目は，図表6-6に示すように，「顧客の満足」が第一位，「高品質の実現」が第二位，「利益確保」が第三位，「低コストの実現」が第四位である。これらは輸出競争力に関連する指標である。製品の輸出競争力を高めるためには，高品質で低コストの製品を提供することによって顧客を満足させることが重要である。このことが実現すれば，製品の輸出競争力は高まり，意図した利益が確保されやすくなる。

図表 6-6 現地事業戦略（2つ以内回答）

(単位：%)

	繊　　維			電　機
	合弁	独資	合計	合計
	n＝11	n＝23	n＝34	n＝42
利益確保	36.4	30.4	32.4	38.1
売上高の拡大	0.0	4.3	2.9	11.9
市場確保	9.1	4.3	5.9	14.3
低コストの実現	9.1	34.8	26.5	21.4
高生産性の実現	9.1	17.4	14.7	9.5
市場占有率の拡大	9.1	4.3	5.9	19.0
高品質の実現	45.5	47.8	47.1	26.2
顧客の満足	63.6	43.5	50.0	28.6
グローバル戦略の一環	18.2	13.0	14.7	28.6

(出所) 筆者作成。

従来からアジアに進出した日系独資は日系合弁よりも「グローバル市場志向戦略」をとる傾向があることが指摘されてきた。中国日系繊維製造企業の場合にも独資の方が合弁よりも「グローバル市場志向戦略」をとる企業が多い。中国の日系独資繊維製造企業は，図表6-6に示すように，日系合弁繊維製造企業

よりも「低コストの実現」を重視している。

中国日系繊維製造企業と中国日系電機製造企業の調査結果を比較すると，図表6-6に示すように，両者ともに「顧客の満足」「高品質の実現」「利益確保」などを重視している点は共通している。しかし，中国日系繊維製造企業は中国日系電機製造企業よりも「売上高の拡大」「市場確保」「市場占有率の拡大」などの市場関連指標を重視する度合いが低い。これは，中国日系繊維製造企業には「グローバル市場志向戦略」をとる企業が多く，中国日系電機製造企業には「現地市場＋海外市場志向戦略」をとる企業が多いことに起因していると考えられる。

(2) 競争戦略
①競争状況の認識

一般に「グローバル市場志向戦略」をとる企業の場合には競争が相対的にマイルドとなり，「現地市場志向戦略」をとる企業の場合には日系企業や現地系企業との競争が熾烈になるという傾向が見受けられる[19]。従来から北米に進出した日系製造企業の競争状況の認識は厳しいことが指摘されてきた。これは北米に進出した日系製造企業には「現地市場志向戦略」をとる企業が多いことによるものである。中国日系繊維製造企業の競争状況の認識は，図表6-7に示すように，5段階評価の平均値が3.4であるから，それほど「厳しい」という認識はもたれていない。これは，中国日系繊維製造企業には「グローバル市場

図表 6-7　競争状況の認識

(単位：％・平均値)

	繊　　維			電　機
	合弁	独資	合計	合計
	n = 11	n = 23	n = 34	n = 42
非常に緩い	18.2	13.0	14.7	2.4
緩い	9.1	0.0	2.9	2.4
多少は厳しい	9.1	34.8	26.5	28.6
厳しい（日本国内並み）	54.5	26.1	35.5	35.7
非常に厳しい	9.1	26.1	20.6	31.0
競争状況の認識（平均値）	3.3	3.5	3.4	3.9

(出所) 筆者作成。

志向戦略」をとる企業が多いことによるものである。

　一般にアジアに進出した日系企業の場合には，合弁は「現地市場＋海外市場志向戦略」をとる企業が多いために独資よりも競争状況の認識が厳しくなるという傾向が見受けられる。しかし，中国日系繊維製造企業の場合には，図表6-7に示すように，合弁は独資よりも競争状況の認識が若干緩い。これは，中国日系合弁繊維製造企業には「グローバル市場志向戦略」をとる企業が多いという特異な状況が一因になっていると考えられる。

　中国日系繊維製造企業と中国日系電機製造企業の調査結果を比較すると，図表6-7に示すように，中国日系繊維製造企業は中国日系電機製造企業よりも競争状況の認識が緩い。これは，中国日系繊維製造企業には「グローバル市場志向戦略」をとる企業が多く，中国日系電機製造企業には「現地市場＋海外市場志向戦略」をとる企業が多いことによるものである。

②主要な競争相手

　一般に海外に進出した日系企業の主要な競争相手は「日系企業」であることが多い。これは，①日本企業の海外直接投資には他社追随型の海外直接投資が多いこと，②日本企業が束になってほぼ同じ時期・場所に海外直接投資を行う傾向があること，などに起因していると考えられる[20]。中国日系繊維製造企業の主要な競争相手は，図表6-8に示すように，「日系企業」「現地系企業」などである。「現地系企業」という回答は予想していたよりも多かった。これは，

図表6-8　主要な競争相手

(単位：％)

	繊　　維			電　機
	合弁	独資	合計	合計
	n＝11	n＝23	n＝34	n＝42
日系企業	36.4	39.1	38.2	50.0
現地系企業	45.5	34.8	38.2	23.8
アジア企業（日本企業以外）	18.2	21.7	20.6	21.4
アメリカ企業	0.0	4.3	2.9	4.8
ヨーロッパ企業	0.0	0.0	0.0	0.0
合　　計	100.0	100.0	100.0	100.0

(出所）筆者作成。

①中国の繊維製造企業の場合には日系企業と現地系企業との間には技術格差が少ないこと，②現地市場における販売では現地系企業の方がコスト優位をもっていること，などに起因していると考えられる。

一般に合弁は「現地市場＋海外市場志向戦略」をとる企業が多いために，主要な競争相手として「現地系企業」をあげる傾向があり，独資は「グローバル市場志向戦略」をとる企業が多いために，主要な競争相手として「日系企業」をあげる傾向がある。中国日系合弁繊維製造企業は，図表6-8に示すように，主要な競争相手として「現地系企業」をあげており，中国日系独資繊維製造企業は主要な競争相手として「日系企業」をあげている。

中国日系繊維製造企業と中国日系電機製造企業の調査結果を比較すると，図表6-8に示すように，主要な競争相手は現地系企業との技術格差が少ない中国日系繊維製造企業の場合には「日系企業」「現地系企業」などであり，現地系企業との技術格差がまだ大きい中国日系電機製造企業の場合には「日系企業」である。

③収益率を規定する5つの競争要因

周知の如く，ポーターは業界の収益率を規定する5つの競争要因をあげ，「業界によって，競争の第1要因はみなちがう」[21]と述べ，5つの競争要因のうちでどれが決定要因になるかは，多くの重要な経済的技術的特性によって決まると主張した[22]。しかし，ポーターは5つの競争要因を強調するあまり，5つの競争要因の1つである「業者間の敵対関係」，すなわち「産業内の同業者間での競争の激しさ」の重要性を希薄化させているのではないかという疑問がある。

一般にアジアに進出した日系製造企業の場合には，収益率を規定する要因として「産業内の同業者間での競争の激しさ」が決定要因であるという傾向が見受けられる[23]。中国日系繊維製造企業の場合には，図表6-9に示すように，「産業内の同業者間での競争の激しさ」が決定要因となっている。2番目に大きな要因は「買い手の交渉力」である。

図表 6-9 収益率を規定する5つの競争要因（2つ以内回答）

(単位：％)

	繊　維			電　機
	合弁	独資	合計	合計
	n＝11	n＝23	n＝34	n＝42
産業内の同業者間での競争の激しさ	72.7	82.6	79.4	88.1
新規参入の脅威	0.0	4.3	2.9	11.9
代替的な製品・サービスの脅威	9.1	17.4	14.7	4.8
供給業者の交渉力	27.3	17.4	20.6	14.3
買い手の交渉力	54.5	26.1	35.3	38.1
その他	9.1	8.7	8.8	4.8

（出所）筆者作成。

　一般に合弁は「現地市場＋海外市場志向戦略」をとる企業が多いために，独資よりも「産業内の同業者間での競争の激しさ」が相対的に重要である程度が高くなる傾向がある。しかし，中国日系繊維製造企業の場合には，図表6-9に示すように，合弁は独資よりも「買い手の交渉力」によって収益率が影響を受けやすいために，その結果として「産業内の同業者間での競争の激しさ」の重要度が相対的に低くなっている。

　中国日系繊維製造企業と中国日系電機製造企業の調査結果を比較すると，図表6-9に示すように，両者はともに「産業内の同業者間での競争の激しさ」を決定要因と考えており，2番目に大きな要因として「買い手の交渉力」をあげている。

(3) 競争優位

①競争優位の内容

　従来から北米に進出した日系製造企業は競争優位の内容として「品質」をあげる企業が多いことが指摘されてきた[24]。また，アジアに進出した日系製造企業については，「品質」や「コスト」といった一般的な競争優位だけでなく，「製品企画・設計力」といった新製品開発力に競争優位の中心が移動しつつあることが指摘されてきた[25]。中国日系繊維製造企業の場合には，図表6-10に示すように，競争優位の内容は第一位が「品質」，第二位が「生産技術」，第三位

が「納期」である。中国日系繊維製造企業は「グローバル市場志向戦略」をとる企業が多いために,「品質」や「納期」が重要な競争優位の内容となっている。

図表6-10 競争優位の内容（3つ以内回答）

(単位：％)

	繊　維			電　機
	合弁	独資	合計	合計
	n＝11	n＝23	n＝34	n＝42
製品企画・設計力	9.1	34.8	26.5	31.0
品質	90.9	100.0	97.1	90.5
生産技術	72.7	43.5	52.9	23.8
生産規模	9.1	4.3	5.9	19.0
コスト	18.2	17.4	17.6	52.4
納期	36.4	43.5	41.2	19.0
厚い優位技術	18.2	8.7	11.8	21.4
製品開発力	18.2	21.7	20.6	16.7
生産システム	18.2	13.0	14.7	4.8
その他	0.0	0.0	0.0	4.8

(出所) 筆者作成。

　また,中国の繊維製造企業の場合には日系企業と現地系企業との間には技術格差が少ないために,中国日系繊維製造企業では競争優位を確保する上で「生産技術」が重視され,重要な競争優位の内容となっている。

　一般に合弁は「現地市場＋海外市場志向戦略」をとる企業が多く,現地系企業との競争が独資よりも相対的に厳しくなるために,「コスト」が重要な競争優位の内容となる傾向がある。しかし,「グローバル市場志向戦略」をとる企業が多い中国日系繊維製造企業の場合には,図表6-10に示すように,合弁も独資もともに「品質」「生産技術」「納期」などを重要な競争優位の内容としてあげている。合弁は独資よりも「生産技術」を重視する程度が高くなっているが,これは通常合弁の方が独資よりも「生産技術」のレベルが低いので,「生産技術」の重要性を強く自覚しているためであると考えられる。

　中国日系繊維製造企業と中国日系電機製造企業の調査結果を比較すると,図表6-10に示すように,両者は「品質」を重要な競争優位の内容と考えている点が共通している。しかし,両者には相違点も多い。例えば,中国日系繊維製

造企業の場合には「生産技術」や「納期」が重要な競争優位の内容となっており，中国日系電機製造企業の場合には「コスト」や「製品企画・設計力」が重要な競争優位の内容となっている。これらの相違をもたらした原因は，両者の経営戦略の相違にあると考えられる。

②競争優位の水準

　北米日系製造企業を対象とした岡本康雄らの調査結果によれば，マザー工場と対比した場合の北米日系製造企業の競争優位の水準は平均値が3.6で，「高い」水準であった[26]。この平均値の計算方法は前述の5段階評価による平均値の計算方法とは若干異なるものである。すなわち，この平均値は「非常に高い」を5点，「相当に高い」を4点，「高い」を3.5点，「どちらともいえない」を3点，「低い」を2点，「非常に低い」を1点として計算したものである。マザー工場と対比した場合の中国日系繊維製造企業の競争優位の水準は，図表6-11に示すように，平均値が3.1で，中間評価並みであった。しかし，岡本らの調査結果とこの調査結果を比較すると，マザー工場と対比した場合の競争優位の水準は北米日系製造企業の方が中国日系繊維製造企業よりも高かった。これは，世界のグローバル企業が拠点を置く北米市場では競争が激しいために，競争優位の水準をマザー工場に近づける努力がなされていることを示唆している。また，これはアジアに進出した日系製造企業ではその主な進出動機が豊富で安価な労働力の活用である場合が多いので，先進国に進出した日系製造企業よりもマザー工場と対比した場合の競争優位の水準がやや低くなる傾向があることを示唆している。

　一般に合弁は独資よりもマザー工場と対比した場合の競争優位の水準が低くなる傾向が見受けられる。中国日系繊維製造企業の場合には，図表6-11に示すように，合弁の平均値が2.4，独資の平均値が3.3であるから，合弁は独資よりもマザー工場と対比した場合の競争優位の水準がかなり低い。これは，合弁は独資の場合よりも最新鋭の設備・機械が導入される度合いが相対的に低いことを示唆している。

図表 6-11　マザー工場と対比した場合の競争優位の水準

(単位：％・平均値)

	繊　維			電　機
	合弁	独資	合計	合計
	n = 11	n = 23	n = 34	n = 42
マザー工場と対比した場合の競争優位の水準				
非常に低い	0.0	4.3	2.9	0.0
低い	18.2	4.3	8.8	19.0
どちらとも言えない	27.3	34.8	32.4	19.0
高い	9.1	13.0	11.8	19.0
相当に高い（日本国内並み）	18.2	26.1	23.5	35.7
非常に高い	9.1	13.0	11.8	7.1
無回答	18.2	4.3	8.8	0.0
マザー工場と対比した場合の競争優位の水準（平均値）	2.4	3.3	3.1	3.4

(出所) 筆者作成。

　中国日系繊維製造企業と中国日系電機製造企業の調査結果を比較すると，図表 6-11 に示すように，両者にはマザー工場と比較した場合の競争優位の水準に若干の差があり，中国日系繊維製造企業の方が若干低い。これは，中国日系繊維製造企業の場合には前述した如く，合弁の競争優位の水準（平均値が 2.4）がかなり低いことが影響していると考えられる。

　北米日系製造企業を対象とした岡本らの調査結果によれば，現地系企業（アメリカ企業）と対比した場合の競争優位の水準は平均値が 3.8 で，マザー工場と対比した場合の競争優位の水準（3.6）よりも若干高かった[27]。中国日系繊維製造企業の場合には，図表 6-12 に示すように，現地系企業（中国企業）と対比した場合の競争優位の水準は平均値が 3.3 で，マザー工場と対比した場合の競争優位の水準（3.1）よりも若干高かった。

　一般に合弁の場合には独資よりも最新鋭の設備・機械が導入される度合いが相対的に低いために，現地系企業と対比した場合の競争優位の水準は合弁の方が独資よりも低くなる傾向がある。しかし，中国日系繊維製造企業の場合には，図表 6-12 に示すように，合弁と独資の間には差が少なく，独資の平均値が予想していたよりも低かった。これは，独資の場合にも最新鋭の設備・機械が導

入される度合いがそれほど高くないことを示唆している。

中国日系繊維製造企業と中国日系電機製造企業の調査結果を比較すると，図表6-12に示すように，両者の間には差が少なく，両者は似通った状況であることがわかる。

図表6-12　現地系企業と対比した場合の競争優位の水準

(単位：％・平均値)

	繊　維			電　機
	合弁	独資	合計	合計
	n = 11	n = 23	n = 34	n = 42
現地系企業と対比した場合の競争優位の水準				
非常に低い	0.0	4.3	2.9	0.0
低い	9.1	17.4	14.7	11.9
どちらとも言えない	18.2	30.4	26.5	35.7
高い	45.5	17.4	26.5	21.4
相当に高い（日本国内並み）	27.3	17.4	20.6	23.8
非常に高い	0.0	13.0	8.8	7.1
現地系企業と対比した場合の競争優位の水準（平均値）	3.4	3.3	3.3	3.4

(出所) 筆者作成。

5. 結び

まず，5つの研究課題に対する解答を要約する。

第一に，中国日系繊維製造企業は経営戦略（基本戦略）として「グローバル市場志向戦略」をとる企業が70.6％を占め，圧倒的に多い。これが中国日系繊維製造企業の大きな特徴である。中国日系繊維製造企業は現地事業戦略として「顧客の満足」「高品質の実現」「利益確保」「低コストの実現」などの輸出競争力に関連する指標を重視している。

第二に，中国日系繊維製造企業には競争が熾烈となる「現地市場志向戦略」をとる企業が少なく，競争が相対的にマイルドな「グローバル市場志向戦略」をとる企業が多いために，中国日系繊維製造企業の競争状況の認識はそれほど

厳しくはない。中国日系繊維製造企業の主要な競争相手は「日系企業」「現地系企業」などである。ポーターは収益率を規定する要因として5つの競争要因を強調しているが，中国日系繊維製造企業の場合には，「産業内の同業者間での競争の激しさ」が収益率を規定する決定要因である。

第三に，「グローバル市場志向戦略」をとる企業が多い中国日系繊維製造企業の場合には，「品質」や「納期」が重要な競争優位の内容となっている。マザー工場や現地系企業と対比した場合の競争優位の水準はそれほど高くはなかった。

第四に，中国日系繊維製造企業の場合には，合弁は独資よりも「グローバル市場志向戦略」をとる企業が少なく，「顧客の満足」を重視し，主要な競争相手として「現地系企業」をあげる企業が多く，競争要因として「買い手の交渉力」を重視し，競争優位の内容として「生産技術」を重視し，マザー工場と対比した場合の競争優位の水準がかなり低い。また，独資は合弁よりも「グローバル市場志向戦略」をとる企業が多く，「低コストの実現」を重視し，主要な競争相手として「日系企業」をあげ，競争要因として「産業内の同業者間での競争の激しさ」を重視し，競争優位の内容として「品質」や「納期」を重視している。

第五に，中国日系繊維製造企業の場合には，中国日系電機製造企業の場合よりも「グローバル市場志向戦略」をとる企業が多く，「売上高の拡大」「市場確保」「市場占有率の拡大」などの市場関連指標を重視する度合いが低く，競争状況の認識が緩く，主要な競争相手として「現地系企業」をあげる企業が多く，競争優位の内容として「品質」「生産技術」「納期」などを重視し，マザー工場と対比した場合の競争優位の水準が若干低い。

つぎに，本研究結果が示唆している重要な論点は以下の三点である。

第一に，従来競争戦略や競争優位は個別的に分析される傾向があったが，本研究結果は経営戦略が異なれば現地事業戦略も異なり，さらに競争戦略や競争優位も異なることを示唆している。したがって，①経営戦略，②現地事業戦略，③競争戦略，④競争優位の4者を一体的に捉えて分析・研究することが必要である。

第二に，従来から経営戦略は所有政策を規定することが指摘されてきたが，

本研究結果でも「グローバル市場志向戦略」をとる企業には独資企業が多く,「現地市場＋海外市場志向戦略」をとる企業には合弁が多いという傾向が顕著に見られた。したがって,これから対中国直接投資を行う企業は,選択する経営戦略に適合した進出形態（合弁や独資など）を選択すべきである。

　第三に,ポーターは収益率を規定する5つの競争要因を強調するあまり,5つの競争要因の一つである「産業内の同業者間での競争の激しさ」の重要性を希薄化させているということである。本研究結果は「産業内の同業者間での競争の激しさ」が収益率を規定する決定要因であることを示している。

　最後に,中国日系繊維製造企業について今後の展望を述べる。マザー工場や現地系企業と対比した場合の競争優位の水準に関する中国日系繊維製造企業の調査結果から,中国日系繊維製造企業の事業意欲が薄らいできているように感じられる。アンケートに回答した34社の地域別分布をみると,上海市12社,江蘇省12社,山東省3社,浙江省2,広東省2社,北京市1社,遼寧省1社,安徽省1社となり,人件費が高騰している沿海地区に所在する日系企業がほとんどである。筆者の現地訪問調査でも,中国日系企業が直面する最大の問題点は人件費の高騰であった。今後中国日系繊維製造企業の多くは採算がとれなくなった中国から撤退し,人件費の安いベトナムへと生産拠点を移転させる動きを加速化させるであろう。

【引用文献】
(1) M.E. ポーター（2001）,（土岐 坤・中辻萬治・服部照夫訳）『新訂競争の戦略』ダイヤモンド社。
(2) 例えば,筆者の研究をあげると,つぎの通りである。
　　原口俊道（1999）,『経営管理と国際経営』同文舘出版。
　　原口俊道（2000）,『東亜地区的経営管理（中文）』中国・上海人民出版社。
　　蘇勇・原口俊道他主編（2004）,『企業国際経営策略（中文）』中国・復旦大学出版社。
　　唐海燕・原口俊道・黄一修主編（2006）,『中日対照　経済のグローバル化と企業戦略』中国・立信会計出版社。
(3) 岡本康雄編（1998）,『日系企業 in 東アジア』有斐閣。
　　原口俊道（2007）,『アジアの経営戦略と日系企業』学文社。

(4) 財務省（2006年1月),『財政金融統計月報』第645号。
(5) 原口俊道（2007),『アジアの経営戦略と日系企業』学文社, pp.33～54。
(6) 岡本康雄編（1998),『日系企業 in 東アジア』有斐閣, p.1。
(7) 同上書, pp.1～42。
(8) 同上書, p.3。
(9) 同上書, p.16。
(10) 同上書, p.25。
(11) 同上書, p.28に基づき筆者が計算した。
(12) 同上書, pp. 27～28。
(13) 原口俊道（2007),『アジアの経営戦略と日系企業』学文社。
(14) 同上書, pp.33～54。
(15) 同上書, p.51。
(16) 同上書, p.51。
(17) 岡本康雄編（2000),『北米日系企業の経営』同文舘出版, p.20。なお, 本研究ではアンケートの質問項目を作成するに当たって, この著書の巻末に収録されている岡本らの調査票を参考にさせていただいた。ここに記してお礼を申し上げる。
(18) 同上書, p.24。
(19) 原口俊道（2007),『アジアの経営戦略と日系企業』学文社, p.43。
(20) 岡本康雄編（2000),『北米日系企業の経営』同文舘出版, p.26。
(21) M.E. ポーター（2001),（土岐 坤・中辻萬治・服部照夫訳）『新訂競争の戦略』ダイヤモンド社, p.20。
(22) 同上書, p.21。
(23) 原口俊道（2007),『アジアの経営戦略と日系企業』学文社, pp.45～46。
(24) 岡本康雄編（2000),『北米日系企業の経営』同文舘出版, p.29。
(25) 原口俊道（2007),『アジアの経営戦略と日系企業』学文社, p.46。
(26) 岡本康雄編（2000),『北米日系企業の経営』同文舘出版, p.32。ただし, 平均値3.59を四捨五入して平均値3.6として表記した。
(27) 同上書, 32頁。ただし, 平均値3.76を四捨五入して平均値3.8として表記した。

【参考文献】
[1] 芮明杰・原口俊道・王明元主編（2008),『亜洲産業発展與企業発展戦略（中文)』中国・復旦大学出版社。
[2] 原口俊道（2007),『アジアの経営戦略と日系企業』学文社。
[3] 唐海燕・原口俊道・黄一修主編（2006),『中日対照 経済のグローバル化と企業戦略』中国・立信会計出版社。
[4] 蘇勇・原口俊道他主編（2004),『企業国際経営策略（中文)』中国・復旦大学出版社。
[5] 唐海燕・原口俊道他主編（2002),『国際化與現代企業（中文)』中国・立信会計出版社。
[6] 原口俊道・陸留弟・黄澤民主編（2001),『中日経済, 社会, 文化比較研究（中文)』中国・華東師範大学出版社。

- [7] 原口俊道（2000），『東亜地区的経営管理（中文）』中国・上海人民出版社。
- [8] 原口俊道（1999），『経営管理と国際経営』同文舘出版。
- [9] グロービス・マネジメント・インスティテュート編（1999），『MBA経営戦略』ダイヤモンド社。
- [10] 奥村昭博（1989），『経営戦略』日本経済新聞社。
- [11] 伊丹敬之（1981），『経営戦略の論理』日本経済新聞社。
- [12] 青島矢一・加藤俊彦（2003），『競争戦略論』東洋経済新報社。
- [13] M.E. ポーター・竹内弘高（2000），『日本の競争戦略』ダイヤモンド社。
- [14] 黄一修（2000年3月『台湾プラスチック原料産業における競争戦略――奇美実業の事例研究を中心として――』岡山大学大学院経済学研究科修士論文。
- [15] 岸川善光（2006），『経営戦略要論』同文舘出版。
- [16] 石井淳蔵・奥村昭博・加護野忠男・野中郁次郎（1985），『経営戦略論』有斐閣。
- [17] 土屋守章編（1982），『現代の企業戦略』有斐閣。

※付記：本章はすでに中国語簡体字論文として発表済みであるが，出版社の許可を受けて日本語に翻訳し，日本語翻訳として発表するものである。元の中国語簡体字論文については，下記の文献を参照されたい。
亜東経済国際学会研究叢書⑨（2010），『東亜経済発展與社会保障問題研究（中文簡体字）』中国・江西人民出版社，pp.22～44。

（原著者　原口俊道：翻訳者　原口俊道）

第7章 日系サービス企業のマーケティング戦略への影響要因
―中国と台湾の日系サービス企業の比較分析―

【要旨】

　これまで在中・台の日系サービス企業のマーケティング戦略への影響要因を定量的に比較分析した研究はほとんどなかった。本研究では在中・台の日系サービス企業を対象として郵便によるアンケート調査を行い，中国からは63社，台湾からは31社の有効回答を得た。本研究では，8つの仮説を構築し，在中・台の日系サービス企業のマーケティング戦略への影響要因を解明するために，①内部環境，②外部環境，③経営成果および④マーケティング戦略という4つの変数間の関係と影響を定量的に比較分析した。ピアソンの相関分析の結果，在中・台の日系サービス企業では共に①内部環境と外部環境との間，②内部環境と経営成果との間，③外部環境と経営成果との間および④経営成果とマーケティング戦略との間に，正の相関関係があることが判明した。影響力分析の結果，在中・台の日系サービス企業の調査結果を総合すると，①内部環境が外部環境に対して，②内部環境が経営成果に対して，③外部環境が経営成果に対しておよび④経営成果がマーケティング戦略に対して，部分的に影響を与えることが判明した。

【キーワード】：在中・台の日系サービス企業，内部環境，外部環境，経営成果，マーケティング戦略への影響要因

1. はじめに

　現在，日系企業の多くがアジアに進出している。なかでも，近隣国である

中国と台湾を重要な市場として位置づけており、今後更なる市場の発展を見込んでいる。中国と台湾に進出している日系企業は、製造企業だけでなくサービス企業も存在する。最近特に日系サービス企業の進出件数の増加が顕著である。しかし、これまで在中・台の日系サービス企業を対象として研究している事例は極めて少なく、しかも数少ない研究事例が対象としている企業数やサービス分野の種類が少ないので、在中・台の日系サービス企業の研究はまだ十分ではない。さらに、在中・台の日系サービス企業にとって市場でのサービスの販売が重要であるにも関わらず、マーケティング戦略への影響要因を定量的に比較分析した研究はほとんどない。

　本研究の課題は在中・台の日系サービス企業のマーケティング戦略への影響要因を解明するために、①内部環境、②外部環境、③経営成果および④マーケティング戦略という4つの変数間の関係と影響を定量的に比較分析することである。本稿では、まず先行研究とその問題点を明らかにし、つぎに分析モデルと仮説を構築し、在中・台の日系企業を対象としたアンケート調査の結果に基づいて仮説の検証を行い、最後に研究課題に対する解答を述べる。

2. 先行研究とその問題点

　在中・台の日系サービス企業に関する先行研究の問題点として、つぎの3点が挙げられる。まず、在中・台の日系企業に関する先行研究のほとんどは、製造企業を対象としており、サービス企業を対象とした先行研究が少ない。第2に、サービス企業を対象としている研究であっても、対象とする企業数やサービス分野の種類が少なく、十分ではない[1]。第3に、台湾日系サービス企業に関する先行研究には、人的資源管理[2]や経営実態に関する研究が多く[3]、マーケティング戦略への影響要因に関する定量的な研究がほとんどない。

3. 分析モデルと研究仮説

本研究では，つぎのような分析モデルを構築し，それを基に8つの仮説を構築した。これらの仮説を検証するために，中国・台湾双方の日系サービス企業に対してアンケート調査を実施した。

図表 7-1　分析モデル

（出所）筆者作成。

H1：内部環境は外部環境に顕著な影響を与える。
H2：内部環境と外部環境には明らかな相関関係がある。
H3：内部環境は経営成果に顕著な影響を与える。
H4：内部環境と経営成果には明らかな相関関係がある。
H5：外部環境は経営成果に顕著な影響を与える。
H6：外部環境と経営成果には明らかな相関関係がある。
H7：経営成果はマーケティング戦略に顕著な影響を与える。
H8：経営成果とマーケティング戦略には明らかな相関関係がある。

4. アンケート調査の概要

本研究では中国と台湾に進出している日系サービス企業（日系小売企業を含めず）を対象にアンケート調査を行った。

アンケートの調査項目は企業属性に関する項目を除き，「同意する」を5,「同意しない」を1とする5段階評価とした。まず，中国日系企業350社に対し，

2011年9月～12月にかけてアンケート調査票を郵送で発送し，その結果，63社から有効回答を得た（有効回収率：18%）。次いで，台湾日系企業130社に対して，2012年3～4月に同じく郵送でアンケート調査票を発送し，その結果，31社から有効回答を得た（有効回収率：23.8%）。

5. 分析結果

分析ソフトSPSS17.0を用いてデータの統計分析を行い，研究仮説の検証を行う。

(1) 中国日系サービス企業のサンプル分析

回収したサンプルについて，事業内容は「物流」が33.8%を占め最も多く，資本金は「1億～5億円未満」が45.3%で最も多かった。日本側出資比率は「100%」の企業が61.5%で約6割を占めており，次いで「50~100%未満」が29.2%であった。従業員数は「100人以上」が46.2%で最も多く，参入時期は「1993年以前」が27.7%で最も多く，次いで「2001～2004年」が26.2%であった。

(2) 台湾日系サービス企業のサンプル分析

回収したサンプルについて，事業内容は「物流」が21.9%を占め最も多く，資本金は「5000万～1億円未満」が28.1%を占め最も多かった。日本側出資比率は「100%」の企業が65.6%で約6割を占めており，次いで「50～100%未満」が28.1%であった。従業員数は「50人未満」が37.5%を占め最も多く，次いで「50～100人未満」が34.4%であった。参入時期は「1993年以前」が62.5%を占め最も多く，「2001年～2004年」が25.0%であった。

以上の結果から，日系サービス企業は，中国と台湾では，出資比率と事業内容において似通った傾向にあり，資本金や従業員数においては，中国の方が台湾よりも規模が大きいということがわかった。参入時期については，台湾の方が中国よりも早く参入している企業が多いということも判明した。

(3) 信頼性分析

本研究では，呉明隆（2008）の分析方法を参考として信頼性分析を行った。「中国日系サービス企業のマーケティング戦略」の初期の信頼度は 0.779 であり，その数値は Cuieford（1965）基準の信頼性の数値である 0.7 〜 1.0 の間に位置するので，信頼性があると認められる。同じく，「台湾日系サービス企業のマーケティング戦略」の初期の信頼度は，0.856 であり，その数値が信頼性の数値である 0.7 〜 1.0 の間に位置するので，信頼性があると認められる。

(4) 相関分析

①内部環境と外部環境の相関分析

内部環境と外部環境の相関分析では，ピアソンの相関分析を用いて，内部環境と外部環境との相関性を検定した。分析を通して，中国（$p < .01$**）も台湾（$p < .01$**）も共に顕著な相関関係が見られた。つまり，在中・台の日系サービス企業において，内部環境と外部環境には正の相関関係がみられた。

図表 7-2　中国日系サービス企業における内部環境と外部環境の相関分析表（相関係数 [a]）

		内部環境総合	外部環境総合
内部環境総合	Pearson の相関係数	1	.416
	有意確率（両側）		.001
外部環境総合	Pearson の相関係数	.416	1
	有意確率（両側）	.001	

a. リストごと N=63
（出所）筆者作成。

図表 7-3　台湾日系サービス企業における内部環境と外部環境の相関分析表（相関係数 [a]）

		内部環境総合	外部環境総合
内部環境総合	Pearson の相関係数	1	.513
	有意確率（両側）		.002
外部環境総合	Pearson の相関係数	.513	1
	有意確率（両側）	.002	

a. リストごと N=31
（出所）筆者作成。

②内部環境と経営成果の相関分析

内部環境と経営成果の相関分析では，ピアソンの相関分析を用いて，内部環

境と経営成果との相関性を検定した。分析を通して，中国（p＜.001***）も台湾（p＜.01**）も共に顕著な相関関係がみられた。つまり，在中・台の日系サービス企業において，内部環境と経営成果には正の相関関係がみられた。

図表7-4　中国日系サービス企業における内部環境と経営成果の相関分析表（相関係数[a]）

	内部環境総合	経営成果総合
内部環境総合　Pearsonの相関係数	1	.650
有意確率（両側）		.000
経営成果総合　Pearsonの相関係数	.650	1
有意確率（両側）	.003	

a. リストごと N=63
（出所）筆者作成。

図表7-5　台湾日系サービス企業における内部環境と経営成果の相関分析表（相関係数[a]）

	内部環境総合	経営成果総合
内部環境総合　Pearsonの相関係数	1	.491
有意確率（両側）		.003
経営成果総合　Pearsonの相関係数	.491	1
有意確率（両側）	.003	

a. リストごと N=31
（出所）筆者作成。

③外部環境と経営成果の相関分析

外部環境と経営成果の相関分析では，ピアソンの相関分析を用いて外部環境と経営成果との相関性を検定した。分析を通して，中国（p＜.001***）も台湾（p＜.01**）も共に顕著な相関関係がみられた。つまり，在中・台の日系サービス企業において外部環境と経営成果には正の相関関係がみられた。

図表7-6　中国日系サービス企業における外部環境と経営成果の相関分析表（相関係数[a]）

	外部環境総合	経営成果総合
外部環境総合　Pearsonの相関係数	1	.497
有意確率（両側）		.000
経営成果総合　Pearsonの相関係数	.497	1
有意確率（両側）	.000	

a. リストごと N=63
（出所）筆者作成。

図表 7-7　台湾日系サービス企業における外部環境と経営成果の相関分析表（相関係数[a]）

	外部環境総合	経営成果総合
外部環境総合　Pearson の相関係数	1	.560
有意確率（両側）		.001
経営成果総合　Pearson の相関係数	.560	1
有意確率（両側）	.001	

a. リストごと N=31
（出所）筆者作成。

④経営成果とマーケティング戦略の相関分析

　経営成果とマーケティング戦略の相関分析では，ピアソンの相関分析を用いて経営成果とマーケティング戦略との相関性を検定した。分析を通して，中国（$p < .05^*$）も台湾（$p < .01^{**}$）も共に相関関係がみられた。つまり，在中・台の日系サービス企業において，経営成果とマーケティング戦略には正の相関関係がみられた。

図表 7-8　中国日系サービス企業における経営成果とマーケティング戦略の相関分析表（相関係数[a]）

	内部環境総合	マーケティング戦略総合
経営成果総合　　Pearson の相関係数	1	.310
有意確率（両側）		.013
マーケティング戦略総合 Pearson の相関係数	.310	1
有意確率（両側）	.013	

a. リストごと N=63
（出所）筆者作成。

図表 7-9　台湾日系サービス企業における経営成果とマーケティング戦略の相関分析表（相関係数[a]）

	経営成果総合	マーケティング戦略総合
経営成果総合　　Pearson の相関係数	1	.429
有意確率（両側）		.008
マーケティング戦略総合 Pearson の相関係数	.429	1
有意確率（両側）	.008	

a. リストごと N=31
（出所）筆者作成。

(5) 影響力分析

①内部環境が外部環境に与える影響力分析

本研究では，研究仮説に基づき，重回帰分析を通して強制投入法で回帰方程式モデルを作りあげた。内部環境を予測変数とし，外部環境を従属変数として回帰分析を行った。図表 7-10 の結果から，外部環境に対する内部環境の重判定係数（R^2）は 0.173 で，これは内部環境が外部環境の 17.3% を説明できることを表している。また，標準化回帰係数によりわずかに内部環境は外部環境に対して影響力があることがわかる（β 値＝ 0.416, t 値＝ 3.603, P 値＝ 0.001**）。回帰分析の結果から，中国日系サービス企業において，内部環境は外部環境に対して部分的に影響力があることがわかった。

図表 7-11 の結果から，外部環境に対する内部環境の重判定係数（R^2）は 0.263 で，これは内部環境が外部環境の 26.3% を説明できることを表している。また，標準化回帰係数によりわずかに内部環境は外部環境に対して影響力があることがわかる（β 値＝ 0.513, t 値＝ 3.215, P 値＝ 0.003**）。回帰分析の結果から，台湾日系サービス企業において，内部環境は外部環境に対して部分的に影響力があることがわかった。

図表 7-10　中国日系サービス企業において内部環境が外部環境に与える影響力分析表（係数 [a]）

モデル	標準化されていない係数		標準化係数	t 値	P 値
	B	標準偏差誤差	β 値		
1　（定数）	1.554	.604		2.572	.013
内部環境総合	.601	.167	.416	3.603	.001

a. 従属変数：外部環境総合
F 値＝ 12.978**
R^2 値＝ 0.173
注：**p<.01
（出所）筆者作成。

図表 7-11　台湾日系サービス企業において内部環境が外部環境に与える影響力分析表（係数[a]）

モデル	標準化されていない係数		標準化係数	t 値	P 値
	B	標準偏差誤差	β値		
1　（定数）	2.324	.447		5.198	.000
内部環境総合	.430	.134	.513	3.215	.003

a. 従属変数：外部環境総合
F 値＝ 10.335**
R^2 値＝ 0.263
注：**p<.01
（出所）筆者作成。

②内部環境が経営成果に与える影響力分析

本研究では，研究仮説に基づき，重回帰分析を通して強制投入法で回帰方程式モデルを作り上げた。内部環境を予測変数とし，経営成果を従属変数として回帰分析を行った。

図表 7-12 の結果から，経営成果に対する内部環境の重判定係数(R^2)は 0.422 で，これは内部環境が経営成果の 42.2％を説明できることを表している。また，標準化回帰係数により，わずかに内部環境は経営成果に対して影響力があることがわかる（β値＝ 0.650, t 値＝ 6.621, P 値＝ 0.000***）。回帰分析の結果から，中国日系サービス企業において，内部環境は経営成果に対して影響力があることがわかった。

図表 7-13 の結果から，経営成果に対する内部環境の重判定係数(R^2)は 0.241 で，これは内部環境が経営成果の 24.1％を説明できることを表している。また，標準化回帰係数により，わずかに内部環境は経営成果に対して影響力があることがわかる（β値＝ 0.491, t 値＝ 3.038, P 値＝ 0.005**）。回帰分析の結果から，台湾日系サービス企業において，内部環境は経営成果に対して部分的に影響力があることがわかった。

図表 7-12 中国日系サービス企業において内部環境が経営成果に与える影響力分析表（係数 [a]）

モデル	標準化されていない係数		標準化係数	t 値	P 値
	B	標準偏差誤差	β 値		
1 （定数）	.674	.437		1.541	.129
内部環境総合	.798	.121	.650	6.621	.000

a. 従属変数：経営成果総合
F 値＝ 43.834***
R^2 値＝ 0.422
注：***p<.001
（出所）筆者作成。

図表 7-13 台湾日系サービス企業において内部環境が経営成果に与える影響力分析表（係数 [a]）

モデル	標準化されていない係数		標準化係数	t 値	P 値
	B	標準偏差誤差	β 値		
1 （定数）	2.433	.476		5.107	.000
内部環境総合	.433	.143	.491	3.038	.005

a. 従属変数：経営成果総合
F 値＝ 9.227**
R^2 値＝ 0.241
注：**p<.01
（出所）筆者作成。

③外部環境が経営成果に与える影響力分析

本研究では，研究仮説に基づき，重回帰分析を通して強制投入法で回帰方程式モデルを作り上げた。外部環境を予測変数とし，経営成果を従属変数として回帰分析を行った。

図表 7-14 の結果から，経営成果に対する外部環境の重判定係数（R^2）は 0.247 で，これは外部環境が経営成果の 24.7％を説明できることを表している。また，標準化回帰係数により，わずかに外部環境は経営成果に対して影響力があることがわかる（β値＝ 0.497，t 値＝ 4.470，P 値＝ 0.000***）。回帰分析の結果から，中国日系サービス企業において，外部環境は経営成果に対して影響力があることがわかった。

図表 7-15 の結果から，経営成果に対する外部環境の重判定係数（R^2）は 0.313 で，これは外部環境が経営成果の 31.3％を説明できることを表している。また，

標準化回帰係数により,わずかに外部環境は経営成果に対して影響力があることがわかる(β値＝0.560, t値＝3.638, P値＝0.001**)。回帰分析の結果から,台湾日系サービス企業において,外部環境は経営成果に対して部分的に影響があることがわかった。

図表7-14　中国日系サービス企業において外部環境が経営成果に与える影響力分析表(係数[a])

モデル	標準化されていない係数		標準化係数	t 値	P 値
	B	標準偏差誤差	β値		
1　(定数)	2.034	.344		5.919	.000
外部環境総合	.410	.092	.497	4.470	.000

a. 従属変数:経営成果総合
F値＝19.984***
R^2値＝0.247
注:***p<.001
(出所)筆者作成。

図表7-15　台湾日系サービス企業において外部環境が経営成果に与える影響力分析表(係数[a])

モデル	標準化されていない係数		標準化係数	t 値	P 値
	B	標準偏差誤差	β値		
1　(定数)	1.660	.609		2.725	.011
外部環境総合	.588	.162	.560	3.638	.001

a. 従属変数:経営成果総合
F値＝13.235
R^2値＝0.313
注:**p<.01
(出所)筆者作成。

④経営成果がマーケティング戦略に与える影響力分析

本研究では,研究仮説に基づき,重回帰分析を通して強制投入法で回帰方程式モデルを作り上げた。経営成果を予測変数とし,マーケティング戦略を従属変数として回帰分析を行った。

図表7-16の結果から,マーケティング戦略に対する経営成果の重判定係数(R^2)は0.096で,これは経営成果がマーケティング戦略の9.6%を説明できることを表している。また,標準化回帰係数により,わずかに経営成果はマーケティング戦略に対して影響力があることがわかる(β値＝0.310, t値＝2.549, P値＝0.013*)。回帰分析の結果から,中国日系サービス企業において,経営成

果はマーケティング戦略に対して部分的に影響力があることがわかった。

図表 7-17 の結果から，マーケティング戦略に対する経営成果の重判定係数（R^2）は 0.184 で，これは経営成果がマーケティング戦略の 18.4％を説明できることを表している。また，標準化回帰係数により，わずかに経営成果はマーケティング戦略に対して影響力があることがわかる（β値= 0.429, t 値= 2.556, P 値= 0.016*）。回帰分析の結果から，台湾日系サービス企業において，経営成果はマーケティング戦略に対して部分的に影響力があることがわかった。

図表 7-16　中国日系サービス企業において経営成果がマーケティング戦略に与える影響力分析表（係数 [a]）

モデル	標準化されていない係数		標準化係数	t 値	P 値
	B	標準偏差誤差	β値		
1　（定数）	2.186	.713		3.067	.003
経営成果総合	.507	.199	.310	2.549	.013

a. 従属変数：マーケティング戦略総合
F 値= 6.498**
R^2 値= 0.096
注：*p<.05
（出所）筆者作成。

図表 7-17　台湾日系サービス企業において経営成果がマーケティング戦略に与える影響力分析表（係数 [a]）

モデル	標準化されていない係数		標準化係数	t 値	P 値
	B	標準偏差誤差	β値		
1　（定数）	1.496	.822		1.821	.079
経営成果総合	.540	.211	.429	2.556	.016

a. 従属変数：マーケティング戦略総合
F 値= 6.534**
R^2 値= 0.184
注：*p<.05
（出所）筆者作成。

(6) 仮説検証の結果と考察

仮説検証の結果を整理すると，次のようになる。ここで中国とは中国日系サービス企業を，台湾とは台湾日系サービス企業を指している。在中・台の日系サービス業ではともに仮説 2，仮説 4，仮説 6 および仮説 8 は支持されたが，在中・台の日系サービス業の調査結果を総合すると，仮説 1，仮説 3，仮説 5 および

仮説7は部分的に支持された。中国も台湾も同じ日系サービス企業であることから，仮説検証の結果はかなり似通っている。

しかし，中国と台湾の結果には相違点もある。仮説3は中国では支持され，台湾では部分的に支持された。また，仮説5は中国で支持され，台湾では部分的に支持された。これらの差異が生じた原因として，中国と台湾の間では資本金や従業員数などの企業規模が異なることを挙げることができる。つまり，企業規模が大きいほど経営成果は内部環境や外部環境から影響を受けやすいことが考えられる。台湾は中国よりも資本金や従業員数などの企業規模が相対的に小さいために，経営成果が内部環境や外部環境から受ける影響が相対的に小さいことが考えられる。

	中国	台湾
H1：内部環境は外部環境に顕著な影響を与える。	△	△
H2：内部環境と外部環境には明らかな相関関係がある。	○	○
H3：内部環境は経営成果に顕著な影響を与える。	○	△
H4：内部環境と経営成果には明らかな相関関係がある。	○	○
H5：外部環境は経営成果に顕著な影響を与える。	○	△
H6：外部環境と経営成果には明らかな相関関係がある。	○	○
H7：経営成果はマーケティング戦略に顕著な影響を与える。	△	△
H8：経営成果とマーケティング戦略には明らかな相関関係がある。	○	○

(注) ○：成立，△：部分成立，×：不成立

6. 結び

中国と台湾の日系企業に関する研究の多くは，製造企業を対象にしたものがほとんどで，在中・台の日系サービス企業のマーケティング戦略への影響要因を定量的に比較分析した研究はほとんどなかった。そこで，本稿では在中・台の日系サービス企業を対象としてアンケート調査を行い，在中・台の日系サービス企業のマーケティング戦略への影響要因を解明するために，①内部環境，②外部環境，③経営成果及び④マーケティング戦略という4つの変数間の関係と影響を定量的に比較分析した。

ピアソンの相関分析の結果，在中・台の日系サービス企業では共に①内部環境と外部環境との間に，②内部環境と経営成果との間に，③外部環境と経営成果との間に及び④経営成果とマーケティング戦略との間に，正の相関関係があることが判明した。

　影響力分析の結果，在中・台の日系サービス業の調査結果を総合すると，①内部環境が外部環境に対して，②内部環境が経営成果に対して，③外部環境が経営成果に対しておよび④経営成果がマーケティング戦略に対して，部分的に影響を与えることが判明した。

　本稿では，在中・台の日系サービス企業を対象として，マーケティング戦略への影響要因を解明するために，①内部環境，②外部環境，③経営成果および④マーケティング戦略という4つの変数間の関係と影響を比較分析したが，企業属性の相違がこれらの変数間の関係と影響に差異を生じさせる可能性がある。

　そこで，今後企業属性を含めたより包括的な分析モデルと仮説を作り，分析してみたいと考えている。

【引用文献】

(1) 川井伸一（1995），「中国企業調査記録（6）」『経営総合科学』65号，pp.103～115。
(2) 廣瀬俊（2011），「国際人的資源管理と日系企業の台湾活用に関する研究」『日本大学大学院総合社会情報研究科紀要』11巻，pp.173～181。
(3) 鈴木滋（1994），「台湾における日系企業の経営」『大阪経大論叢』45巻（4），pp.49～70。

【参考文献】

［1］Cuieford, J.P.(1965), *Fundamental Statistics in Psychology and Education* 4th ed., McGraw Hill, NY.
［2］呉明隆（2008），『SPSS操作興応用問卷統計分析実務』台北，五南。

（國﨑歩）

第8章　中国日系小売企業の経営現地化の重視度※
——中国日系自動車部品製造企業との比較——

【要旨】

　中国日系小売企業の経営現地化の重視度に関する分析から，①「経営戦略」として「現地型（現地市場志向戦略）」をとる中国日系小売企業は経営現地化の重視度が最も高い，②「進出形態」として合弁形態をとる中国日系小売企業は経営現地化の重視度が最も高い，③中国日系小売企業は中国日系自動車部品製造企業よりも経営現地化の重視度がやや高い，などが判明した。これらの結果は，「経営戦略」「進出形態」「業種」などが経営現地化の重視度に影響を及ぼす要因であることを示唆している。従来の研究は中国日系企業の経営現地化への影響要因として「経営戦略」「進出形態」「業種」などを挙げる研究は非常に少なかったが，本研究の結果は中国日系企業の経営現地化への影響要因として「経営戦略」「進出形態」「業種」などが重要であることを示唆している。

【キーワード】：中国日系小売企業，経営現地化，経営戦略，進出形態，業種

1．はじめに

　海外の日系企業は，投資受入国からみれば外国企業である。海外の日系企業が外国企業の性格を弱め，投資受入国の企業の性格を強めることを現地化と呼んでいる[1]。一般に経営現地化という場合には，人（特に幹部），モノ，カネ，販売市場，研究開発などの現地化が含まれる。これまで海外の日系企業は人（特に幹部），モノ，カネなどの経営現地化をかなり進めてきたが，販売市場，研

究開発などの経営現地化についてはかなり遅れていると言われてきた。

　日本企業の有望な直接投資先として中国が挙げられるようになってから既に久しい。しかし，中国日系企業の経営現地化に関する先行研究は意外に少なく，しかもこれまでの先行研究には幾つかの問題点がある。本章の目的は筆者が行った中国日系小売企業と中国日系自動車部品製造企業を対象としたアンケート調査に基づいて，まず中国日系小売企業の経営現地化の重視度について進出形態別分析を行うことによって，合弁や独資といった進出形態による差異を明らかにし，つぎに中国日系小売企業の経営現地化の重視度について経営戦略別分析を行うことによって，「現地市場志向戦略」「現地市場＋海外市場志向戦略」「グローバル市場志向戦略」などの経営戦略のタイプによる差異を明らかにし，さらに中国日系小売企業と中国日系自動車部品製造企業の経営現地化の重視度について業種別比較分析を行うことによって，業種による差異を明らかにすることにある。

　2001年に中国はWTOへの加盟を契機として外資流通業へ門戸を開放した。外資流通業は沿海地区に集中的に進出したために，すでに沿海地区では外資流通業は過当競争に陥り，最近では外資流通業は成長が著しい東北地区や内陸地区への進出を加速させている。日本小売企業にも概ね同じような投資行動が見られる。これから中国の東北地区や内陸地区に進出する日本の小売企業はますます増加することが予想される。

　しかし，これまで日本小売企業の中国への進出企業数がまだ80社程度で少ないこともあり，中国日系小売企業に関する定量的研究は驚くべきことに本格的な研究がなかった[注-1]。本研究の結果は，中国への進出を計画している日本小売企業に対して経営現地化の面で実践的インプリケーションを与えるであろう。

2.　中国日系企業の経営現地化に関する先行研究とその問題点

(1) 原口俊道の研究（「日系企業の現地化―中国とフィリピンの日系企業の分析―」『経営管理と国際経営』同文舘，1999年6月）[2]

　この研究は中国日系企業とフィリピン日系企業を対象として現地化の現状に

ついてアンケート調査し，両者の結果を比較分析している。中国日系企業の調査は1996年に行われ，195社にエアメールを使ってアンケートを郵送し，41社からこれを回収した（回収率は21％）。フィリピン日系企業の調査は1997年に同様の方法で行われ，148社にアンケートを郵送し，37社からこれを回収した（回収率は25％）。日系企業の現地化の現状に関するこれら2つの調査から，原口俊道は①日系企業は社長の現地化には消極的である，②日系企業は経営幹部の現地化には必ずしも積極的でない，③現地人幹部の要件として，「実務能力」や「人柄」が重視されている，④現地人幹部は重要な意思決定に参加する機会が増えている，などが判明したと述べている。原口の研究は日本において中国日系企業の経営現地化を定量的に研究した最初の事例である。

（2） 関満博らの研究（『現地化する中国進出日本企業』新評論，2003年9月）[3]

　関満博らは「進出企業の現地化は，中国での事業展開の成否を決定づける重要なポイントであり，『現地』に対するもう一歩の踏み込みが求められている」[4]と述べている。関満博らは日本企業の中国事業展開に関わる現地化問題を，①経営戦略，②生産・調達，③研究開発，④ヒトの現地化と人材戦略などの側面に分けて考察している。関らの研究は2次的な資料や事例研究に依拠して中国日系企業の経営現地化を分析した定性的研究である。

（3） 古田秋太郎の研究（『中国における日系企業の経営現地化』税務経理協会，2004年4月）[5]

　古田秋太郎は「在中日系企業は，目下，中国国内市場販売重視という新事業戦略展開のために，経営方式変革に取り組まざるを得なくなっている[6]」と述べている。古田は中国内販事業で最大の激戦区である上海地区や江蘇省に進出している日本企業の本社100社と中国子会社135社を対象として，経営現地化に関するアンケート調査を行った。本社から38社（回収率は38％），中国子会社から40社（回収率は29.6％）の回答が寄せられた。本社の回答を分析した結果，①中国子会社への経営現地化政策の導入が徐々に進められているこ

と，②中国子会社への本社のコントロールも徐々に弱められていること，などが判明した。また，中国子会社の回答を分析した結果，中国子会社は現地での競争激化の中で，経営現地化志向がさらに高いことが判明した。古田の研究は中国全土の日系企業を対象とした研究でないので，分析結果を一般化できないことは留意すべきである。古田の研究も中国日系企業の経営現地化を定量的に研究した事例である。

(4) 喬晋建の研究（「中国における日系企業の経営現地化」唐海燕・原口俊道・黄一修『中日対照 経済のグローバル化と企業戦略』中国立信会計出版社，2006年9月）[7]

喬晋建は，「経営現地化という問題は，企業の経営活動のすべての側面に関わりを持ち，多岐にわたる奥深い問題である[8]」と述べている。喬は中国日系企業における経営現地化の問題を①研究開発，②資材調達，③販売市場，④人的資源という4つの側面に限定して分析している。喬は結論として，①全体的な状況として，日系企業の経営現地化は遅れている，②研究開発，資材調達，販売市場に関して，全力を尽くすように本格的な現地化を早急に推し進めていく必要がある，③ヒトの現地化について，ブルーカラーを対象とする労務管理の現地化が非常に進んでいるのに対して，ホワイトカラーを対象とする人事管理の現地化があまり進んでいない，などと主張している[9]。喬の研究は中国日系企業の経営現地化を分析した定性的研究である。

(5) 原口俊道・戦俊の研究（「中国における日系自動車部品製造企業の経営現地化に関する現状分析――アンケート調査を中心として――」原口俊道・劉成基主編『東亜産業発展與企業管理（中文繁体字）』台湾暉翔興業出版，2009年9月）[10]

原口俊道と戦俊は，中国日系自動車部品製造企業を対象としたアンケート調査に基づいて，中国日系自動車部品製造企業の経営現地化に関する進出形態別分析を行い，合弁や独資といった進出形態による差異を明らかにし，その差異の原因を分析した。全体としてみれば，中国日系自動車部品製造企業は経営現地化についてあまり熱心ではない。合弁と独資の結果を比較すると，経営現地

化については，合弁のほうが独資よりもやや熱心である。逆に，独資は合弁よりも経営現地化にやや熱心ではない。原口と戦はこのような差異をもたらした原因として，①経営現地化への要求が合弁と独資では異なること，②合弁と独資の経営戦略が異なること，③合弁と独資の原材料・部品の現地調達比率が異なること，などを挙げている[11]。原口と戦は結論として，従来の研究は中国日系企業の経営現地化への影響要因として「進出形態」や「経営戦略」を挙げるものは皆無であったが，本研究の結果は経営現地化への影響要因として「進出形態」や「経営戦略」の重要性を示唆していると主張している[12]。原口と戦の研究は中国日系企業の経営現地化を分析した定量的研究である。

(6) 5つの先行研究の問題点

以上，中国日系企業の経営現地化に関する5つの先行研究を紹介した。これらの先行研究を概観してみて気づいたことは，中国日系企業の経営現地化への影響要因を明らかにした研究が非常に少ないために，どのような要因が中国日系企業の経営現地化に影響を及ぼしているかがまだ十分に解明されていないことである。

本章は，この問題点を解明するために，中国日系小売企業と中国日系自動車部品製造企業を対象として実施した筆者のアンケート調査によって分析を行う。以下では，まず中国日系小売企業の経営現地化の実態を明らかにし，つぎに中国日系小売企業の経営現地化の重視度に関する分析を行う。

3. 中国日系小売企業の経営現地化の実態

(1) 調査の方法

筆者は2010年11月に中国日系小売企業77社を対象としてエアメールを使ってアンケートを郵送し，20社からこれを回収した（回収率は26.0%）（図表8-1）[注-2]。アンケートを回収した20社の内訳は合弁が9社，独資が11社である。なお，筆者はこの調査に先立って2008年8月に中国日系自動車部品

製造企業197社を対象としてエアメールを使ってアンケートを郵送し，59社からこれを回収した（回収率は29.9%）。アンケートを回収した59社の内訳は合弁が21社，独資が38社である。以下では，両者の調査結果を比較する。

図表8-1　アンケートの回収状況

(単位：企業数・%)

中国日系企業	調査時期	配布数	回収数	回収率
日系小売企業	2010年11月	77	20	26.0
日系自動車部品製造企業	2008年8月	197	59	29.9

(注) アンケートの配布先は，日本人派遣社員のいる中国日系企業である。

(2) 最も進めている経営現地化の側面

最も進めている経営現地化の側面は全体では「人（特に幹部）の現地化」であり，6割を占めている（図表8-2）。ついで「商品開発の現地化」が15.0%を占めている。合弁も独資も「人（特に幹部）の現地化」を最も進めている。合弁は独資よりも「人（特に幹部）の現地化」を進めており，独資は合弁よりも「販売市場の現地化」を進めている。日系小売企業は日系自動車部品製造企業よりも「人（特に幹部）の現地化」と「モノの現地化」が少ない。これは「商品開発の現地化」が15.0%を占めていることが影響している。

図表8-2　最も進めている経営現地化の側面

(単位：%)

	中国日系小売企業			中国日系自動車部品製造企業
	合弁 n=9	独資 n=11	全体 n=20	全体 n=59
商品開発の現地化／研究開発の現地化	11.1	18.2	15.0	1.7
モノの現地化	0.0	9.1	5.0	20.3
販売市場の現地化	0.0	18.2	10.0	8.5
人（特に幹部）の現地化	66.7	54.5	60.0	69.5
その他	11.1	0.0	5.0	0.0
無回答	11.1	0.0	5.0	0.0

(注1) 商品開発の現地化は日系小売企業の選択肢，研究開発の現地化は日系自動車部品製造企業の選択肢を示す。
(出所) 筆者作成。

(3) 社長の現地化

①海外子会社の社長（図表8-3）

海外子会社の社長については，全体では「社長として適任であるかが重要」という回答が60.0%，「日本人のほうがよい」が25.0％を占めている。注目すべきことは，海外子会社の社長については，合弁も独資も「日本人のほうがよい」という回答が第2位であり，「現地人がよい」という回答が第3位を占めていることである。これは，合弁も独資も日本人が総経理を務める割合が高いことが影響していると考えられる。しかし，日系小売企業は日系自動車部品製造企業よりも「日本人のほうがよい」という回答が少なく，「現地人のほうがよい」という回答が多い。つまり，業種により海外子会社の社長に差異がみられる。

②現地人社長の長所（図表8-3）

現地人社長の長所については，全体では「現地社会との関係がうまくいく」という回答が6割を占め，最も多い。独資は合弁よりも「現地社会との関係がうまくいく」という回答が多く，合弁は独資よりも「現地従業員のモラールが上がる」という回答が多い。これは，予想された通りである。日系小売企業は日系自動車部品製造企業よりも「現地社会との関係がうまくいく」という回答が多く，「現地従業員のモラールが上がる」という回答が少ない。つまり，業種により現地人社長の長所に差異がみられる。

③現地人社長の短所（図表8-3）

現地人社長の短所については，全体では「日本の親会社の方針や戦略に従わないことがある」という回答が6割を占め，最も多い。ついで多いのは「日本人出向社員との関係に問題が生じる」という回答である。注目すべきは，合弁は独資よりも「日本の親会社の方針や戦略に従わないことがある」という回答が多いことである。これは，合弁企業の総経理には日本人が多いことが影響している。日系小売企業は日系自動車部品製造企業よりも「日本の親会社の方針や戦略に従わないことがある」「日本人出向社員との関係に問題が生じる」などの回答が多い。つまり，業種によって差異がみられる。

図表 8-3　社長の現地化

(単位：％)

	中国日系小売企業			中国日系自動車部品製造企業
	合弁 n=9	独資 n=11	全体 n=20	全体 n=59
海外子会社の社長				
日本人のほうがよい	33.3	18.2	25.0	42.4
現地人のほうがよい	22.2	9.1	15.0	0.0
社長として適任であるかが重要	44.4	72.7	60.0	55.9
その他	0.0	0.0	0.0	0.0
無回答	0.0	0.0	0.0	1.7
現地人社長の長所				
業績がよくなる	11.1	0.0	5.0	3.4
現地従業員のモラールが上がる	22.2	0.0	10.0	27.1
現地社会との関係がうまくいく	33.3	81.8	60.0	27.1
現地政府との関係がうまくいく	11.1	9.1	10.0	16.9
現地化を進めているとのイメージができる	11.1	9.1	10.0	10.2
その他	0.0	0.0	0.0	6.8
無回答	11.1	0.0	5.0	8.5
現地人社長の短所				
業績が悪くなる	0.0	0.0	0.0	3.4
日本の親会社との関係がうまくいかない	11.1	9.1	10.0	27.1
日本人出向社員との関係に問題が生じる	11.1	36.4	25.0	11.9
日本の親会社の方針や戦略に従わないことがある	77.8	45.5	60.0	30.5
現地人の従業員のモラールが下がる	0.0	9.1	5.0	3.4
その他	0.0	0.0	0.0	13.6
無回答	0.0	0.0	0.0	10.2

(出所)　筆者作成。

(4) 経営幹部の現地化

①幹部の現地化が困難な理由 (図表 8-4)

　幹部の現地化が困難な理由として, 全体では「日本企業は人的コントロールへの依存度が高いことからある程度の人数の日本人出向社員が必要なため」「能力のある現地人が少ないから」などの回答が多い。合弁では「能力のある現地

人が少ないから」という回答が最も多く，独資では「日本企業は人的コントロールへの依存度が高いことからある程度の人数の日本人出向社員が必要なため」という回答が最も多い。つまり，進出形態によって差異がみられる。日系小売企業と日系自動車部品製造企業との間には第1位と第2位の回答項目が同じであり，差が少ない。

図表8-4 経営幹部の現地化

(単位：％)

	中国日系小売企業			中国日系自動車部品製造企業
	合弁 n=9	独資 n=11	全体 n=20	全体 n=59
幹部の現地化が困難な理由（2つ以内回答）				
日本企業は人的コントロールへの依存度が高いことからある程度の人数の日本人出向社員が必要なため	44.4	45.5	45.0	49.2
日本語の特殊性のため	0.0	9.1	5.0	20.3
給与が比較的低いと思われることから優秀な現地人を確保するのが難しいから	22.2	27.3	25.0	25.4
現地人にとって日本的経営より現地的経営のほうが好まれるから	33.3	27.3	30.0	13.6
能力のある現地人が少ないから	55.6	18.2	35.0	45.8
その他	11.1	27.3	20.0	5.1
現地人幹部の問題点（3つ以内回答）				
愛社心が不足	55.6	9.1	30.0	23.7
個人プレーが多い	22.2	36.4	30.0	42.4
日本の親会社の方針や戦略に従わない	22.2	18.2	20.0	1.7
日本理解が不足	0.0	63.6	35.0	13.6
仕事が残っていても残業しないで家に帰る	22.2	9.1	15.0	22.0
給与が高すぎる	0.0	0.0	0.0	3.4
仕事の能力が不十分	22.2	36.4	30.0	57.6
日本人出向社員との関係がよくない	0.0	0.0	0.0	1.7
日本の親会社との関係がよくない	11.1	0.0	5.0	0.0
モラールが低い	33.3	9.1	20.0	23.7
いつ辞めるか不安がある	33.3	45.5	40.0	50.8
人柄に問題がある	0.0	9.1	5.0	5.1
その他	0.0	9.1	5.0	6.8

現地人幹部の要件（2つ以内回答）				
日本語能力	11.1	0.0	5.0	23.7
日本理解	0.0	36.4	20.0	13.6
実務能力	66.7	63.6	65.0	78.0
人柄（信頼できるなど）	77.8	81.8	80.0	55.9
愛社心	22.2	9.1	15.0	23.7
その他	11.1	0.0	5.0	1.7
現地人幹部登用の成功に必要な準備（2つ以内回答）				
日本の親会社の経営理念及び方針を現地人の幹部候補に理解させること	77.8	54.5	65.0	37.3
職責と業績評価の明確化	55.6	54.5	55.0	52.5
有利な給与体系の整備	22.2	18.2	20.0	10.2
現地人管理者に日本語を知ってもらうこと	11.1	9.1	10.0	5.1
日本の親会社での研修	0.0	27.3	15.0	20.3
優秀な現地人の採用	33.3	18.2	25.0	50.8
日本的経営でなく現地的経営を実施すること	0.0	9.1	5.0	3.4
その他	0.0	0.0	0.0	3.4

（出所）筆者作成。

②現地人幹部の問題点（図表8-4）

現地人幹部の問題点として，全体では「いつ辞めるか不安がある」「日本理解が不足」などの回答が多い。合弁では「愛社心が不足」，独資では「日本理解が不足」という回答が最も多い。つまり，進出形態によって差異がみられる。日系小売企業では「いつ辞めるか不安がある」という回答が最も多く，日系自動車部品製造企業では「仕事の能力が不十分」という回答が最も多い。つまり，業種によって差異がみられる。

③現地人幹部の要件（図表8-4）

現地人幹部の要件として，全体では「人柄（信頼できるなど）」「実務能力」などの回答が多い。合弁と独資の間には大差がない。しかし，日系小売企業では「人柄（信頼できるなど）」という回答が最も多く，日系自動車部品製造企業では「実務能力」という回答が最も多い。つまり，業種によって差異がみられる。

④現地人幹部登用の成功に必要な準備（図表8-4）

現地人幹部登用の成功に必要な準備として，全体では「日本の親会社の経営

理念及び方針を現地人の幹部候補に理解させること」「職責と業績評価の明確化」などの回答が多い。現地人幹部登用の成功に必要な準備については，合弁と独資の間に大差がない。しかし，日系小売企業では「日本の親会社の経営理念及び方針を現地人の幹部候補に理解させること」という回答が最も多く，日系自動車部品製造企業では「職責と業績評価の明確化」という回答が最も多い。つまり，業種によって差異がみられる。

4. 中国日系小売企業の経営現地化の重視度

中国日系小売企業20社がとる経営戦略の内訳は「現海型（現地市場＋海外市場志向戦略）」が10社，「現地型（現地市場志向戦略）」が7社，「グロ型（グローバル市場志向戦略）」が3社である。図表8-5に示すように，「経営戦略」として「現地型（現地市場志向戦略）」をとる企業は経営現地化の重視度が最も高い。この結果は，「経営戦略」が経営現地化の重視度に影響を及ぼす要因であることを示唆している。

図表8-5 経営現地化の重視度

(単位：平均値)

	中国日系小売企業				中国日系自動車部品製造企業
	グロ型 n＝3	現海型 n＝10	現地型 n＝7	全体 n＝20	全体 n＝59
経営現地化の重視	4.0	3.5	4.3	3.9	3.5

(注1) グローバル市場志向戦略を「グロ型」，現地市場＋海外市場志向戦略を「現海型」，現地市場志向戦略を「現地型」と略記する。

また，図表8-6に示すように，「進出形態」として合弁形態をとる企業は経営現地化の重視度が最も高い。この結果は，「進出形態」が経営現地化の重視度に影響を及ぼす要因であることを示唆している。一般に経営現地化への要求が合弁企業と独資企業とでは異なるために，合弁企業は独資企業よりも経営現地化にやや熱心であるという傾向が見受けられる。中国日系小売企業の結果は

こうした傾向と符合している。

図表 8-6　経営現地化の重視度

(単位：平均値)

	中国日系小売企業			中国日系自動車部品製造企業
	合弁 n = 9	独資 n=11	全体 n=20	全体 n = 59
経営現地化の重視度	4.1	3.7	3.9	3.5

(出所) 筆者作成。

さらに，図表8-6に示すように，中国日系小売企業は中国日系自動車部品製造企業よりも経営現地化の重視度がやや高い。この結果は，「業種」が経営現地化の重視度に影響を及ぼす要因であることを示唆している。これは，「業種」によって経営現地化の必要度が異なることに起因している。現地市場での販売が多い中国日系小売企業のような業種の場合には，当然経営現地化の必要度が高くなる。

5. 結び

中国日系小売企業の経営現地化の重視度に関する分析から，①「経営戦略」として「現地型（現地市場志向戦略）」をとる中国日系小売企業は経営現地化の重視度が最も高い，②「進出形態」として合弁形態をとる中国日系小売企業は経営現地化の重視度が最も高い，③中国日系小売企業は中国日系自動車部品製造企業よりも経営現地化の重視度がやや高い，などが判明した。これらの結果は，「経営戦略」「進出形態」「業種」などが経営現地化の重視度に影響を及ぼす要因であることを示唆している。

従来の研究は中国日系企業の経営現地化への影響要因として「経営戦略」「進出形態」「業種」などを挙げる研究は非常に少なかったが，本研究の結果は中国日系企業の経営現地化への影響要因として「経営戦略」「進出形態」「業種」などが重要であることを示唆している。

【注釈】

(注 -1) 最近の筆者の中国日系企業に関する研究にはつぎのような研究がある。

原口俊道（2007），「第2章中国日系電機製造企業の競争戦略と競争優位――タイ日系電機製造企業との比較――」原口俊道『アジアの経営戦略と日系企業』学文社，pp.33 〜 54。

原口俊道（2008），「日本的経営の中国日系繊維製造企業への移植――中国日系電機製造企業との比較」鹿児島国際大学経済学部学会『鹿児島経済論集』第49巻第1号，pp.125 〜 166。

なお，現在までのところ，中国日系小売企業を対象とした本格的なアンケート調査は筆者が調べた範囲内ではまだ見つからない。

(注 -2) 筆者は日系企業の経営現地化に関するアンケート調査票を作成するに当たっては，参考引献［1］の吉原英樹の著書に示されているアンケート調査の内容を参考にさせていただいた。記して謝意を表する次第である。

【引用文献】

(1) 吉原英樹（1996），『未熟な国際経営』白桃書房，p.3。
(2) 原口俊道（1999），『経営管理と国際経営』同文舘出版，pp.221 〜 232。
(3) 関満博・範建亭編（2003），『現地化する中国進出日本企業』新評論。
(4) 同前書，p.215。
(5) 古田秋太郎（2004），『中国における日系企業の経営現地化』税務経理協会。
(6) 同前書，p.4。
(7) 喬晋建（2006），「中国における日系企業の経営現地化」唐海燕・原口俊道・黄一修主編『中日対照 経済のグローバル化と企業戦略』中国・立信会計出版社，pp.393 〜 412。
(8) 同前書，p.393。
(9) 同前書，pp.410 〜 411。
(10) 原口俊道・戦俊（2009），「中国における日系自動車部品製造企業の経営現地化に関する現状分析――アンケート調査を中心として――」原口俊道・劉成基主編『東亜産業発展與企業管理（中文繁体字）』台湾・暉翔興業出版，pp.224 〜 234。
(11) 同前書，p.233。
(12) 同前書，p.233。

【参考文献】

［1］吉原英樹（1996），『未熟な国際経営』白桃書房。
［2］石田英夫（1985），『日本企業の国際人事管理』日本労働協会。
［3］片岡信之・三島倫八編（1997），『アジア日系企業における異文化コミュニケーション』文眞堂。
［4］島田晴雄・本田敬吉編（1991），『国際経営と異文化コミュニケーション』東洋経済新報社。

[5] 吉原英樹 (1997),『国際経営』有斐閣。
[6] 吉原英樹編 (1992),『日本企業の国際経営』同文舘出版。
[7] 原口俊道 (1999),『経営管理と国際経営』同文舘出版。
[8] 蘇勇・原口俊道他主編 (2004),『企業国際経営策略 (中文)』中国復旦大学出版社。
[9] 原口俊道 (2007),『アジアの経営戦略と日系企業』学文社。
[10] 関満博・範建亭編 (2003),『現地化する中国進出日本企業』新評論。
[11] 古田秋太郎 (2004),『中国における日系企業の経営現地化』税務経理協会。
[12] 唐海燕・原口俊道・黄一修主編 (2006),『中日対照 経済のグローバル化と企業戦略』中国・立信会計出版社。
[13] 原口俊道・戦俊 (2009),「中国における日系自動車部品製造企業の経営現地化に関する現状分析――アンケート調査を中心として――」原口俊道・劉成基主編『東亜産業発展與企業管理 (中文繁体字)』台湾・暉翔興業出版。
[14] 芮明杰・原口俊道・王明元主編 (2008),『亜洲産業発展與企業発展戦略 (中文)』中国・復旦大学出版社。
[15] 廖暁明・原口俊道主編 (2010),『東亜経済発展與社会保障問題研究 (中文)』中国・江西人民出版社。
[16] 原口俊道・劉成基主編 (2010),『亜洲産業経営管理 (中文・繁体字)』台湾・暉翔興業出版。
[17] 原口俊道・黒川和夫他編 (2011),『アジアの産業発展と企業経営戦略』五絃舎。
[18] 原口俊道・張慧珍・劉水生主編 (2011),『東亜産業與管理問題研究 (中文・繁体字)』台湾・暉翔興業出版。

※付記：本論文はすでに中国語繁体字論文として発表済みであるが，これに大幅な修正と加筆を加え，出版社の許可を受けて日本語で発表するものである。元の中国語繁体字論文については，下記の文献を参照されたい。
亜東経済国際学会研究叢書⑬ (2011),『東亜産業與管理問題研究 (中文・日文・英文)』(台湾・暉翔興業出版), pp.165〜177。

(原口俊道)

第9章 日本の自動車生産における非常時対応について
——非常事態への対処にみる生産ネットワークと企業間信頼——(注-1)

【要旨】

　本稿は，非常時に停止した自動車生産の復旧活動に着目し，その復旧支援体制が生産ネットワークに由来するものであり，生産システムの紐帯が「企業間信頼」に基づくものであることを前提とする。非常時におけるアセンブラーやサプライヤーの協力関係について，これを一般化して捉えた場合，筆者は継続的な取引関係における情報交換の恒常性の効果（＝社会的不確実性を低下させるインセンティブ）と信頼性における結びつきの逆転（合理的信頼から関係的信頼への結びつきの強さの転移）の表出と捉える。西口が指摘したネットワークの関係性（近隣で繋がる企業と遠距離関係にある企業との紐帯）と共に，筆者が本稿で指摘した情報交換の緊密性から生じる「信頼」と平常時から非常時への「場の転換」に符号した関係性の変化は，非常時における企業組織の意思決定のあり方や行動要因の分析に有用であると考えられる。

【キーワード】：平常時，非常時，社会的不確実性，合理的信頼，関係的信頼，場の転換

1．はじめに

　日本の自動車生産はアセンブラーがサプライヤーを組織化して実施されている。代替性がないタイトな取引関係と代替性の効く緩やかな取引関係が混ざった分業生産体制であるが，筆者はその取引関係には企業間の「信頼」が，特に日本では重要な要因であると考えている。

「信頼」の概念については社会心理学分野で，山岸（1998）が整理を行っている。山岸は「自然の秩序に対する期待」とともに「道徳的（社会）秩序に対する期待」に区分し，後者について「相手が自分を搾取しないだろうとする期待」を広義の「信頼」としている。そしてこの広義の「信頼」は，相手の能力に対する期待と意図に対する期待とで構成されると説く。強調されるべき論点のひとつとして，信頼は社会的不確実性が存在している文脈でのみ重要であり，社会的不確実性を低下させるための方法として，特定の相手との安定的かつ親密なコミットメント関係（継続的相互協力関係）が形成されることを指摘している。なおコミットメント関係について，真鍋（2002）らは行動主体を企業に拡張して，信頼概念を合理的信頼と関係的信頼に区分している（後述）。

社会心理学の知見を企業行動に当てはめるならば，東日本大震災で被災したサプライヤーの工場復旧に関連会社が参集し，復旧支援を行った企業行動の理解の一助となるのではないかということである。自動車生産におけるコミットメント関係の形成のあり方は，その分業体制に起因するものであると考えられ，このような分業体制は，企業間取引における相手側に対する信頼性に依拠しているものであると判断できよう。

本稿では「信頼」概念をもとに，これまでの平常時における生産供給の分析から，分析の射程を非常時における生産活動にまで広げ，その生産支援体制が生産分業体制（生産ネットワーク形成）に由来するものであり，生産システムの紐帯が「企業間信頼」に基づくものであることを明らかにする。

2. 平常時の生産とサプライチェーン

日本の自動車産業は，アセンブラーによりサプライヤーが組織化され，いわゆる「系列」なるものが出来上がっている。その特徴は，エンジンなど基幹部品はアセンブラー自身が内製化し，それ以外の部品はサプライヤーに外注するものである。サプライヤーから供給される部品の善し悪しが，最終組み立て段階で「摺り合わせ」を行う際に大きな影響を与えることになるので，アセンブ

ラー側からすれば，サプライヤーの選別と育成は重要な問題である。アセンブラーとサプライヤーの部品取引に着目すると，情報の非対称性を少なくするべく，両者は一定の関係をもちながら継続的な取引を成立させている。大雑把に分類すれば，アセンブラーと1次サプライヤーとの取引は「承認図」方式により，下層のサプライヤーとの関係は「貸与図」方式により部品が生産され，構成部品が供給される傾向がある。

特にトヨタ自動車を筆頭に，自動車生産ではアセンブラーがなるべく在庫をもたないような生産管理が行われている。トヨタは，「カンバン」を通して生産情報の交換を行うトヨタ生産システム（TPS）を構築し，サプライヤーにも同様の生産管理を求めている（生産における同期化）。

これは，在庫をもたず，生産する分だけサプライヤーからの部品納入を同期させていくため，平常時には効率的な生産が可能となるが，事故や災害などの非常時には，在庫をもたない分，生産への影響が大きいものとなる。

そのため平常時の生産から非常事態に発展した時に，元の平常時における水準にまで，どれだけ迅速に生産を回復させることができるかが当該サプライチェーン維持の焦点となる。

アセンブラーは，生産計画に対し組立部品の供給が断絶しないように，一方の部品供給が断絶した場合に別のサプライヤーに部品を発注できるよう複数発注が可能な体制を確保しておくべきであり，個々のサプライヤーは資材の調達先の確保はもちろん，部品工場の生産ラインに支障が生じた場合は，予め復旧プランを策定しておく必要がある。これは表面的には企業毎に設定しておくべきリスク管理としての事業継続計画の範囲の話であるが，別の側面として見ると，自動車生産における生産ネットワークの中断と再開の問題として捉えられる。

3. ネットワークと企業間信頼

平常時における企業間の取引は，契約履行の確実性を判断するものとして，実績や支払能力にかかわる市場での評価を指標として考慮して締結される。スポッ

ト契約と比較すると，長期に亘る継続的な取引関係は，互いの契約履行の期待値を高めるとともに，取引相手に対する信頼関係も強化されると考えられる。

自動車産業をベースにして企業間信頼に焦点を当てた先行研究は，真鍋・延岡らによる幾つかの論文がある。真鍋・延岡らによる信頼の定義は「信頼対象が，自らにとって肯定的な役割を遂行する能力と意図に対する期待」であるとしている[1]。信頼の形成と根拠についての「源泉」を「関係特殊的」「社会普遍的」の2区分に分類し，信頼形成メカニズムを3つの特性区分（直接的・間接的・多義的）のマトリクスとして表現している。真鍋・延岡は「能力」と「意図」に着目しているが，信頼関係には，何らかの「依存関係」が伴うと仮定すれば，相手の「能力」と「意図」に関する情報を高いレベルで獲得していることが前提となる。総じて言えることは，繰返しの取引により依存関係が生じ，情報が生産され，その情報の入手の頻度が高まるとともに信頼関係も強化されることになる。

真鍋（2002）は，取引相手の市場での評判や製品の品質を基とした経済的合理性に由来する「信頼」を合理的信頼，取引相手との関係性（社会的関係性）に由来する「信頼」を関係的信頼として，下記による表のように区分している（図表9-1）。

図表 9-1　合理的信頼と関係的信頼

	背景	視野	信頼の根拠
合理的信頼	経済的合理性	短期的自己利益	市場・製品 客観的事実
関係的信頼	社会的関係性	継続的共存共栄	関係特殊性 主観的判断

（出所）真鍋（2002），p.4。

平常時の取引では，合理的信頼を前提とする一方，関係的信頼は補完的な役割が期待されているが，真鍋・延岡らの信頼区分による解釈を非常時に拡張すると，この関係が逆転すると筆者は考えている。それは，JIT（Just In Time）方式による在庫管理のあり方から説明できる。平常時の自動車生産は，カンバン方式で「ほぼ在庫ゼロ」のもとで部品供給体制が構築され，自己の利益の最

大化行動を原理として各企業間での「生産の同期化」が達成されている（経済的合理性の論理の貫徹）。ところが非常時では，生産ネットワークでコアとなる企業の生産部門が停滞（操業停止）した場合，「ほぼ在庫ゼロ」の部品供給体制がリスク要因（ボトルネック）となって顕在化する。構築された既存の分業体制は，平常時ではコスト要因でなかったが，非常時における分業生産体制（生産ネットワーク）分断の結果，ネットワーク構成員としてネットワーク全体からのリスクを負担する立場に転換することとなる。すると日ごろの経済的合理性に依拠した合理的信頼から，一転してネットワーク維持が優先されるため，関係的信頼へと結びつきの強さが転移した結果，関連企業による支援活動（利他的行動）が生起したと推察できよう。

　換言すれば，自動車産業での継続的な取引関係や系列の組織化が，企業間の接触の頻度を高め，企業間の信頼を醸成する情報生産機能を担っていたが，アセンブラーによる組織化は緩やかなものであったため，平常時における分業生産参加企業の行動基準は「関係的信頼での結びつき」より「合理的信頼関係の結びつき」の要因が強かったと考えられる。平常時から非常時への外部環境の変化に伴い「関係的信頼」＞「合理的信頼」へと転移し，生産ネットワーク復旧にかかる関連会社の個別の支援行動が生じたのではないかと推察される。これは，被災企業からの支援要請以前に支援部隊の提供の提案を行うことや，先遣隊を送り被害状況の確認とアドバイスを行うなどの支援活動は契約外の企業活動であり，「関係的信頼」に依拠したものと考えられる。

4．事故や災害等に伴う生産中止事例

　自動車生産ネットワークが危機にさらされた事例の中で，事故や災害等に伴う大きな自動車生産中止事例はいくつか挙げられる。1979年7月に東名高速道路日本坂トンネル（下り）事故で約1週間にわたり通行不能となり，部品流通に支障を来たした。1995年の阪神大震災により部品調達ができず，トヨタなど自動車工場の生産ラインが停止した。2001年9月にはアメリカで同時多

発テロが発生し，連邦航空局（FAA）はアメリカ国内の民間航空路を封鎖した。これらの措置は数日間続き規制対象はアメリカ本土のみならず，アメリカ航空管制下にあるグアムやパラオ周辺などの南太平洋の一部地域や，北大西洋の一部地域など広範囲に及んだため，海外の現地自動車生産工場での生産にも影響を与えた。

　日本国内で自動車生産が停止した初めての大きな事故としては，アイシン精機の「刈谷第一工場」で発生した火災（1997年2月）がある[注-2]。以下，アイシン精機を含む3つの事例を紹介する。

　① 1997年2月1日の午前4時過ぎ，アイシン精機刈谷第一工場（タンデムマスターシリンダー，クラッチマスターシリンダーおよびプロポーショニング・バルブを生産）で，小休憩していた従業員が戻ってきた際に，ドリルから飛び散った火花が中央ラインのプラットフォームに引火しているのを確認したが，初期対応が遅れ火災が拡大した。同日8時52分に鎮火。タバコ箱大のプロポーショニング・バルブ（Pバルブ）の製造用精密工作機械約500台が火災によりほぼ全壊状態に陥った。この高い加工精度が要求されるPバルブは，車種ごとに形状が微妙に異なる問題もあり，他工場での代替生産が難しいものであった。

　トヨタ車のPバルブは，アイシン精機のほかアイシン新和，自動車機器など複数の部品メーカーに発注していることになっていた。しかし，Pバルブはいくつかの小部品を組み合わせて作るため，組合せ部品の一部についてアイシン精機「刈谷第一工場」がほぼ独占的に製造していた。このため，JIT方式により在庫を極力持たないトヨタの工場や同製品供給先の三菱自動車工業の主力工場も操業停止となった。

　2月1日，アイシン精機はアイシングループ4社，仕入先会社22社，系列企業2社等へ遊休生産設備借用・代替生産を要請し，翌2日には，トヨタ協豊会メーカーに代替生産の即時開始を要請した。2月3日，操業不能となった第一工場の生産補充のため，他工場の生産ラインを24時間体制で稼動することなど復旧作業に向けた作業が本格化するも生産再開のめどがたたず，トヨタ

車を生産している30ラインの約7割にあたる12工場のラインが操業を停止した。これによりトヨタほか（ダイハツ工業池田工場を除く）19工場での4日の自動車生産は全面操業停止となった。

　アイシン精機が生産を再開するには，工作機械の手配と作業場所の確保に数ヶ月かかると見込まれたが，トヨタ・グループが部品の代替生産に協力した結果，トヨタは2月7日に全20工場30ラインで操業再開することができた。

　② 2007年7月16日に発生した新潟県中越沖地震でリケンの2つの工場（柏崎市）の設備が被災し，国内で高い販売シェアをもつ自動車部品のピストンリングが生産停止となった(注-3)。このため，国内の主要な自動車完成車メーカーのほとんどが生産中止に陥った。リケンの工場は，半数程度の加工設備の位置ずれ，鋳造部門でのサンドビンの破損，金型ラックの倒壊，金型・ゲージの落下，仕入先のシェル砂再生装置の倒壊などの被害を被った。

　震災翌日には，自動車メーカーなどの先遣隊が駆けつけ，加工設備の位置ずれや転倒を起こしたラインを視察し，復旧の手はずを相談している。復旧目標を1週間として，復旧のための資材と人を確保するために，自動車メーカーなどが関係業者に声をかけ復旧活動に入った。

　リケンと支援部隊とで1日3回ミーティングが行われ，作業の進捗状況など情報共有が図られ，その中で，支援部隊から量産可能の指示をもらい，生産が復旧していく。7月23日には操業を再開し，1週間後の30日には全ラインが生産復旧となる（この間2週間）。

　自動車メーカーらの支援は先遣隊の後，重機が入り，さらに保全の支援隊，最後に品質確認の支援隊が交替で入り，その人員は最大840人を数えた。8月10日ごろには支援隊は撤収した。リケン側は「今回，お客様の支援隊がいたからこそ，復旧が可能となり，その高度な技と実行力は驚嘆に値した。我々としても大きな勉強となった。特に問題の把握，方策の検討，手順の決定，実行，検証が素早く正確だった。後から，災害・地震に詳しい精鋭部隊を送っていただいたと聞いて合点がいった。」と感想を述べている。

③ 2011年3月11日に発生した東日本大震災で，東北・関東地域の自動車関連企業の工場が被災し，半導体メーカーの「ルネサス　エレクトロニクス」においても，半導体前工程工場6拠点，半導体後工程工場3拠点が生産停止に至った。被災した工場のうちルネサスの那珂工場（茨城県ひたちなか市）は半導体前工程工場で，自動車向けマイコンの生産主力工場であった。この工場は自動車向けマイコンの世界シェア4割を占め，他社への代替性が困難な製品のため，トヨタやホンダなどへの供給停止に至る。この工場の復旧のために，1997年のアイシン精機工場火災と同様に自動車メーカーなどが結集し，復旧支援を行った。

　震災の数日後，自動車業界の側からルネサンスへの支援を要請し，3月28日には技術者を那珂工場へ送っている(注-4)。

　震災以降，ルネサス・グループ，建設会社，設備会社，自動車メーカーなどからの混成部隊が24時間体制の復旧作業を行った。これはルネサス側が，要請したわけではなく，関係者が続々と集まったものであるという。その数は，4月には最大2500人/日の人員になったという。

　人海戦術によって，震災から1カ月後の4月10日にクリーン・ルームやインフラ設備が復旧し，23日には自動車向けマイコンなどを生産する200mmライン「N2棟」で試験生産が開始された(注-5)。

5.　非常時の支援と生産ネットワーク機能

　以上のように，自動車生産にかかわる生産分業体制（生産ネットワーク）が非常事態に見舞われた際に，関連企業に自生的・自然発生的に支援の動きが現れ，短期間での生産復旧に貢献している事例のいくつかを俯瞰した。ここでは，この企業間の支援行動をどのようにとらえるかについて，いくつかの既存の理論と本稿での理論的な枠組みとの比較をもとに考察する。

　第一に，事業継続計画（Business Continuity Plan：BCP）または事業継続マネ

ジメント（Business Continuity Management：BCM）の一環として，個別企業が夫々の計画に基づき活動した結果であるとする見方である。BCP は，地震や水害などの自然災害や事故が発生した際に，業務について予め目標とする復旧期間を設定し，事業再開に向けて，事前の対策と事後の行動計画，計画遂行能力を用意するものである。先の3つの事例では，関係会社が参集し連携をとりながら生産ネットワークの回復に取り組んでいる。BCP は自社の事業継続が第一であり，関連会社への支援は間接的な性格を伴うとすれば，支援部隊レベルの結集までの動きを説明しにくい。あくまでも自社レベルの復旧メニューであり，本稿の理論枠組みでは「合理的信頼」レベルの活動である。

　第二に，自動車産業における系列組織化の観点からの説明も可能である。系列の階層の中で上位のサプライヤーは重要部品，代替性の利かない部品を製造している場合が多いので，それだけ系列組織の結合を保持しようとするだろう。アイシン精機の場合はこの条件に該当しそうだが，ルネサスへの支援については「系列組織化論」からは説明しにくい。コミットメント形成は，系列組織化のみに限定されないためである。

　第三に，企業の組織デザインと「ケーパビリティ」の観点から，谷口（2005）は，「経営者は，資源の拡張に向けて，補完的な企業制度の複合体（システム）としてデザインせねばならず，その際，従業員に明確な目的を植えつけ，（中略）自生的な協力を志向する組織をつくりあげねばならない。」としてトヨタ・アイシン危機の事例を挙げ，「迅速な回復は，トヨタによる命令なしに，トヨタ・グループ各社の自生的な協力，および分権的な資源の再配置とコミュニケーションによって可能になった。」としている[(2)]。これは，「企業の境界」問題と関連し，実態として現代の企業組織とりわけ自動車産業について，今井らの「中間組織」論のように外延的に拡張している中での経営資源の配分問題と捉えることができる。限定的に捉えれば，このことは経営資源の内製化と外注化の選択の問題として言い換えられ，選択の基準のひとつに「信頼」概念が関与することになろう。

　第四に，「スモールワールド・ネットワーク」により説明される。西口によれば，北米でのサプライヤー・ネットワークが規則的で放射状の「レギュラー・

ネットワーク」であるのに対して，トヨタとサプライヤーとの系列関係は，一部にランダム接続をもつ「スモールワールド・ネットワーク」になっているという(3)。先のアイシン精機の工場火災での対応として，トヨタ周辺のサプライヤー220社が自律的にPバルブ代替生産に協力したことを挙げ，「トヨタ系の『自主研究会（自主研）』に代表される，選ばれたサプライヤー同士の交流によって日常から『スモールワールド化』していたネットワークへ，一時的に強いショックが加わり機能停止に陥ったが，平時の活動のちょっとした拡張でロバストネス（頑健性）を取り戻すとともに，サプライチェーン全体に長年蓄積された潜在能力が一気に呼び起こされ，迅速なリワイヤリングによる代替生産を経て壊れたトポロジーが修復され，現状復帰した」と結論付けている(4)。

　西口は，事例での企業の支援行動基準として，トヨタ生産方式に基づく価値観の共有化にあることを指摘している。筆者の立場は西口に近いが，この場合，アイシン精機工場火災の事例に当てはまっても，それはトヨタとの関係に限定されよう。より一般化して捉えた場合，筆者は継続的な取引関係における情報交換の恒常性の効果と信頼性における結びつきの逆転（合理的信頼から関係的信頼への結びつきの強さの転移）に着目したい。企業間信頼が，互いの社会的不確実性を低下させるために，相互の情報交換の継続により規定されるとするなら，真鍋・延岡の指摘した「信頼」の概念を非常時に拡張して，筆者が強調する企業間信頼における結びつきの一時的転移が，非常時の復旧支援行動の説明をする上で重要な要因となると考えられる。

　復旧支援では，製品の代替性がきかないため「やむをえず」といった消極的な企業支援活動も想定されるが，非常時にこそ長期の取引を見据えた積極的な支援が求められており，実態面から分析した西口のネットワークの関係性（近隣で繋がる企業と遠距離関係にある企業との紐帯）に対し，筆者は企業の意思決定の基準のひとつである「企業間信頼」に着目して，情報交換の緊密性（＝社会的不確実性を低下させるインセンティブ）から生じる「信頼」と平常時から非常時への「場の転換」に符号した関係性の変化を指摘したが，いずれも非常時における企業組織のあり方の分析に有用であると考えられる。

6. 結びに代えて

　本稿では，日本での自動車分業生産体制が比較的緩やかなネットワークを形成していることに着目し，非常時における生産施設復旧への支援を通じて，自動車産業の結集力を「企業間信頼」の視点からひとつの考察を試みた[注-6]。「企業間信頼」を基にした結びつきは，企業間における継続的な取引関係を通じた情報交換（＝社会的不確実性を低下させるインセンティブ）により醸成されるもので，これが日本のものづくりの強さのひとつであると筆者は考えている。さらに信頼は，企業の内部組織における労使間の関係にも視点を向けることができる。

　この「企業間信頼」の概念はとらえどころがなく，直接的な計測も困難であるが，先の議論から筆者は，企業における行動基準のひとつとして「信頼」基準が設定され，その「信頼」のあり方が，非常時では生産活動の結束力の大きな要因であると推測するものである。

【注釈】

(注-1) 本稿は，経営行動科学学会第14回年次大会で著者が発表した原稿を一部修正したものである。
(注-2) 以下の事故に関する記述については，西口，2007，の他，WEBサイト「失敗百選」(http://www.sydrose.com/case100/315/)，「仙台リスクマネジメント」(http://bcp-pl.com/)を参考とした。
(注-3) リケンの被害についての記述は，http://www.nikkeibp.co.jp/sj/2/special/325/ を参考とした。
(注-4) 2011年9月19日付『日本経済新聞』
(注-5) この記事については，http://www.nikkeibp.co.jp/article/reb/20110613/273768/?HYPERLINK "http://www.nikkeibp.co.jp/article/reb/20110613/273768/?ST=rebuild" HYPERLINK "http://www.nikkeibp.co.jp/article/reb/20110613/273768/?ST=rebuild" ST=rebuild を参考とした。
(注-6) 本稿では，工場単独被災等のアクシデントに限定して議論している。2011年の東日本大震災のような広域災害の場合は，生産立地と産業集積の観点から別途，考察が必要となる。

【引用文献】

(1) 真鍋・延岡（2003），p. 54。
(2) 谷口（2005），p. 304。

(3) 西口 (2007), pp. 88-89。
(4) 西口 (2007), p. 123。
　西口は「アイシン精機の火災事故ケースのように，トヨタやアイシン精機がパニックに なっても，サプライチェーンの各ロケーションでほとんど自律的に合目的な情報をあっという間に検索して横展開し，10日で原状復帰したということで，近所づきあいと遠距離交際のバランスのよいネットワークがここに現出している」「最も重要だったのはトポロジカルなアドバンテージです。遠距離交際と近所づきあいのバランスのよいトポロジーが平時からすでにそこにあって，優れた価値観が共有されていました。この場合，その価値観はトヨタ生産方式であり，この常に進化して改善を促す方式が浸透していたことが功を奏したと考えられます。」と述べている（西口敏宏「成功するネットワーク戦略とフォーラム活動」[宇宙航空研究開発機構講演]）。

【参考文献】
[1] 今井賢一・伊丹敬之・小池和男 (1982), 『内部組織の経済学』東洋経済新報社。
[2] 谷口和弘 (2005), 「企業は戦略を補う」『三田小商学研究』第48巻第1号。
[3] 西口敏宏 (2007), 『遠距離交際と近所づきあい―成功する組織ネットワーク戦略』NTT出版。
[4] 西口敏宏 (2009), 『ネットワーク思考のすすめ―ネットセントリック時代の組織戦略』東洋経済新報社。
[5] 西口敏宏・アレクサンダー・ボーデ (1999), 「カオスにおける自己組織化：トヨタ・グループとアイシン精機火災」『組織科学』第32巻第4号。
[6] 真鍋誠司 (2002), 「企業間信頼の構築：トヨタのケース」『Research Institute for Economics and Business Administration, Kobe University, Discussion Paper Series』No.J42, 神戸大学経済経営研究所。
[7] 真鍋誠司・延岡健太郎 (2002), 「組織間学習システムとネットワーク信頼」『Research Institute for Economics and Business Administration, Kobe University, Discussion Paper Series』No. J44, 神戸大学経済経営研究所。
[8] 真鍋誠司・延岡健太郎 (2003), 「信頼の源泉とその類型化」『国民経済雑誌』第187巻第5号。
[9] 真鍋誠司・延岡健太郎 (2003), 「ネットワーク信頼：構築メカニズムとパラドクス」『Research Institute for Economics and Business Administration, Kobe University, Discussion Paper Series』No.J50, 神戸大学経済経営研究所。
[10] 真鍋誠司 (2004), 「企業間信頼の構築とサプライヤーシステム：日本自動車産業の分析」『横浜経営研究』第25巻第2・3号。
[11] 山岸俊男 (1998), 『信頼の構造―こころと社会の進化ゲーム』東京大学出版会。

（石田幸男）

第10章　警備員の生理的ストレス反応と職務満足
―― 第二報 ――

【要旨】
　明確に警備業を研究対象とした論文は未だ希少である。岩崎龍太郎（2013）は，部分的ではあるが実証的研究によって，交通誘導警備業務（以後，「交通誘導警備」と称す）による生理的ストレスの上昇を明らかにし，警備員の劣悪かつ苛酷な労働実態を明らかにした。本研究（第二報）では，標本数を拡大し，日本国鹿児島県で交通誘導警備に従事する3事業者の交通誘導警備員を対象に，労働実態と職務満足を解明するために実証的研究を行った。生理指標は唾液アミラーゼモニタを用いた生理的ストレス反応の測定，主観的評価法は新職業性ストレス簡易調査票にモデレーター要因の「生きがい」と「基本属性」を追加した無記名自記式調査票（以後，「調査票」と称す）を作成し回答を得た。

　この結果，生理指標の測定では交通誘導警備の従事によって生理的ストレスが有意に上昇した。主観的評価法では警備員のダブルバインド状況の発生や，劣悪かつ苛酷な労働実態を改めて検証したことは成果といえる。畢竟するに，「ハードワーク」や「オーバーワーク」を少なくし，法令遵守や内部統制の強化など事業場レベルでの改善を図ることが，職務満足度と，心の健康に大いに影響することが明らかとなった。

【キーワード】：職務満足，警備業，交通誘導警備業務，労働実態，ダブルバインド，唾液アミラーゼ，バイオマーカー，職業性ストレス，モデレーター要因，ワークライフバランス

1. はじめに

　明確に警備業を研究対象とした論文は未だ希少である。岩崎龍太郎（2013）は，部分的ではあるが実証的研究によって，「交通誘導警備業務による生理的ストレスの上昇」や「警備員の劣悪かつ苛酷な労働実態」を明らかにした[1]。しかし，岩崎龍太郎の第一報は標本数が少なく，研究目的に対する成果も限定的であった。

　本研究（第二報）は，警備業法第2条第1項第2号に規定される警備業務のひとつである交通誘導警備を対象とする。交通誘導警備は，手旗や誘導灯を用いて通行人や通行車両，工事車両を誘導することを主な業務とする。交通誘導警備の現場の多くは，公道において実施され，公道では常に何らかの変化が生じるなど，警備員に臨機応変な対応が望まれる警備業務である。

　岩崎龍太郎（2013），青木卓（1995），手塚正巳（2011）が指摘するように，「交通誘導警備に従事する警備員の多くは日雇い労働者で，公共工事が少ない閑散期と，逆に多い繁忙期の就労頻度の差が激しい」[2][3]ため，他産業と比較して低賃金であり（厚生労働省が行った平成24年賃金構造基本統計調査[4]による），長時間労働であり（警備業における労働時間改善調査研究委員会（1990）[5]による），かつ不安定な労働実態（国土交通省が行う公共工事設計労務費調査（平成24年10月調査）[6]による）がある。

　そこで，本研究では，警備業に従事する警備員の労働実態と職務満足要因の更なる解明のため，標本数を拡大し，鹿児島県内で交通誘導警備に従事する3事業者65名の警備員を対象に，生理指標として唾液アミラーゼモニタを用いた生理的ストレス反応の測定を行い，また主観的評価法を採用して調査票によるアンケート調査を実施した。

2. 評価指標

(1) 唾液アミラーゼ活性

　「ストレス」という用語は，もともと「圧力」という意味の工学用語である。Hans Selye（1936）は動物実験の結果から，「生体は外界からの刺激（ストレッサー）に直面した時，自らの破綻を回避する目的で全身反応を起こす…ストレッサーに対する生体の反応は，個々の生体に特有なものではなく，ある一定の防御のパターン（ときには疾病のパターン）をとること」[7]を明らかにした。ストレスを評価するには問診やアンケート調査による主観的評価法，血液のノルエピネフリンやコルチゾールを測定する生化学的方法（最もよく用いられる），脳波のα波や心拍数の変動などを用いた生理学的評価法などがある。しかし，警備が終わって事業所に戻ったら血液を抜かれたという話になっては，そのこと自体が警備員のストレスとなりかねない。

　そこで，本研究の生理指標では生化学的方法の唾液アミラーゼモニタ（ニプロ社製）を用いる。山口ら（2001）は，生理指標として「心的ストレス（交感神経緊張状態）に対し，唾液アミラーゼ活性が変動すること」[8]を見出し，唾液アミラーゼ活性が心的ストレスマーカーになることを報告した。この方法は唾液を検体とするため，非侵襲性，随時性，即時性，簡便性，携帯性，経済性に優れる。注意点として，その瞬間のストレスを示すため，調査票を記入した後や，勤務終了時に心理ゆとりが生まれたりすると，アミラーゼ活性が大きく変化する。したがって，警備による正確なストレス値を計測するには，測定環境・測定条件・分析方法などに十分留意しなければならない。また，飲食後30分以内は唾液中のアミラーゼ活性が意図的に上昇するため，採取を避けなければならない。

(2) 調査票

　主観的評価法には，交通誘導警備に従事する警備員の労働実態と職務満足を解明するために，新職業性ストレス簡易調査票[9]に，モデレーター要因の「生

きがい」と「基本属性」を追加した合計96項目の無記名自記式調査票を用いた。

①新職業性ストレス簡易調査票

新職業性ストレス簡易調査票は，川上憲人 (2012) の「労働者のメンタルヘルス不調の第一次予防の浸透手法に関する調査研究」によって，職場のメンタルヘルスの第一次予防の日本型枠組みとして提案された。「仕事の負担」と「作業，部署，事業場レベルでの仕事の資源」が，労働者の心身の健康，仕事へのポジティブな関わり（ワーク・エンゲイジメント），職場の一体感（職場のソーシャルキャピタル），職場のハラスメント，労働者の満足・幸福（職務満足度，家庭満足度）などのアウトカムを予測するという。警備員への身体的・精神的な負担を考慮し，短縮版を採用した。

②モデレーター要因

原口俊道 (1995) は，「組織要因の『部門の性格』と『仕事の性格』がモチベーターとなり『性別』（基本属性）によって有意に異なる」[10]といい，小曽木加奈子 (2010) は，介護老人保健施設のケアスタッフの「職務満足度」と「転職」の要因が「業務の内容」（基本属性）と「労働条件」（組織要因）にあるという[11]。

本研究においても，モデレーター要因によって結果が有意に異なると仮定して研究を行った。第一モデレーター要因を，「生きがい」と「基本属性」とした。「基本属性」は，性別，年齢，最終学歴，雇用形態，職種，業務内容，勤続年数，加入保険，起床からの時間，残業時間を含む一週間の労働時間の10項目とした。

第一報では，交通誘導警備前後の「生理状態の安定（ストレス差）」と，「心の健康」，「職務満足度」との間に相関がみられなかった。そこで，本研究では「ストレス差」を第二モデレーター要因として別個に設け，「健康いきいき職場環境」と「第一モデレーター要因」への効果を検証する。

3. 研究目的

先行研究の整理から，筆者は以下の研究目的を設定する。

① 唾液アミラーゼなどのバイオマーカーと職業性ストレスとの関係に関す

る方法論に関する研究をすること。
② 交通誘導警備員の劣悪かつ苛酷な労働実態を実証的研究によって明らかにすること。
③ 交通誘導警備員の職務満足要因を明らかにすること。

4. 研究方法

(1) 研究仮説

筆者は研究目的を解決するために、以下のとおり研究仮説と分析モデルを設け検証を行う（図表10-1）。

図表10-1　警備員の生理的ストレス反応と職務満足度に関する分析モデル

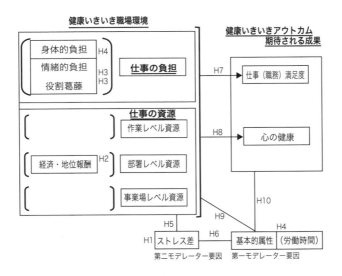

(出所) 筆者作成。

仮説H1：交通誘導警備に従事することで「生理的ストレス」が上昇する。
仮説H2：「経済・地位報酬」の全国平均値と警備員の平均値を比較して，警備員の得点が悪い。
仮説H3：「情緒的負担・役割葛藤」の全国平均値と警備員の平均値と比較して，警備員の得点が悪い。
仮説H4：「身体的負担・労働時間」の全国平均値と警備員の平均値と比較して，警備員の負担が大きい。
仮説H5：「ストレス差」と「健康いきいき職場環境」に効果がある。
仮説H6：「ストレス差」と「第一モデレーター要因」に効果がある。
仮説H7：「健康いきいき職場環境」は「職務満足度」に影響を与える。
仮説H8：「健康いきいき職場環境」は「心の健康」に影響を与える。
仮説H9：「第一モデレーター要因」は「健康いきいき職場環境」に効果がある。
仮説H10：「第一モデレーター要因」は「健康いきいきアウトカム」に効果がある。

(2) 対象

　調査対象は，鹿児島県で交通誘導警備に従事する3事業者65名の警備員を対象とした。対象者には研究の主旨を理解し同意を得た。調査期間は，2013年8月1日から2013年8月31日及び，2014年2月1日から2014年2月28日までとした。

(3) 研究デザイン

　研究デザインを図表10-2に示す。岡本博照（2012）によれば，「勤務終了後ではなく，勤務終了直前に唾液アミラーゼを測定することが望ましい」[12]という。勤務終了時に心理ゆとりが生まれると，アミラーゼ活性が大きく変化するためである。よって，勤務時間内の交通誘導警備前と，警備後に唾液を採取しその変化を測定した。調査票は，唾液アミラーゼ活性に影響がでないよう

に，2回目の唾液採取後に記入させた。また，唾液中のアミラーゼ活性の意図的な上昇を防ぐため，唾液採取の直前に10分間の安静時間を設けた。

図表10-2　研究デザイン

（出所）筆者作成。

(4) 統計解析

資料の解析は，統計ソフトSPSS17.0を使用して，記述統計，t検定，因子分析，クラスター分析，相関分析及び重回帰分析を行った。

5. 分析結果

(1) 回答者（被験者）の基本情報

唾液アミラーゼ活性の測定の結果，警備員65名（男性53名，女性3名，有効標本数56名，有効標本率86.2％）の標本を得た。年齢は20～71歳，平均年齢が45.2歳であった。調査票の結果では，警備員65名（男性62名，女性3名，有効回答数65名，有効回答率100.0％）の標本を得た。20歳代21.5％，30歳代18.5％，40歳代13.8％，50歳代26.2％，60歳代18.5％，平均年齢が45.0歳であった。雇用形態は，正社員46.2％，非正規社員53.8％であった。勤続年数は，1年未満15.4％，1年以上3年未満18.5％，3年以上7年未満29.2％，7年以上36.9％であった。一週間の労働時間の平均は55.1時間であった。

しかし，このような長時間労働の実態があるにもかかわらず，公的加入保険は，社会保険52.3％，国民健康保険36.9％，無保険10.8％であるなど，警備員の労働環境の劣悪性と苛酷性を表す労働実態が明らかとなった。

(2) 唾液アミラーゼ活性の結果

図表10-3に交通誘導警備前後の警備員の唾液アミラーゼ活性の変化を示す。

交通誘導警備をする前の唾液アミラーゼ活性の平均値は41.36 kIU/L，警備した後の平均値は75.14 kIU/Lと，平均値が33.79 kIU/L上昇した。t検定の結果，唾液アミラーゼ活性の上昇に有意な差が認められた（t（55）=4.29,p<.01）。唾液アミラーゼ活性の上昇は生理的ストレスの上昇を表す。よって，仮説H１の「交通誘導警備に従事することで生理的ストレスが上昇する」は成立した。

図表10-3　警備員の交通誘導警備前後の唾液アミラーゼ活性

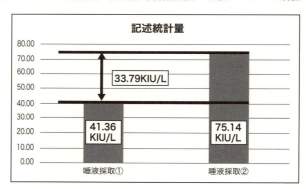

（出所）筆者作成。

(3) 調査票の結果

調査票の新職業性ストレス簡易調査票部分の尺度は，高い得点の方が良好な状態を表す。図表10-4は，警備員の平均値と全国平均値を比較したものである。

まず，図表10-4の全国平均値および業種別平均値と比べ警備員の平均値が有意に高い尺度は，「上司のリーダーシップ」（t（63）=2.44,p<.05），「失敗を認める職場」（t（64）=3.75,p<.01），「個人の尊重」（t（63）=2.28,p<.05），「キャリア形成」（t（64）=3.22,p<.01）などであった。仕事の努力や達成度に対し金銭・処遇を適切に受けていることを表す「経済・地位報酬」では，警備員の平均値は全国平均値と比べ0.03点低い2.22点で有意な差はみられなかった（t（64）=−0.33,ns）。よって，

第 10 章　警備員の生理的ストレス反応と職務満足　161

図表 10-4　警備員の平均値と全国平均値

変数グループ	尺度名	現行＋標準版			
		全国平均		警備員	
		人数	平均	人数	平均
仕事の負担	仕事の量的負担	1,621	2.14	65	2.34
	仕事の質的負担	1,617	2.17	65	2.05
	身体的負担度	1,625	2.49	65	2.02 △
	職場での対人関係	1,610	2.88	65	2.77
	職場環境	1,627	2.78	65	2.65
	情緒的負担	1,628	2.65	65	2.32 △
	役割葛藤	1,628	2.87	65	2.29 ▲
	ワーク セルフ バランス（ネガティブ）	1,625	2.84	65	2.69
	仕事の負担合計	1,570	2.60	65	2.39
仕事の資源（作業レベル）	仕事のコントロール	1,618	2.53	65	2.31
	仕事の適性	1,628	2.92	65	2.72
	技能の活用	1,625	3.00	65	2.63 △
	仕事の意義	1,627	2.87	65	2.23 ▲
	役割明確さ	1,628	3.41	65	3.34
	成長の機会	1,626	2.62	65	2.78
	作業レベルの仕事の資源合計	1,603	2.89	65	2.69
仕事の資源（部署レベル）	上司のサポート	1,612	2.37	64	2.44
	同僚のサポート	1,615	2.68	65	2.56
	家族友人のサポート	1,619	3.31	65	3.03
	経済・地位報酬	1,625	2.25	65	2.22
	尊重報酬	1,621	2.59	64	2.58
	安定報酬	1,622	2.84	65	2.85
	上司のリーダーシップ	1,623	2.25	64	2.52 ＋
	上司の公正な態度	1,623	2.65	64	2.70
	ほめてもらえる職場	1,624	2.58	64	2.59
	失敗を認める職場	1,622	2.45	65	2.85 ＋
	部署レベルの仕事の資源合計	1,584	2.52	65	2.64
仕事の資源（事業場レベル）	経営層との信頼関係	1,621	2.58	65	2.66
	変化への対応	1,621	2.35	65	2.46
	個人の尊重	1,621	2.14	64	2.38 ＋
	公正な人事評価	1,616	2.04	64	2.22
	多様な労働者への対応	1,619	2.72	65	2.55
	キャリア形成	1,619	2.23	65	2.54 ＋
	ワーク セルフ バランス（ポジティブ）	1,625	2.08	65	2.14
	事業場レベルの仕事の資源合計	1,596	2.30	65	2.42
いきいきアウトカム	ワーク・エンゲイジメント	1,622	2.51	65	2.47
	職場の一体感	1,627	2.66	65	2.46
心身の健康	活気	1,616	2.26	64	2.42
	イライラ感	1,618	2.70	65	2.70
	疲労感	1,624	2.70	65	2.54
	不安感	1,623	2.87	65	2.76
	抑うつ感	1,618	3.27	65	3.17
	心理的ストレス反応合計	1,590	2.85	65	2.72
	身体愁訴	1,610	3.22	65	3.18
職場のハラスメント	職場のハラスメント	1,626	3.70	65	3.66
満足度	仕事満足度	1,630	2.60	65	2.68
	家族満足度	1,629	3.06	65	2.97

(注1) 高得点ほど良好な状態を示すように変換している。
(注2) 得点を項目数で除している。
(注3) ※は推奨尺度以外。仕事の負担・資源の合計得点の計算には使用していない。
(注4) NA＝短縮版では採用していない尺度。
(注5) ＋は有意に高い　▲は平均より0.5以上低い　△は平均より0.3以上0.5未満低い

(出所) 筆者作成。

仮説 H2 の「経済・地位報酬の全国平均値と警備員の平均値を比較して，警備員の得点が悪い」は不成立となった。感情面での業務負担を表す「情緒的負担」では，警備員の平均値は全国平均値と比べ 0.33 点低い 2.32 点で有意な差があった（t(64)=-3.25,p<.01）。これは他の業種と比較して最も低い値であった。合わせて，方針や要求が相容れないため業務遂行が困難となる負担を表す「役割葛藤」では，全国平均値と比べ 0.58 点低い 2.29 点と有意に低得点で（t(64)=-5.10,p<.01），他の業種と比較して最も低い値であった。よって，仮説 H3 の「情緒的負担・役割葛藤の全国平均値と警備員の平均値と比較して，警備員の得点が悪い」は成立した。身体的業務負担を表す「身体的負担度」では，警備員の平均値は全国平均値と比べ 0.47 点低い 2.02 点で有意な差があった（t(64)=-4.37,p<.01）。合わせて，警備員の一週間の労働時間は 55.1 時間で，厚生労働省「毎月勤労統計調査・平成 24 年分結果確報（一般労働者）」（2012）の労働時間 39.0 時間と比べ非常に長時間であった（t(64)=7.44,p<.01）。よって，仮説 H4 の「身体的負担・労働時間の全国平均値と警備員の平均値と比較して，警備員の負担が大きい」は成立した。

この他，警備員の「技能の活用」や「仕事の意義」の平均値が，全国平均値と比べ何れも有意に低得点であった（t(64)=-3.40,p<.01，t(64)=-6.40,p<.01）。各尺度の説明文章によれば，「仕事にもっている技術が生かされず，仕事の意義が認識できない」という警備員の労働価値観を表した。

(4) 唾液アミラーゼ活性と調査票の関連結果

交通誘導警備前後の「ストレス差」と，調査票の「心理的ストレス反応合計」，「職務満足度」をそれぞれ相関分析した結果，有意な相関はみられなかった。「ストレス差」と「健康いきいき職場環境」の関係をみると，「ストレス差」と，「仕事のコントロール」，「役割葛藤」でそれぞれ逆相関がみられた（r=-.33,p<.01，r=-.22,p<.05）。つまり，仕事がコントロールでき，役割が明確であるほど，ストレス差が小さくなった。よって，仮説 H5 の「ストレス差と健康いきいき職場環境に効果がある」が成立した。「ストレス差」と「第一モデレーター要因」の関係をみると，「ストレス差」と，「勤続年数」に逆相関がみられた（r=-

.23,p<.05)。つまり,勤続年数が長くなるほど,ストレス差が小さくなった。よって,仮説 H6 の「ストレス差と第一モデレーター要因に効果がある」が成立した。

(5)「健康いきいき職場モデル」の検証

「健康いきいき職場モデル」が警備員に当てはまるか相関分析をした。その結果,警備員の「職務満足度」と,「仕事の負担合計」,「作業レベルの仕事の資源合計(以後,「作業レベル合計」と称す)」,「部署レベルの仕事の資源合計(以後,「部署レベル合計」と称す)」,「事業場レベルの仕事の資源合計(以後,「事業場レベル合計」と称す)」との関係のすべてにおいて相関がみられた(r=.34,p<.01,r=.40,p<.001, r=.66,p<.001, r=.71,p<.001)。加えて,従属変数を「職務満足度」とした重回帰分析の結果,説明力があった(R^2=.63 (p<.001)。また,このときの共変関係(相関)は「仕事の負担合計」と「事業場レベル合計」に相関がみられ(r=.31,p<.01),「部署レベル合計」と「事業所レベル合計」に相関がみられた(r=.76,p<.001)。

つぎに,「心の健康(以後,「心理的ストレス反応合計」と称す)」と「健康いきいき職場環境」との相関は,警備員の「作業レベル合計」を除く,「仕事の負担合計」,「部署レベル合計」,「事業場レベル合計」において相関がみられた(r=.46,p<.001, r=.50,p<.001, r=.55,p<.001)。また,従属変数を「心理的ストレス反応合計」とした重回帰分析の結果,説明力があった(R^2=0.42,p<.001)。また,このときの共変関係(相関)は「仕事の負担合計」と「事業場レベル合計」に相関がみられ(r=.31,p<.01),「部署レベル合計」と「事業所レベル合計」に相関がみられた(r=.76,p<.001)。他にも,「職務満足度」と「心理的ストレス反応合計」に相関がみられた(r=.54,p<.001)。よって,仮説 H7 の「健康いきいき職場環境は職務満足度に影響を与える」と仮説 H8 の「健康いきいき職場環境は心の健康に影響を与える」が成立した。

(6) モデレーター要因の検証

モデレーター要因の尺度の信頼性は,ρ=0.944 以上と高い内的整合性が認

められた。モデレーター要因「生きがい」6項目から、2つの因子を抽出したが、項目数の少なさからα係数が低くなり、尺度として利用することができなかった。個々のモデレーター要因みれば、「一週間の労働時間」と「仕事の負担合計」、「事業場レベル合計」、「職務満足度」および「心理的ストレス反応合計」とが逆相関となり（r=−.43,p<.001, r=−.263,p<.05, r=−.23,p<.05, r=−.31,p<.01）、仮説 H9 の「第一モデレーター要因は健康いきいき職場環境に効果がある」及び、仮説 H10 の「第一モデレーター要因は健康いきいきアウトカムに効果がある」は成立した。

6. 結果の考察

以上、研究仮説の検証結果を図表10-5に示し、警備員の生理的ストレス反応、労働実態及び職務満足要因について考察する。

図表 10-5 研究仮説の検証結果

研 究 仮 説		実証結果
仮説H1	:交通誘導警備に従事することで生理的ストレスが上昇する。	○
仮説H2	:経済・地位報酬の全国平均値と比較してマイナス差がある。	×
仮説H3	:情緒的負担・役割葛藤の全国平均値と比較してマイナス差がある。	○
仮説H4	:身体的負担・労働時間の全国平均値と比較してマイナス差がある。	○
仮説H5	:ストレス差と健康いきいき職場環境に効果がある。	○
仮説H6	:ストレス差と第一モデレーター要因に効果がある。	○
仮説H7	:健康いきいき職場環境は職務満足度に影響を与える。	○
仮説H8	:健康いきいき職場環境は心の健康に影響を与える。	○
仮説H9	:第一モデレーター要因は健康いきいき職場環境に効果がある。	○
仮説H10	:第一モデレーター要因は健康いきいきアウトカムに効果がある。	○

○は成立、△は不明、×は不成立を表す。
（出所）筆者作成。

生理指標では、交通誘導警備に従事することによって生理的ストレスが上昇したため、仮説 H1 が成立した。次に、生理指標と主観的評価法との関連性を調べたが、一部の尺度において相関関係がみられた。よって、仮説 H5 と仮説 H6 が成立した。

平成24年賃金構造基本統計調査では警備員の低賃金の実態があったものの、

調査票の「経済・地位報酬」では，全国平均値と比較して大きな差は無く，仮説 H2 は不成立となった。

「情緒的負担」と「役割葛藤」の警備員の平均値は，全国平均値と比べ低得点で，仮説 H3 が成立した。結果，警備員のダブルバインド状況の発生が再度確認される結果となった。警備員が現場で臨機応変な対応を求められる反面，依頼主から『余計なことをするな』と叱責されるといった，警備員のダブルバインド状況は，田中智仁（2012）が質的調査で明らかにしたが[13]，本研究では実証的研究によって明らかとなった。

「身体的負担度」の警備員の平均値は，全国平均値と比べ有意に低得点で，警備員の一週間の労働時間は 55.1 時間と長時間労働であった。よって仮説 H4 は成立した。

新職業性ストレス簡易調査票の「健康いきいき職場モデル」において，仮説 H7 と仮説 H8 が成立し，モデルを支持することが明らかとなった。特に，警備員の「職務満足度」では「事業場レベル合計」との相関が高かった。一方，「一週間の労働時間」と「健康いきいき職場環境」，「職務満足度」，「心理ストレス反応合計」との間にそれぞれ相関があることが明らかとなり，仮説 H9 及び仮説 H10 が成立した。また，このとき「職務満足度」と「心理的ストレス反応合計」に相関がみられた（$r=.54, p<.001$）。畢竟するに，「ハードワーク」，「オーバーワーク」を少なくし，法令遵守や内部統制の強化など事業場レベルでの改善を図ることが，職務満足度と心の健康に大いに影響することが明らかとなった。

7. 結び

本研究（第二報）の実証的研究おいても，交通誘導警備による生理的ストレスの上昇が有意に明らかとなった。加えて，警備員の劣悪かつ苛酷な労働実態を明らかにしたことは大きな研究成果であった。

先行研究において，原口俊道（1995）は，鹿児島県内における実証的研究で Herzberg, F.（1966）の動機づけ - 衛生理論[14]を支持した。国内外の大規

模標本の調査をみれば，田村輝之（2010）は，OECD 諸国を対象として，「職務満足度を引き下げる共通要因は，『ハードワーク』，『オーバーワーク』，『転職が困難』である」[15]という。田中規子（2009）は，日本全国を対象として，「ストレスは達成感や職務満足度に正の影響を与える」[16]が，過度なストレスは職務満足度を引き下げると推察している。

本研究（第二報）の結果も，Herzberg, F. の動機づけ - 衛生理論でいうところの不満の解消すなわち，警備員の「ハードワーク」，「オーバーワーク」を少なくすることや，社会保険3保険の加入などの法令遵守が職務満足度と心の健康に大いに貢献すると考えられる。

ただし，現時点において，標本数が少なく，対象範囲も鹿児島県内と狭いため，さらに標本数，対象範囲を拡大し研究を進める必要がある。

【引用文献】
(1) 岩崎龍太郎（2013），「警備員の生理的ストレス反応と職務満足に関する一考察（第一報）」『亜東経済国際学会研究叢書⑯ 東亜社会発展興産業経営』台湾・暉翔興業出版社。
(2) 青木卓（1995），『夜路のガードマン―日雇い日払い棒ふり物語』技術と人間。
(3) 手塚正巳（2011），『警備員日記』太田出版。
(4) 厚生労働省統計情報部（2013），『賃金センサス〈第 1 巻〉平成 24 年賃金構造基本統計調査』労働法令。
(5) 警備業における労働時間改善調査研究委員会（1990），『警備業における労働時間短縮の現状と今後の方向：労働時間改善のための経営上の対策に関する実践的研究報告』大蔵省印刷局。
(6) 土地・建設産業局，2013 年 5 月 9 日，「公共事業労務費調査（平成 24 年 10 月調査）における社会保険加入状況調査結果について」http://www.mlit.go.jp/common/000997140.pdf
(7) Selye HA. (1936), "A syndrome produced by diverse nocuous agents", *Nature*, Vol.138, No.32, Nature Publishing Group.
(8) 山口昌樹（2007），「ストレスと生活2 唾液マーカーでストレスを測る」『日本薬理学雑誌』第 129 巻，第 2 号，pp.80～84。
(9) 川上憲人（2012），「労働者のメンタルヘルス不調の第一次予防の浸透手法に関する調査研究 平成 23 年度総括・分担研究報告書」厚生労働省。
(10) 原口俊道（1995），『動機づけ - 衛生理論の国際比較』同文舘。
(11) 小曽木加奈子（2010），「介護老人保健施設におけるケアスタッフの仕事全体の満足度・転職・離職の要因：職務における 9 つの領域別満足度との関連を中心に」『社会福祉学』第 51 巻，第 3 号，pp.103～118。

(12) 岡本博照（2012），「都市部救急隊員の疲労と唾液アミラーゼ活性値」『民族衛生』第78巻，第3号，pp.61〜75。
(13) 田中智仁（2012），『警備業の分析視角』明石書店。
(14) Herzberg, F. (1966), *Work and the Nature of Man*, Cleveland and New York: The World Publishers.（フレデリック・ハーズバーグ，北野利信訳（1968），『仕事と人間性 動機づけ―衛生理論の新展開』東洋経済新報社）。
(15) 田村輝之（2010），「OECD諸国における職務満足度の決定要因について」行動経済学会。
(16) 田中規子（2010），「職務満足の規定要因―フレデリック・ハーズバーグの『動機づけ衛生理論』を手がかりとして」『人間文化創成科学論叢』第12巻，第12号，pp.257〜266。

（岩崎龍太郎・難波礼治）

第2編

東アジアの社会・観光・企業（英文）

Chapter 11 The Cross-cultural Conflicts at Sino-foreign Enterprises in China

【Abstract】

Due to the differences of cultural background and experience in business management between foreigners and Chinese, cross-cultural conflicts are likely to occur at Sino-foreign enterprises in China. What conflict of ideas and conduct has already occurred? What are the hidden causes for the conflicts? Why must we bring harmony to the cross-cultural conflicts? How can we bridge the gap? This paper tries to expound one issue - the possibility of harmonizing the different cultures at Sino-foreign enterprises in China. The course of harmonizing will lead to a new enterprise culture and management mode. The key to success resides in the people's psychology breeding from a particular culture and the associated conducts.

【Keywords】: the cross-cultural conflicts; Sino-foreign enterprises in China; the hidden causes for the conflicts; the possibility of harmonizing the different cultures

1. Introduction

Sino-foreign enterprises in China include Sino-foreign joint ventures, Sino-foreign cooperative ventures, and foreign-funded enterprises. As a kind of beneficial means to balance differences between different countries and racial groups, many countries in the world welcome these enterprises. This kind of international economic cooperation has contributed a great deal to the development of the world economy in the past 30 years, and will be a beneficial factor to retain a rapid growth of the global economy in the future.

Since Mainland China implemented the Policy of "opening-up" and reform in the late 1970's, international financial and technological exchanges have been expanding continuously. "By the end of 2012, the total number of employees are 12,460,000 at Sino-foreign funded enterprises and 9,690,000 at the enterprises with funds from Hong Kong, Macao & Taiwan in China." [1] Together with those Sino-foreign funded enterprises, the western ideology and values come to China that clashed inevitably with both traditional and modern Chinese ideology in business administration. Culture has the most important effect on the enterprise management in a diverse environment with intertwining social factors. In practice, the foreign investors have gradually come to realize that importance of getting a clear understanding of the cultural differences in Chain, or their business can go nowhere. However, so long as the investors understood the importance of above task and tried to do their best, they are very likely to find a way to success. The key to success resides in the people's psychology breeding from a particular culture and the associated conducts.

2. The Conflicts between the Two Sides of Sino-foreign Enterprises

At Sino-foreign enterprises in China, owing to the differences of cultural background and experience between foreign and Chinese employees, cross-cultural conflicts are likely to occur in their cooperative process. You may get some understanding of this problem from some cases as shown in the following.

(1) Illusions of the Foreign Staffs

Case 1: A young Chinese female worker asked for leave but her foreign boss refused without asking for an explanation and told that the company was too busy getting the ordered goods ready. The upset girl handed in her letter of resignation immediately. After hearing about it a Chinese manager talked with the girl and found out that the reason for leave was that the girl's parents had arranged her marriage against her wish. She had to go home to persuade her parents to cancel the marriage arrangement. The Chinese manager explained to the foreign boss this situation and suggested that the request for leave to be approved. With the permission to leave, the girl went home and succeeded in persuading her parents. Soon she returned and a valuable staff is being retained.

A Chinese old saying goes, "human beings are neither grass nor wood, so how can they be free from feelings?" If a manager cares about nothing but the business, he is most likely to incur displeasure in China where personal feelings are highly respected.

Case 2: Some Chinese workers complained to a foreign general manager about

---

(1) http://data.stats.gov.cn/workspace/index?m=hgnd

the rude manner of a foreman, and they also asked negotiate for higher wages, but the general manager did not respond at all. Later the workers went into the manager's office arguing for answer, and the general manager was terribly annoyed by their behavior of getting together to making trouble during working time. He threatened to fire them if they didn't go back to work immediately. Unexpectedly, the whole Chinese workers at the plant went on strike for two days to support those threatened workers, causing great loss to the enterprise.

Chinese workers have long been regarded as a leading class in Mainland China, and have a strong sense of self-respect. No wonder foreign manager's impertinence arose hostility among Chinese workers who are more accessible to sympathy and friendly feelings.

(2) Illusions of the Chinese Staffs

Case 1: Some Chinese staff members are not so careful when handling the property of the enterprise. They would take small pieces of property from the enterprise into their own possession, such as a pen from the office or a nice coffee-cup at the meeting room. It is not that these people are morally corrupted, but more due to their habit had been with state-owned enterprises where such actions are common. However, foreign staffs regard such a habit as no less serious than theft and show great contempt for those who have committed it.

In Mainland China, due to certain social factors there is no clear demarcation between public property and private property. This has a great effect on people's ideas and behaviors. Workers at the state-owned enterprises have long been accustomed to the idea of owning enterprise property. However, such behavior is surely intolerable for foreigners and they naturally draw the conclusion that those who are tainted with such a fault should not be trusted.

Case 2: A senior Chinese manager often acted like a father figure before his young foreign subordinates. He paid close attention not only to their work but also to their personal affairs, such as their friends and style of dress. The foreign staffs often became angry at his intrusive superiority and respected him no more.

In Mainland China, it had almost been a duty of the manager to care for the personal life of his subordinates and to make sure that they led a "correct" life, but for foreigners it was an intrusion upon their privacy. They felt insulted by such unwanted care.

(3) The Illusions of Both Sides

Case 1: A foreign manager passed by a workshop, which was in the charge of a Chinese manager. He caught a glimpse that a worker left the workshop after giving a very precious product sample to another worker. He stopped the worker and asked him to lock the sample in the safe and reprimanded him for violation of the regulations. However, the Chinese manager was not pleased with his foreign colleague as he thought that everyone should only mind his own business rather than poke his nose into other people's business.

Foreign staffs don't think there is a demarcation between "my duty" or "others duty" in the same enterprise whereas Chinese staffs are accustomed to mind their responsibilities in a certain department and to stand aloof no mater what happens in others' departments.

Case 2: In a meeting attended by all the department managers, a foreign manager made unfavorable remarks about a department, which was under the charge of a Chinese manager. The latter immediately took it as a sign of hostility, so he tried hard to find the foreign manager's fault at work. After the meeting foreign manager still considered this Chinese manager as a friend, but the latter had lost all positive feelings towards him for talking about his friend's fault on a public occasion.

Whether business relationships and personal relationships should be mingle together or not, Chinese and foreign employees have different views on how to solve these problems. We can see through the appearance to get the essence, it clearly reflect their different value composition in the interpersonal relationships.

(4) Cultural Differences Have Been the Cause of Many Conflicts

At Sino-foreign enterprises both sides that have high expectations of cooperation might be disappointed. On one hand foreign investors and managers lack adequate preparation to acknowledge the great difference between two cultures. On the other hand, Chinese employees also feel that they have not adapted to accommodate the difference between two cultures. In short, both sides have great expectation, but the results turn out to be unsatisfactory. The reason lies in the fact that neither part has, from the onset, paid enough attention to the promotion of mutual understanding on the cultural level. Instead, both sides have focused too much attention to the direct economic benefit that they can get from each other. Neither part has tried seriously to bridge the gap. As a result, the co-operation gradually erodes and many intangible problems occur concerning the enterprise management.

These conflicts have shown clearly that there are sharp contrasts between the two cultures. So much time and energy has been wasted on such problems and conflicts. It is really a disharmonious note in the whole melody of the organizational culture management in which people as the most importance resource. The two parts, in the same boat, may face the sinking of the boat if they do nothing to change the whole situation of cultural conflicts.

As a Chinese idiom puts it, "a small ant hole may cause the collapse of a thousand mile long dike." From the cases mentioned above we can see that such "ant holes" do exist widely at Sino-foreign enterprises. An analysis of the conflicts between two cultures is therefore very essential to mend the "ant hole". The discussion on the importance of human characters below will be useful to both sides in a new environment.

3. The Hidden Causes for the Conflicts

Geert Hofstede has done comprehensive analysis of cultural diversity. [2] In contrast to most of the previous organizational studies where only a limited number of countries were included or small numbers of enterprises in different countries, Hofstede surveyed over 116,000 employees in 40 countries who all worked for a multinational corporation. This extensive database eliminated any differences that might be attributable to varying practices and policies at different companies. So any variations that he found between countries could reliably be attributed to national culture. What did Hofstede find? His huge database confirmed that national culture had a major impact on employee's work-related values and attitude. To find the causes of the conflicts between two sides of the cooperative entity, we need to acknowledge and study closely the special features of the two associated cultures as well as the differences between them.

As might be seen from the cases in the above-mentioned, Mainland China employees have displayed distinct features of its traditional culture. Ever since 1949, the state-owned enterprises have annexed private businesses step by step and made competition impossible. A state-owned enterprise is just like "a big family" which

---

(2) See Hofstede, Geert (1993), "Cultural Constraints in Management Theories", *Academy of Management Executive*, February, pp. 81-94.

every member's work and life is regulated by a certain routine. They do not have to use their brains because everything has been arranged for them, including their daily life and welfare. The workers, as well as their leaders, all operate mechanically at a very slow pace. Under such circumstances, many intelligent and dexterous Chinese workers have lost the sense of competition and adopted a rather passive attitude toward their work. The traditional notion of "worrying not about poverty but about the unequal distribution of wealth" is very popular among them, and whoever wants to show more talents than others do will most probably give up his efforts at last under extensive pressure. They also hold the old Chinese saying that a man can sacrifice his life for someone who really understands him. So if someone can win their heart, Chinese employees will display great loyalty in working for him. The brief analysis above helps us to understand the past and current psychological conditions of the workers in Mainland China.

However what foreign investors bring into Mainland China is the scientific methods of business administration of advanced western society. They try to regulate every worker's conduct by setting up strict regulations and stimulate them to work hard with high pay. Such measures might take effect at the beginning, but will have unfavorable consequence in the long run. Chinese workers show great respect for personal relationships and are reluctant to do anything to harm such relationships. Yet the varied salaries may instill a grievance among workers. Besides, they think it unfair for foreign managers and technicians who are no more capable to enjoy much higher salaries. What is more, in Mainland China workers are very sensitive to their status hate foreigners who hurt their pride. As we have mentioned in the above cases, it will make the matter worse.

Fundamentally speaking, what have caused so many problems are the differences in the cultures. When speaking about cultural differences existing at Sino-foreign enterprises, Peter F. Drucker, a famous American scholar on business administration has pointed out: "Joint ventures are the most flexible instruments for making fits out of misfits, which will become increasingly important. At the same time joint ventures are the most demanding and difficult of all models of business operation not to mention the fact that they are the least understood." [3] The difficulty here lies in

---

(3) Drucker, Peter F. (1973), *Management: Tasks, Responsibilities, Practices*, Harper and Row, New York, p. 720.

the improbability for two sides getting used to each other's culture, especially when the traditional preferences and value concepts cause the differences. Naturally every culture has a great cohesive force, but such a force can be very hostile to anything from outside the community.

With the trend towards internationalization of business administration, workers from different cultures mixed in the same enterprise, bringing with them their own value concepts and behavioral modes. This is why many conflicts have occurred. In fact, at Sino-foreign enterprises, employees at all rank often lack the skills of communication, which cause so many unpleasant incidents of misunderstanding. For example, neither side is active, cooperative, even at a time when communication is possible and advisable. No one is willing to clarify what problem is troubling him and what help he needs. Instead, both parties seek to excuse and defend themselves, pouring out their complaints on the other party and turning the chance for communication into a debate.

At some enterprises, foreign staffs keep a lot of information about production and management only to themselves and the Chinese staffs conceal certain information about the government policy, which would often be helpful to foreigners. The operating workers at the basic level receive orders from Chinese managers and report to the latter concerning their work. Getting too little information about the plan of production and the market condition of the enterprise, Chinese manager finds it difficult to decide the best interests of the enterprise. On the other side, foreign manager has no knowledge of how the business is going for no feedback can be gotten from the workers. They make decisions and plans that are invariably incompatible with the real situation of production.

Thus, the lack of communication has been a main cause between the conflicts of two parts. Just as Stephen P. Robbins said in his book: "A review of the research suggests that semantic difficulties, insufficient exchange of information, and noise in the communication channel are all barriers to communication and potential antecedent conditions to conflict." [4]

---

(4) Robbins, Stephen P. (1996), *Organizational Behavior*, Seventh Edition, Prentice-Hall, Inc., p. 508.

4. How to Bridge the Gap

To translate into reality the possibility coordinating and harmonizing different cultures at Sino-foreign enterprises in China, the theoretical basis, methods and approaches must be studied carefully. Recent studies in cultural anthropology have proven that although culture can maintain relatively stable, it is changeable as well. American scholars Carol R. Ember and Melvin Ember argue that culture undergoes constant change and point out that culture has both adaptability and unity. Cultural adaptation is, in fact, cultural changes according to environmental variation. At the beginning, it is regarded as abnormal and unusual. But later, as the environment changes, people would learn from it and adapt themselves to the new situation. When most people have learned from this change, it will be considered normal again. [5] According to their theory, the bridging of the cultural gap is always preceded by the cross-cultural conflicts. Such theory opens up an optimistic outlook for bridging of the cultural gap. As Chinese saying goes, "without step by step, how can one tread a thousand mile long", Sino-foreign enterprises should deal with the problems by one step followed by another one patiently and find the way to bridge the gap in the course of practice so that two parts can both achieve prosperity.

However, all cultures are nurtured by history and its great inertia makes any change difficult. Besides, to substitute one culture with another can only succeed at the price of deleting the former one. Such one-sided emphasis is sure to cause drastic reaction. Therefore, in facing so many conflicts in the climate of internationalizing business administration, it is impossible and also unnecessary to force one side of the cooperation to submit to the other side. What should be emphasized are forbearance, mutual understanding and tolerance when you have studied and acknowledged the differences between two cultures. It is highly advisable to accept each other's cultural patterns and pay less attention to the fact that it is Chinese or foreigner that issues the orders, so that a harmonious cooperation can be achieved.

Tracing back to the mainstream of traditional Chinese culture, Confucianism has made it a principle to achieve success in such a process. Firstly, it perfects one's own personality; secondly, it builds harmony in one's own family; then, it prospers one's own country; and finally, it achieves peace in the whole world. This process shows

---

(5) Ember, Carol R. & Ember, Melvin (1999), *Cultural Anthropology*, Ninth Edition, Prentice Hall, Upper Saddle River, New Jersey, pp26-30.

evidently that Chinese people have always paid great attention to human nature; it is why the characteristic of Chinese culture laid too much stress on the personal relationships. Form this point of view, it is advisable to take into consideration the objectives of the employees when making a plan for the enterprise, and, if possible, to satisfy the employee's needs to the greatest extent so that the individual objective can be combined harmoniously with that of the enterprise.

However, a manager is not expected to be as tolerant and indulgent as to sacrifice the interest of the enterprise as a whole. Pay attention to personal relationships at the risk of damaging the production and management is senseless. Regulations should be observed strictly and can never be neglected in consideration of personal relationship. Negligence toward or excessive emphasis on either regulations or personal relationship can result in the imbalance of management. Here is the delicate matter of "degree", and to test whether the degree is proper, harmony in management is the standard.

The "Z Theory" proposed by William Ouchi is now popular with the managers all over the world. What the theory advocates is a harmonious environment inside enterprises. Only when work and life have been combined and Chinese and foreign staffs have gotten accustomed to each other's cultural characteristics can the management stimulate the inner creative power of the cultures. To put the essence of the theory into practice at Sino-foreign enterprises management can likely lead us to overcome many difficulties and to find a way to success. In the concept of the so-called "Z-Type Culture", the culture of an enterprise is composed of its tradition and its own established practice, also including its values.

Following this approach, Sino-foreign enterprises should attempt to identify the value of the enterprise with that of employees'. On this basis, they can unite all forces within the enterprise so that a peculiar enterprise culture — concepts, moral codes, working regulations, and operation modes can be formed and then accepted by all the employees at the enterprise. Members of the enterprise can, in this way, unite more closely and the enterprise can have more enduring and centripetal forces.

It is high time then we have a review of Danish scholar Neil Bohr 's words. He argues, "We may truly say that different human cultures are complementary to each other. Indeed, each such culture represents a harmonious balance of traditional conventions by means of which latent potentialities of human life can unfold themselves in a way that reveals to us new aspects of its unlimited richness and variety. Of course, there cannot, in this domain, be any question of such absolutely exclusive relationships as those between complementary experiences about the behavior of well-defined atomic objects, since hardly any culture exists which could be said to be fully self-contained. On the contrary, we all know from numerous examples how a more or less intimate contact between different human societies can lead to a gradual fusion of traditions, giving birth to a quite new culture." [6] The message carried in these words also applies to the areas where the conflicts occur as a result of the differences between two cultures. However, two parts of the conflict do not only repel each other, in reality, they also make up for each other.

Therefore, it is not surprising that foreign and Chinese employees will have different opinions about certain affairs at Sino-foreign enterprises. What is important is that we should have an insightful understanding of the areas where the differences come up and that we should find out the individual and personal causes of the differences. As Hedlund Gunner said, "More efforts should be made to enable all staffs to communicate assumptions about the conditions underlying certain plans and proposals." [7] To bridge the gap of different cultures, we propose here the following approaches for discussion.

(1) Foreign investors are more important in two parts of the co-operation because their decisions decide the future at Sino-foreign enterprise. In view of this, the managers sent to Mainland China should have these qualifications: ① A comprehensive knowledge about China that will enable them to get along with the local people. ② A flexible working method that deals with persons and business in accord with certain circumstances. ③ An upright patient and warmhearted manager who cares his fellow workers. ④ Acute insight and skill in finding talented local people.

Chinese members of Sino-foreign enterprise should try their best to create a benign investment environment for foreign investors and managers and to adjust their original concept to adapt themselves to a foreign system of management. They should understand that there will be no "gain" without "giving others" and

---

(6) Bohr, Niel (1958), *Atomic Physics and Human Knowledge*, John Wiley and Son, Inc., New York, pp. 30-31.
(7) Gunnar, Hedlund (1980), "The Role of Foreign Subsidiaries in Strategic Decision—Making in Swedish Multinational Corporations", *Strategic Management Journal*, 1, p. 33.

only when foreign investors get their investment profitable can they have satisfy their own interest. If possible, those who have a mind to enter Sino-foreign enterprises should receive special training arranged by relative agencies, so that the mutual adaptation process can be shortened.

(2) A consulting system should be set up. For a considerable number of foreign managerial staffs, their strong point lies in their technical knowledge rather than in their ability of management. These people can be technical consultants so that they can bring into full play their ability in technical affairs and avoid daily involvement in matters they are not familiar with. The administrative positions should be offered to those local people, who have high intelligence, high moral principle and keen sense of management. This kind of "feeling investment" can save a lot of trouble in dealing with some knotty problems.

(3) A trade union should be set up at the enterprise. Detailed regulations concerning the interests of both parts should be made up. Both parts should strictly observe the regulations about labor protection, rights and responsibilities of staffs at all level. Whenever conflicts occur, the trade union can serve as the mediator. The representatives from the union will talk with both sides, so that an agreement can be reached without a face-to-face conflict between the two parts. The members of the union are elected from Chinese and foreign staffs. They are not released from their regular work, yet they receive a token allowance from the union.

(4) Mutual trust should be built up between both sides. They should follow the rules and regulations of the enterprise and try their best to fulfil their own responsibilities for the mutual benefit of the whole enterprise. In the course of the cooperation, mutual understanding, mutual respects and mutual concerns should be strengthened for the benefit. It is not wise for foreign staffs to complain all the time or to act as teachers. They should understand the role personal feelings play in the enterprise management so long as such a personal concern does not go against the principles. Simultaneously, Chinese staffs should, in view of working for the benefit as well as for them, follow the instructions of the manager. If they have different opinions about the instructions they should speak their minds in proper ways. They should not echo other people's views thoughtlessly

and they should be bold enough to air their different views about unreasonable management. If their suggestions are not adopted immediately, they should give the manager time to consider the matter and should not be so impatient as to slow down with their work.

(5) Both parts should support the managing system directed by the general manager. The system should be formed in the spirit of efficiency and within each department there should be one person who is responsible. Training of the workers and the managerial staffs at all level should be strengthened so that their skill will be raised and their concepts be refreshed. Management should be carried out on the basis of statistics and management-on-the-spot should be emphasized. Workers should be highly conscious of the product quality.

(6) In order to urge the staffs to follow the regulations strictly, such economic measures as reward and punishment could be taken. One thing is to be noted: the income and other material interests entitled to a worker cannot be withheld as a punishment. Reward does not only have one form in bonus but can also be given in a more moral way, for example, to praise the worker orally, to list the name on the honor board or allow the worker more holidays with no deduction of payment. Neither is punishment exercised in only one way. Punishment does not necessarily mean the deduction of bonus, or the firing of the wrong doer. Criticism, instructions and tolerance for mistakes and failures sometimes might be surprisingly effective. Do not hurt the self-respect of an employed person, even when they decided to fire or punish him. Try to reason with him so that he will accept the punishment without unnecessary grievances.

There are certainly many means to bridge the gap between the different cultures at Sino-foreign enterprises. The above are just a few remarks by way of introduction so that others may come up with more valuable suggestions and opinions.

5. Conclusions

The sources of the cross-cultural conflicts at Sino-foreign enterprises in China can take various forms. Management can use quick conflict resolution techniques that seek to resolve the conflicts but do not deal with the causes – like a doctor treating the symptoms but not the diseases. However, these conflicts will break out in a different form if the causes are not treated. To effectively deal with the cross-cultural conflicts, it is essential to study the cultural backgrounds and value systems of both Chinese employees and the foreign colleagues within the enterprise. A thorough and frank discussion is encouraged of the sources and types of conflict and the achievement of a resolution that is in the best interest of the enterprise. This study provides a valuable guidance for both employees and managers of a Sino-foreign enterprise. The cross-cultural conflicts are not necessarily bad for Sino-foreign enterprises in China, even though they may waste valuable managerial effort and organizational resources. Conflicts can release creative problem-solving energies and lead to genuine innovation within the enterprises. Management should regard conflict as a constant force within the enterprises and seek to manage it in a beneficial manner.

【References】

[1] Benedict, Ruth (1953), *Patterns of Culture*, George Routledge & Sono, Ltd., London.
[2] Bohr, Niel (1958), *Atomic Physics and Human Knowledge*, John Wiley and Son, Inc., New York.
[3] Drucker, Peter F. (1999), "Selected Essays of Peter Drucker", *The Founder of Modern Management*, Mechanical Industry Press House.
[4] Drucker, Peter F. (1973), *Management: Tasks, Responsibilities, Practices*, Harper and Row, New York.
[5] Ember, Carol R. & Ember, Melvin (1999), *Cultural Anthropology*, Ninth Edition, Prentice Hall, Upper Saddle River, New Jersey.
[6] Gunnar, Hedlund (1980), "The Role of Foreign Subsidiaries in Strategic Decision—Making in Swedish Multinational Corporations", *Strategic Management Journal*, 1.
[7] Hofstede, Geert (1993), "Cultural Constraints in Management Theories", *Academy of Management Executive*, February.
[8] Hood, Neil & Vahlne, Jan – Erik (ed.) (1988), "Strategies in Global Competition", *Selected Papers form the Prince Bertil Symposium at the Institute of International Business*, Stockholm School of Economics, Croom Helm Ltd.
[9] Killing, Peter J. (1983), *Strategies for Joint Venture Success*, Croom Helm Ltd., London & Canberra.
[10] Robbins, Stephen P. (1996), *Organizational Behavior*, Seventh Edition, Prentice-Hall, Inc.

[11] Senge, Peter M. (1994), *The Fifth Discipline: The Art and Practice of the Learning Organization*, Commonwealth Publishing Co., Ltd.

[12] Valsiner, Jaan (1989), *Human development and culture: the social nature of personality and its study,* Lexington Books.

[13] Wang Zhizhang (1991), *The Theory of Harmony,* Shanghai Society & Science Press House.

Jin Yu
Toshimichi Haraguchi

Chapter 12 Competitiveness in the Reception of Mainland Tourists in Taiwan's Travel Industry

【Abstract】

In recent years, the central and local governments for the development of Taiwan's tourism has left no stones unturned to promote Taiwan's tourism industry to flourish to its strong economic development and the growing attention of people seeking tourism for leisure purposes. In 2013, the government continues to promote the "Tourism Pilot Program" and to implement "Economic Momentum to Push Forward" and "Optimized to Enhance the Quality of Tourism" to strive and build the quality of Taiwan's tourism environment. With the catchphrase of "Travel in Taiwan is Now" spun for marketing, Taiwan has proclaimed to the world of its fine food, beauty, virtue and culture.

China's rapid economic development in recent years both supports and shows the willingness and financial ability of consumers to travel abroad. This trend has increased significantly. Meanwhile, the loosening of policy opens up travelers to Taiwan reaching an unprecedented number in guests. In 2012, the total number of travelers exceeded 7.3 million people, which 2.58 million were of mainland origins, accounting for more than 35%. Group tours from the mainland also reached a record high of 1.78 million people. Thus, the reception of mainland tourists to Taiwan tourism market shows its prospects.

Tourism includes integration, packaging, marketing, resources and other functions. The emphasis of this study is to explore its internal competitive relationships with relevant external demand. To analyze the competitiveness of Taiwan's tourism providing a reference value of the proposal with its supply and demand. The result shows three main factors with firstly being that the strength of Taiwan's travel industry's competitiveness lies within the corporate culture of innovation and spirit of cooperation. Secondly, companies embark on a mentality of "continuous innovative", which increase the awareness level of talent. Therefore it not only raises the Taiwan travel industry with corporate cultural but also to improve staff quality resulting in lower turnover rate. Thirdly, corporate culture and service relationships has a direct correlation. As explained above that the corporate culture affects service awareness. The strength of the travel industry is the organization's ability to learn which increase the "Service" awareness. In other words, companies must constantly train employees to improve the quality of service in order to increase their service capacity and service quality optimization. These findings are expected to provide a reference to propel Taiwan travel industry into a more management direction.

【Keywords】: Taiwan, Travel Agencies, Mainland Tourists, Competitiveness, Tourism

1. Introduction

According to the Taiwan Tourism Bureau statistics, it showed that in 2010 visitors to Taiwan reached more than 5.56 million people, of whom mainland tourists consisted of 1.63 million (29.3%); 2011 visitors to Taiwan climbed to 6.08 million people, including mainland tourists of 1.78 million (29.3%); By 2012, more than 7.3 million tourists visited Taiwan, which accounted for 2.58 million mainland tourists (more than 35%). The above statistics shows that the number of tourists visiting Taiwan increases yearly. Therefore, the travel agencies who are charged with the integration, packaging, marketing Taiwan's tourism resources, will need to shift the focus from internal organization to external environment as two main aspects, in order to change the face of large environmental trends and to meet customer demand for diversity of challenges.

With the trend of internationalization and globalization, business and industrial management model is thus affected. In this era of rapid changes in the environment, customer demand tends to lean on diversity and customization. The tourism industry relating business environment is facing great changes. In response to the complex changes in the external environment, organizations should have the flexibility to adjust to fit. When effective response of organization desires while the external environment changes, companies are bound to face the challenges of change within the organization to be more agile than flat organizational structure within the organization, or to provide employees adequate authorization and education needed in response to changes in environmental policy. Colin Leys means that in order to seek technological development to the competitiveness of enterprises, the diversity of products and services to customers and international distribution, the ultimate goal is to obtain a place in the international market. Therefore, companies must pay attention to their "management" level. Simultaneously through overseas expansion with its country's experience, Visible International economic activity focuses on a particular country or region, the formation of geographic concentration of production activities, etc. Most of the production is to gather local natural resources including population density, transportation, and even complex geography and history combined to form the advantages. The companies will also produce innovative agglomeration effects. Most cases are within the enterprise of external knowledge. Enterprises attach importance to products and services, thus, bringing added value to the customer service is ever more so necessary to be met. In the meantime, the staff of the enterprise in terms of innovation and creativity is competitiveness. When enterprises are formed during the organization of strategic alliances will prone to lead to innovation. In order to serve our customers and create business value, inter-organizational cooperation such as complementary goods and services, innovation is created but not deliberately formed in the case. The East Asia region with the factors of production to the company's internal structure adjustment, one can create and sustain high economic growth advantage. Meanwhile, the company's continuous innovation and R&D products or services will be led toward a new stage of development of enterprise as an important factor. The innovative capability of enterprises to form agglomeration, inter-banking cooperation is a mutual learning and imitation model, and its corporate know-how and their experience with the company's organizational learning will constantly be pushed forward to meet production efficiency improvement and to increase market share and other effects. In addition Kale & Singh pointed out that companies need to focus on strategic alliances, while "knowledge sharing" in order to enhance the competitiveness of the whole industry.

Comprehensive travel industry is divided into three main categories. Type A specializes only in domestic travel. Then there is type B which serve both domestic and international travel but with limited specialties. The last type includes services of both type A and B with the addition of travel liaison, promotion, pricing and other services limited to the first two types. It acts as a delegate to cover all bases to encompass an inclusive travel industry. This study will show the Taiwan travel industry's point of view to explore the travel industry competitiveness. Obtaining first-hand information to the questionnaire sent to Taiwan integrated travel agency, in order to understand the internal structures of Taiwan travel agency and a competing trend, and analysis to provide recommendations.

2. Literature Review
(1) Definition of Competitiveness

The so-called competitiveness, this term risen in the 1980s, nearly 20 years to pursue global business enterprises are inherent competitiveness. Concept of competitiveness stems from competition. Darwin's "natural selection, survival of the fittest" theories emphasize competition dominated the direction of evolution of species, between species through competition to compete for the resources necessary to their survival; but only those who were able to survive has an advantage not eliminated by the environment. The concept of competition is also to expand the application in sociology, economics and management science is used to describe the individual, group, organization development in order to survive among the various activities. Competitive conduct complex, according to their purpose, scope, objects, methods, rules are different and have different meanings. Competition may be a means to a certain environment (including the natural environment and social system) with restrictions in result. The scope of competition and the object whose wide-ranging, probably competition between people, between species or species within the competition, but also may be competition between units of the organization (including the organization of small groups within each sub-business, industry, or even a national competition). The need in a competitive process to obtain survival or favorable position, one must have a competitive advantage, which is the basic concept of competitiveness.

Competitiveness is usually divided into three layers of businesses, industries and national competitiveness and have different objectives and by means of pursuing different research. The competitiveness of enterprises is concerned about profitability and market share, often as indicator to be measured. Industrial competitiveness research topic is the industrial productivity, technological innovation capability and Industry life cycle. Competition is targeted at industries in other countries, and thus the competitiveness of the industry level is more concentrated on an international trade performance; such industries in the export price, quantity and quality of other aspects of performance. The National Competitiveness considerations are in addition to the economic level, with its emphasis on social welfare enhancement. Industry composed by the enterprise, but also exists in the country among the three are actually linked together and influence each other. In order to explore any level of competitiveness, one should also consider factors from other levels of the potential impact thus deepened to investigate the competitiveness of complexity. But regardless of what level of competitiveness is underlined, a persistent advantage prevails. This three-level, where the concept of national competitiveness becomes most vague, especially in doing international comparisons often due to subjective values, cultural differences, political and economic situation and many other factors, so it is not a truly objective metrics and definitions. According to M.E. Porter is to determine the competitiveness of the core business success. Competitiveness determines the appropriateness of the activities of enterprises, while the company's core resources such as personnel innovation, service, corporate culture or brand's performance can be a good measure of competitiveness. For enterprises, competitive strategy is fundamentally wrestling to find the most favorable position. While the competitive policy goal is to establish a profitable and sustainable management of the environment in order to determine the competitiveness of enterprises to overcome the external ambient pressure.

Core resources included tangible and intangible assets, and intangibles assets including the capital, intellectual property, etc. And the core capabilities include personnel, individuals and organization's unique capabilities. Based on the output of the resource basis of enterprise business strategy, we know that products and services affect the enterprise's major core factors. Resource-based theory of the firm measured on that description having other competing companies that cannot be imitated, scarce, valuable and irreplaceable resources or ability to support the strategy adopted, and thus establishing a long-term and sustained competitive advantage. In regards to resource-strategy focus, companies must first focus on a variety of different angles in observation of its resources purposes and portfolio review and evaluate resource quality. Evaluate the strategy behavior in conducting policy-making which can be considered of its further decision of the outcome to create a performance resource advantages.

(2) **Competing Relationship**

The more the global market moves towards internationalization activities, the more the need of organizations to achieve their business goals. Therefore in the late 1970s, companies began to make strategic alliances. Strategic alliances between enterprises produced and redefined the relevant rules and governing policies for the enterprise, and allowing enterprises to rethink the positioning of business organizations, including the way they compete and cooperation patterns. Appropriate strategies and alliances take quite a long period of time; assuming cooperation on related products or services of similar products or services are part of the state of competition, then one needs a strategic alliance agreement clearly stipulated in the contract. In addition, this may bring a long-term cooperation between the insecurity caused due to distrust. It is recommended to certain items as short-term cooperation; or between the two companies of a product must be made with a different future goals and vision plan which will not overlap and do not cross to the other side of the related fields. This goal is difficult to make plans, but in any case, the two companies entered into a strategic alliance in order to achieve different objectives alliance efficacy.

The heart of the strategic alliance to attract more than two enterprises in their resources with each other is the willingness to cooperate on the basis of funds. In other words, two or more enterprises strategic alliance involves cooperation and competition policy (competing strategies) and to avoid falling into the trap of the other party. According to the above literature, this study is defined as between enterprises competing strategy (travel agency) how competition and cooperation with other travel agencies in order to achieve a win-win profit. In recent 20 years, the global economic arena has become increasingly uncertain and complex, and as more and more participants from different cultures step onto the world economic stage, the stage has been accepted by many changing ideas, competitiveness and economic theory has gradually emerged. Companies have adopted new measures to face the climate change impact. They seek new ways to reduce costs, improve efficiency, reduce debt, improve competitiveness, while conserving resources and reducing waste. Competitive strategy is simply to find a market for wrestling tournament of the most favorable position. Competing policy goal is to establish a sustainable profitable environment to overcome the external pressure. This goal determines the company's competitiveness. Therefore, the success of an alliance, like its original plan would mostly depends on partners and expanding relationships among them. The initial agreement is only an alliance to provide development opportunities which brings to its partners declaring the relationship between the growth and the value of the basic rules. Unfortunately, the development trend of alliance will lead to even more great changes over time. It is often misinterpreted as a weakness nonetheless. In extreme cases, the change may result in the withdrawal of a member resulting in a high dropout rate alliance. However, this concern may ultimately be a mute point as the instability should not be regard as a priority. Alliance stability should not be the purpose of its existence, but rather the success of its coalition policy content.

The core of the strategic alliance with resources companies to attract other partners to each other using the resources and capabilities. In other words, enterprises are to compete and cooperate rather than competition and cooperation in order to avoid. In this study, we have listed previously for strategic alliances are defined as follows:

Table 12-1 Definition of Experts on Strategic Alliances

Scholar	Content
James (2002)	Strategic alliances are a mutually profitable process, from two or more groups for commitment in dependence and maintenance.
Porter & Fuller (1986)	The original method by contact between two or more businesses creates a long term relationship, but not a merger.
Grant (1991)	Sustainable development and organization's strength to create sustainable competitiveness are of two major components.
Barney(1991)	Strategic alliance refers to as two companies in the development, manufacture and marketing services to work together with the aim of having a source of competitive advantage.
Kale & Singh (2007)	Knowledge sharing within the union learning process helps build their skills of enterprise alliance in creating a more successfully managed alliance.

Source: This Study

According to most references, this study defines competitiveness and strategic alliance partners as a strategy applied to independent innovation and technical cooperation in partnership in order to create each mutual benefit competition. At the same time, companies must apply their core values in order to be upgraded to a partnership for an added value.

According to Rosabeth argument, the alliance between two companies, whether they come from different regions in the world, shares a similar standards of today business life. Some alliances exist only for a very short time, only to maintain its partners to establish a presence in the emerging markets of the time required for the other league to say that two or two mentioned company's technology and the ability to fully merge as a prelude. As partners, it is importantly crucial to have the ability to learn and to cooperate. Moreover, the different operational needs between companies will generate un-exception to resolve. It is important to build relationships between many partners to help wrinkle out the differences before it becomes inexplicable. According to many references to the literature, this study will be based on competitiveness with competing policy as defined how companies use their own limited resources, strategic alliances with industry, to compete in a globalized market as a key capability.

3. Research Methods

Under Haraguchi Jun Tao professor guidance, in January 2013, questionnaires were sent out to all 300 of Taiwan travel agencies (including the ones which only cater to mainland tourists). Questionnaires containing competitiveness-related issues (including personnel, services, corporate culture, and competing relationship as four constitutive surfaces) were used. Feedback of 138 in which only 117 are of validity. The effective rate was 39.0%. Lee Curtis' five measurements (Cronbach's Alpha) were 0.711, 0.793, 0.880, 0.766, and 0.728. According to Cuieford proposed reliability, any index of above 0.7 is considered as a high reliability.

This study is divided into descriptive statistics and inferential statistics. SPSS17.0 version of the questionnaire inferential statistical analysis of the Pearson correlation and linear regression analysis is used to understand the talent, services, corporate culture, and competing relationship as four dimensions of relevance and impact significance. The study hypothesis and the model showed in Fig. 12-1.

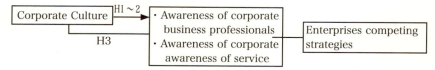

Fig.12-1 Model in this Study

Hypotheses described as follows:

H1: Corporate culture has a significant impact on human cognition.

H2: Corporate culture awareness of its services have a significant impact.

H3: Corporate culture affects business professionals and service awareness, thereby affecting the business of competing strategies.

4. Results of Research and Analysis

117 valid and comprehensive questionnaires were sent out to 63 travel agencies and 52 specialized agencies (2 missing values). The basic profiles are summarized as follows in Table 12-2.

Table12-2 List of Taiwanese Travel Agencies Profile

Project	Number	Percentage
Capital		
Less than NT$30 Million	31	26.50%
NT$30M – 60M	7	6.00%
NT$60M – 90M	15	12.8%
NT$90M – 120M	23	19.7%
NT$120M and above	24	20.5%
Unanswered	17	14.5%
Years in Business		
Before 1950	10	8.6%
1951 - 1980	26	22.2%
1981 - 1990	52	44.4%
2000 and after	25	21.4%
Unanswered	4	3.4%
Number of Employees		
Less than 20	24	20.5%
21 - 50	10	8.5%
51 - 100	16	13.7%
101 - 200	16	13.7%
Above 201	51	43.6%

Source: This Study

From Table 12-2, the majority of enterprises in capital were under NT$30 millions (31%), but 24% of enterprises showed capital above NT$120 millions. Most of the enterprises established from 1981 to 1990 showed the number of employees of more than 200 people, belonging to large enterprises. The four dimensions of the mean and standard deviation are shown in Table 12-3.

Table 12-3 Facets of Mean and Standard Deviation List

Questions	Mean	Standard Deviation
Talent		
1. The company's employees were good (high quality)	2.85	0.706
2. Employees are the most important asset	3.28	0.585
3. New staffs are often able to get started without training	3.94	0.837
4. The company emphasizes importance to education and training of employees on a regular basis	2.85	0.761
5. The company employee turnover rate is very low	2.53	0.934
6. The company pays attention to language skills of staff	2.48	0.831
(Overall average)	2.99	
Corporate Culture		
1. Organizational learning is a key competitive advantage	3.11	0.856
2. The Company believes that education and training of employees is an investment	3.34	0.960
3. Continuous innovation is one of the Company's corporate culture	3.93	0.966
4. The company has internal cross-organizational (department) cooperation and coordination	3.72	0.849
5. The company acknowledges there is a difference in product design for mainland sightseeing tourists than with customers from other countries	2.83	0.712
6. The company like to host group of mainland tourists more than travelers from other countries	3.16	0.945
7. The Company considers inter-organizational knowledge management is very important	3.39	0.710
8. Organization team of mutual cooperation is one of your company's culture	3.77	0.731
(Overall average)	3.41	
Services		
1. The company pays attention to let customers know the contents of goods and services	3.85	0.988
2. Endless training of staff to continuously improve service quality is very important	3.83	0.782
3. Due to the company's high service quality, many customers return	3.28	0.863
4. The company provides customers with diversified and customized selection of products	3.48	0.831
5. The company's service quality is better than others in the industry	3.35	0.772
6. The Company considers Taiwan travel industry service types	2.48	0.832

(hospitality) to emulate Japan (Overall average)		3.38
Competing Relationship		
1. The Company will cooperate with others in the industry to expand the mainland market	3.58	0.758
2. The Company's products and services are different from others in the industry	3.63	0.873
3. Travel industry price competition will be a way to attract customers (R)	2.72	0.899
4. The company cooperates with peers in reception to mainland tourists	3.18	0.682
5. A fierce competitive travel industry (R)	3.33	0.882
6. Good potential for the future development of the industry (reception of mainland tourists)	2.52	0.832
7. The company cooperate with the mainland travel agency in reception of mainland tourists traveling to Taiwan	3.20	0.723
8. The Company has leadership over its products and services	3.17	0.813
(Overall average)	**3.17**	

Source: This Study Note: R represents a negative list

Table 12-4 Summary of Results of Correlation Analysis

		Talent	Service	Corporate Culture	Concurrence Tactics
Talent	Person Related		0.533	0.616	0.342
	P Value		0.000*	0.000*	0.001*
Services	Person Related	0.533		0.675	0.253
	P Value	0.000*		0.000*	0.007*
Corporate Culture	Person Related	0.616	0.675		0.520
	P Value	0.000*	0.000*		0.000*
Concurrence Tactics	Person Related	0.324	0.235	0.520	
	P Value	0.001*	0.007*	0.000*	

Source: This Study (* represents p <0.05, with significance)

Table 12-5 Verification of Hypothesis 1 (Linear Regression Analysis)

Dimensions	Non standardized Coefficient		Standardized Coefficient Beta Allocation	T Value	Significant (p)	VIF
	B Estimated Value	Standard Error				
(Constant)	1.209	0.168		7.188	0.000*	
1. Organizational learning is a key competitive advantage	0.022	0.066	0.028	0.331	0.741	1.463
2. The Company believes that education and training of employees is an investment	0.100	0.063	0.154	1.594	0.114	1.905
3. Continuous innovation is one of the Company's corporate culture	0.237	0.061	0.352	3.888	0.000*	1.666
4. The Company has internal cross-organizational (department) cooperation and coordination	0.161	0.049	0.318	3.297	0.001*	1.890
5. The company acknowledges there is a difference in product design for mainland sightseeing tourists than with customers from other countries	-0.015	0.047	-0.024	-0.318	0.751	1.200
6. Your company likes to host group of mainland tourists more than travelers from other countries	0.086	0.033	0.190	2.603	0.011*	1.084
7. The Company considers inter-organizational knowledge management is very important	-0.040	0.072	-0.063	-0.548	0.585	2.726
8. Organizational team of mutual cooperation is one of your company's culture	0.017	0.068	0.029	0.252	0.801	2.741

R^2=0.494   Adj-R^2=0.454   F=12.559   Significant (p)=0.000   D-W=2.062

Note: * indicates p less than 0.05, a statistically significant.
Dependent variables: the awareness level of talent

From Table 12-3, the highest level of corporate awareness of the two projects are "corporate culture" and "enterprise services."

(1) Hypothesis Verification:

Pearson correlation analysis discussed four degree of correlation between dimensions, and its results are summarized below in Table 12-4.

The above table shows four inter-related dimensions are having a significant extent, and are positively correlated. It is worth mentioning that among the largest correlation coefficient are "corporate culture" and "Services" (0.675). Linear regression was used to verify the hypothesis 1 (H1): its corporate culture has a significant impact on human cognition.

D-W value of 2.062 nearing 2, which means that there is major correlation in the error term, In addition, VIF values is less than 10, which means that each variable has no collinearity problems. The estimated regression equation is: talent level of knowledge (Y) = 1.209 +0.237* (continued innovation is one of the Company's corporate culture) +0.161* (company internal cross-organizational department cooperation and coordination) +0.086* (company likes to host group of mainland tourists more than other countries travelers). In other words, the degree of attention of business professionals by the corporate culture of innovation, enterprise capabilities and cooperation with interdepartmental group of mainland tourists received the highest degree of positive impact. Among which "innovation" is the ability to forward the highest coefficient. Therefore, hypothesis 1 is partially substantiated. From Table 12-3, the average talent of this dimension is only 2.99. From the linear regression analysis, results can be explained when the company embarked on "continuous innovation", one can increase the awareness level of talent. Therefore the recommendation is that Taiwan travel industry should be "innovative" to raise its corporate culture to enhance staff quality and to reduce turnover rates. Meanwhile, the study found that Taiwan travel industry does not value their foreign language skills (average of only 2.48), the reason is "like to host group of mainland tourists more than travelers from other countries," only need to benefit from the advantage of language - Chinese. , The following table shows Hypothesis 2 concerning the validation results.

Hypothesis 2 (H2): Corporate culture awareness of its services has a significant impact. Its authentication is analyzed as follows in Table 12-6.

Table 12-6　Verification of Hypothesis 2 (Linear Regression Analysis)

Dimensions	Non standardized Coefficient		Standardized Coefficient Beta Allocation	t Value	p Value	VIF
	B Estimated Value	Standard Error				
(Constant)	0.448	0.169		2.653	0.009*	
1. Organizational learning is a key competitive advantage	0.273	0.067	0.326	4.089	0.000*	1.468
2. The company believes that education and training of employees is an investment	0.016	0.064	0.022	0.250	0.803	1.859
3. Continuous innovation is one of the cultures of the company	0.195	0.061	0.269	3.166	0.002*	1.666
4. The Company has internal cross-organizational (department) cooperation and coordination	0.154	0.050	0.278	3.081	0.003*	1.884
5. The company acknowledges there is a difference in product design for mainland sightseeing tourists than with customers from other countries	0.005	0.048	0.007	0.103	0.918	1.197
6. Your company likes to host group of mainland tourists more than travelers from other countries	0.011	0.034	0.022	0.322	0.748	1.084
7. The company considers inter-organizational knowledge management is very important	0.051	0.074	0.076	0.695	0.488	2.782
8. Organizational team of mutual cooperation is one of your company's culture	0.055	0.069	0.086	0.787	0.433	2.783

R^2=0.　R^2=549　Adj-R^2=0.515　F=15.842　Significant (p)=0.000　D-W=2.056

Note: * indicates p less than 0.05, a statistically significant.
Dependent variables: the awareness level of service

The estimated regression equation is: service awareness (Y) = 0.448 +0.273* (organizational learning is a key competitive advantage) +0.195* (continued innovation is one of the Company's corporate culture) +0.154 * (the Company has internal cross-organizational (department) cooperation and coordination). In other words, the degree of awareness of the service enterprise by enterprise culture of organizational learning, innovation and enterprise capabilities with the degree of cross-sectoral cooperation effects has a positive influence. Among which "organizational learning" has the highest positive coefficient. Therefore, hypothesis 2 is partially substantiated. From Table 12-3, Taiwan travel industry for "organizational learning is a key competitive advantage," the average of 3.11 for this project, is close to the 'no opinion' level. From the analysis of the results in Table12-6, it shows that when enterprises strengthen the organization's ability to learn can increase the "service" of cognition. It is recommended that companies should proceed to the organization of learning, such as regularly scheduled training courses in order to increase their service capacity and quality of service optimization capabilities. Hypothesis 3 concerning the validation results shows in the following table.

Hypothesis 3 (H3): Corporate culture affects business professionals and service awareness, thereby affecting the business of competing strategies.

Table 12-7 Hypothesis 3 Validation (Human Cognition Linear Regression Analysis)
Note: * indicates p less than 0.05, a statistically significant.

Dimensions	Non standardized Coefficient		Standardized Coefficient Beta Allocation	t Value	p Value	VIF
	B Estimated Value	Standard Error				
(Constant)	1.189	0.161		7.398	0.000*	
Corporate Culture	0.592	0.072	0.616	8.204	0.000*	1.000

R^2=0.380 Adj-R^2=0.374 F=67.299 P=0.000* D-W=2.141
Dependent variables: cognitive talent

Dimensions	Non standardized Coefficient		Standardized Coefficient Beta Allocation	t Value	p Value	VIF
	B Estimated Value	Standard Error				
(Constant)	1.108	0.246		4.507	0.000*	
Corporate Culture	0.550	0.112	0.509	4.901	0.000*	1.578
Cognitive Talent	0.019	0.118	0.016	0.158	0.875	1.578

$R^2=0.269$ Adj-$R^2=0.256$ F=19.720 P=0.000* D-W=2.13

Dependent variables: Enterprise competition

Table 12-8   Hypothesis 3 Validation (Cognitive Services Linear regression Analysis)

Dimensions	Non standardized Coefficient		Standardized Coefficient Beta Allocation	t Value	p Value	VIF
	B Estimated Value	Standard Error				
(Constant)	0.488	0.161		3.035	0.003*	
Corporate Culture	0.698	0.072	0.675	9.638	0.000*	1.000

$R^2=0.456$ Adj-$R^2=0.451$ F=92892 P=0.000* D-W=1.899

Dependent variables: cognitive service

Dimensions	Non standardized Coefficient		Standardized Coefficient Beta Allocation	t Value	p Value	VIF
	B Estimated Value	Standard Error				
(Constant)	1.141	0.203		5.631	0.000*	
Corporate Culture	0.555	0.120	0.518	4.620	0.000*	1.863
Cognitive Service	0.001	0.115	0.001	0.013	0.990	1.863

$R^2=0.270$ Adj-$R^2=0.256$ F=19.949 P=0.000* D-W=2.137

Note: * indicates p less than 0.05, a statistically significant.

Dependent variables: Enterprise competition

Table 12-7 and 12-8 show the direct effects, indirect effects and the total effect of the results are summarized below in Table 12-9.

Table 12-9 Hypothesis 3 Results

Dimensions	Direct Effect	Indirect Effect	Total Effect
Cognitive Talent	0.509	0.616*0=0	0.509
Cognitive Service	0.518	0.675*0=0	0.518

Source: This Study

From Table 12-5, 12-6 and 12-9; the corporate culture will affect business professionals and service awareness, while corporate culture will affect competing strategies. However, the talent level of knowledge and service show no direct effect. Although Hypothesis 3 is not true, nonetheless this study shows that if corporate enterprises have innovation, cross-sectoral coordination and knowledge management as components of its corporate culture, it then ensure that personnel will be equipped with competing strategies while improving the quality of services as a significant positive impact.

5. Conclusions

This study is aimed to investigate the competitiveness in Taiwan travel industry on the mainland tourists after the loosening up of its tourism policy. According to the literature made of the three hypotheses, two are partially substantiated. The other does not hold. The findings of this study and the recommendations conclusion are as the following three factors.

(1) Reception of Taiwan travel industry's competitiveness lies in mainland tourists' corporate culture, among which innovation and organizational cooperation having the highest value. In addition, both Taiwan and the mainland have the same language competitive advantage.

(2) The degree of attention of business professionals by the corporate culture of innovation, enterprise capabilities and cooperation with interdepartmental group of mainland tourists amassed the degree of positive influence. When companies started in "continuous innovation", one can increase the awareness level of talent.

Therefore it is recommended that Taiwan travel industry should be "innovative" to raise its corporate culture to enhance staff quality and reduce turnover rates.

(3) The four dimensions in this study, "service awareness" when "company attention so that customers understand the content of goods and services" and "constantly training staff to enhance service quality is very important." are of the highest average. The study also found that corporate culture and service relationships with significant cognition present positive correlation; and the corporate culture affects service awareness. In the validation of the hypothesis 2, when travel industry strengthen the organization's ability to learn can increase the "Service" awareness. In other words, companies that train employees to improve the quality of service is very important, but will not be adequate. Therefore it is recommended that companies should proceed with the organization of learning, such as regularly scheduled training courses in order to increase their service capacity and service quality optimization.

For the subsequent part of the study, it suggests a consumer satisfaction surveys oriented from the mainland tourists whom visited Taiwan. To use the consumer awareness of travel agents in order to evaluate the actual comparison of differences and satisfaction could be competitiveness for the companies.

(4) Reception of Taiwan travel industry's competitiveness lies in mainland tourists' corporate culture, among which innovation and organizational cooperation having the highest value. In addition, both Taiwan and the mainland have the same language competitive advantage.

(5) The degree of attention of business professionals by the corporate culture of innovation, enterprise capabilities and cooperation with interdepartmental group of mainland tourists amassed the degree of positive influence. When companies started in "continuous innovation", one can increase the awareness level of talent. Therefore it is recommended that Taiwan travel industry should be "innovative" to raise its corporate culture to enhance staff quality and reduce turnover rates.

(6) The four dimensions in this study, "service awareness" when "company attention so that customers understand the content of goods and services" and "constantly training staff to enhance service quality is very important." are of the highest average. The study also found that corporate culture and service relationships with significant cognition present positive correlation; and the corporate culture affects service awareness. In the validation of the hypothesis 2, when travel

industry strengthen the organization's ability to learn can increase the "Service" awareness. In other words, companies that train employees to improve the quality of service is very important, but will not be adequate. Therefore it is recommended that companies should proceed with the organization of learning, such as regularly scheduled training courses in order to increase their service capacity and service quality optimization.

For the subsequent part of the study, it suggests a consumer satisfaction surveys oriented from the mainland tourists whom visited Taiwan. To use the consumer awareness of travel agents in order to evaluate the actual comparison of differences and satisfaction could be competitiveness for the companies.

【Reference】

[1] Andretsch, D.B. and M.P. Feldman(1996), "R&D spillovers and the geography of innovation and production", *American Economic Review*, 86, pp. 630-640.

[2] Balassa, B.(1966), "Tariff Reductions and Trade in Manufactures among Industrial Counties", *American Economic Review*, No. 56, Vol. 3, pp. 466-473.

[3] Barney, J.B.(1991), "Firm Resource and Sustained Competitive Advantage", *Journal of Management*, Vol. 17, pp.99-120.

[4] Buckley, P.J.& M. Chapman(1993), "Bounded Rationality in the International Strategic Alliance", *Paper presented at the EIBA conference*.

[5] Chandler, A.D.(1990), *Scale and Scope: The Dynamics of Industrial Capitalism*, Harvard University, Cambridge, Mass.

[6] Chunwei Lu, Chenghsien Sung, George Y. Wang, Weichin Li, (2012), "A Study of Competitive and Cooperative Strategies on Taiwan Amplifier and Speaker Manufacturers", *Mathematical Models and Methods in Applied Sciences*, Vol. 6, pp. 661-669.

[7] Chunwei Lu(2011), "International Competitiveness of Taiwan Transformer Industry", *International Journal of Education and Information Technology*, Issue 2, Vol. 2, pp. 1-13.

[8] Colin Ley(2001), *Market-Driven Politics, Neo-liberal democracy and the public interest*, London, Verso Books 280.

[9] Cuieford, J.P.(1965), *Fundamental Statistics in Psychology and Education 4th ed.*, McGraw Hill, N.Y.

[10] Dunning, J.H. (1997), *The Changing Nature of Firms and Governments in a*

Knowledge-Based Globalizing Economy, Carnegie Bosch Institute, England.

[11] Grant R.M.(1991), "The Resources-Based Theory of Competitive Advantage: Implications for Strategy Formulation", *California Management Review*, pp. 114-135.

[12] James D.(2002), "Bamford, Benjamin Gomes-Casseres, and Michale S. Robinson", *Mastering Alliance Strategy,* pp. 5-15.

[13] Joan Vuust(1999), *Towards an International Economy of Strategic Alliances*, Kopicentralen, Aalborg Universitet Press.

[14] Kale, P., and Singh, H(2007), "Building firm: Capabilities through learning: The role of the alliance learning process in alliance capability and firm-level alliance success", *Strategic Management Journal*, 28, pp. 981-1000.

[15] Piderit, S.K(2000), "Rethinking resistance and recognizing ambivalence: A multidimensional view of attitudes toward an organizational change", *Academy of Management Review*, No. 25, Vol.4, pp.783-794.

[16] Popescu Delia Mioara, Robescu Valentina Ofelia, Velter Victor, Ion Stegaroiu, Popa Gabriela, GoldbachDumitru(2010), "Innovation Management and Romanian SME's", *Proceedings of the 4th WSEAS International Conference on Business Administration.*

[17] Porter, M. E. & Fuller, R. (1986), *Competition Global Industries*, Harvard Business Press, Boston.

[18] Porter, M.E. (1998), *On Competition.* Cambridge, Mass: Harvard Business School Press.

[19] Rosabeth Moss Kanter (2002), "Collaborative Advantage: The Art of Alliances", *Harvard Business Review on Strategic Alliances.*

[20] http://admin.taiwan.net.tw/public/public.aspx?no=315 Tourism Bureau website

Chienlin, Lee

Chapter 13 Determination and Interpretation of Correlations between Perceived Quality, Relationship Quality and Brand Evaluation among Patrons at Kagoshima Restaurants

【Abstract】

In Japan, research and theoretical knowledge on "restaurant patron actions" is still being developed. There have been few studies on the perceived quality, relationship quality, and brand evaluation of restaurant patrons. Studies of this type are necessary for restaurants to gain a long-term competitive advantage and to understand the relationship between consumers and brand relationships. This study focused primarily on the correlations among internal perceived quality by patrons of Kagoshima restaurants and perceptions such as brand evaluation of relationship quality in order to supplement inadequacies in empirical studies of patron actions. This study conducted convenience sampling on patrons after eating at 10 Kagoshima restaurants between July and September of 2011, with 312 valid questionnaires. Data analysis includes descriptive statistics, factor analysis, Pearson correlation analysis, and regression analysis. The study finds that there is a significant correlation between a patron's perceived quality and relationship quality; there is also a significant correlation between relationship quality and brand evaluation. In addition, a patron's perceived quality has a significant effect on relationship quality; the patron's relationship quality also has a significant effect on brand evaluation.

【Keywords】: Restaurant patron, Perceived quality, Relationship quality, Brand evaluation, Introduction

1. Research Background and Motives

As a result of economic growth factors, changes in social and family structure, and increasing numbers of women in the work force, eating out has gradually become an important part of family life. In exploiting the massive business opportunities in the family eat-out market, a key to increasing the profitability of restaurants is to understand the characteristics of families when dining in restaurants (Chen Zongxuan, 2010). Thus, the first priority of businesses is to understand the demands of their patrons in order to provide good services and to achieve the sustainable development of restaurant brands.

2. Research Purpose

Aoki Yukihiro (2010) pointed out that specific brands would affect the inclination to continue purchasing by consumers. However, consumers have different understandings and perceptions of brands, which make it difficult for managers to maintain long-term relationships with them. Therefore, in order to create a sustainable competitive advantage, it is necessary to research consumers and brand relationships (Sugano Saori, 2011). A review of literature shows that there is still a need for more studies and theoretical knowledge of patron actions; a few studies have focused on consumers at food exhibitions (Huang Huixuan, 2007; Cai Changqing et al., 2009); and consumers at night markets (such as Li Suxin, Li Weizhen, 2007, Cai Mujie, 2009, Wu Jiahua, 2010), followed by those exploring specialty foods in rural tourism (Tang Xingfen, 2007) or food consumers while they traveled (Hall et al., 2003). However, there have been relatively few studies focusing on the perceived quality, relationship quality, and brand evaluation of restaurant patrons. The above studies still do not clearly define the term "restaurant patron." This study adopts the definition of those who "spend money on food and drink outside the home for enjoyment." This study seeks to understand the feelings of patrons while dining at restaurants and to combine their psychological variables to explore the correlations among perceived quality, relationship quality, and brand evaluations so that businesses can improve in multiple dimensions, such as personnel services and core services and thereby improve their interaction with patrons to achieve the sustainable operation of their brands. Thus, the purposes of this study are as follows:

(1) To understand the distribution of Kagoshima patron samples.

(2) To understand whether there are correlations between patrons' perceived quality and relationship quality.

(3) To understand the correlation between patrons' relationship quality and brand evaluation.

(4) To explore the effect of patrons' perceived quality on relationship quality.

(5) To explore the effect of patrons' relationship quality on brand evaluation.

3. Literature review
(1) Perceived quality

Kelly (1987) believed that consumption experience does not only involve feelings, but rather is the cognitive process formed after an individual has experienced something for a period of time or participated in some activity (Grace & O'Cass, 2004). Perceived quality consists of consumer's feelings and perceptions after consuming a product (Iijima Kotono et al., 2009). Grace and O'Cass (2004) pointed out that perceived quality would affect customers' consumption emotions, satisfaction, and brand attitude. In other words, consumers would have different views and feelings about every product. Elevating consumers' perceived quality of products would positively affect satisfaction toward those products (Iijima Kotono et al., 2009). Xue Zhaoyi and Xue Rongtang (2007) found that personnel services and service scenarios have significant positive effects on relationship quality. Fang Jianyi (2010) also found that good perceived quality positively affected consumers' overall valuation of and satisfaction with travel products, which, in turn, affected the image of the scenic spot and the behavioral intentions at those destinations.

(2) Relationship quality

Crosby et al. (1990) believed that relationship quality is the overall evaluation of buyers and sellers of the strength of their relationship. It consists of the emotions formed in the process of interaction between customers and service personnel, so that customers can feel trust and satisfaction toward service personnel. It is necessary to establish good relationships with consumers in order to establish competitive advantages over long-term operations (Sugano Saori, 2011). The strength of interactive relationships between customers and employees would positively affect relationship quality and customer loyalty (Wong & Sohal, 2006). Customer satisfaction affects customer maintenance, so it is necessary to have good quality to elevate customer satisfaction. Customer satisfaction comes from trust in quality, robust corporate systems, and the relationships established with customers (Henning-Thurau, 2000; Iwamoto Toshihiko, 2010).

(3) Brand evaluation

Keller (2000) pointed out that brand image is "an associative memory of consumers about brands" (Tonegawa Koichi, Bai Jingyi, 2008). Wong and Merrilees

(2008) define brand evaluation as how a brand succeeds in the market, and brand evaluation can effectively measure the strategies of a brand (Zeng Junlin, 2010). In related studies, Zeng Junlin (2010) believed that relationship quality is an antecedent variable that effectively influences brand evaluation, which shows that good interaction between businesses and consumers can bring about a better brand image and a positive reputation.

(4) **Summary of questions**
① What are the perceived feelings of Japanese patrons during consumption?
② What are the factors that affect Japanese patrons' brand evaluation?
③ What are the relationships among perceived quality, relationship quality, and brand evaluation?

4. Research Design
(1) Research Framework
Based on an exploration of domestic and foreign literature, the model in this study primarily refers to work by Gracea and O'Cass (2004), Wong and Sohal (2006), Xue Zhaoyi and Xue Rongtang (2007), and Zeng Junlin (2010) as foundations for the consumption behaviors of patrons in this study. The research framework in this study is shown in Figure 13-1.

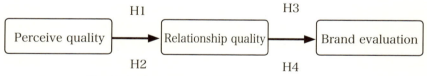

Fig. 13-1 The research framework in this study

(2) Research Hypotheses
Based on the above literature review and framework, the hypotheses for this study are thus constructed:

H1: there is a significant correlation between patrons' perceived quality and relationship quality.

H2: there is a significant correlation between patrons' perceived quality and relationship quality.

H3: there is a significant correlation between patrons' relationship quality and brand evaluation.

H4: patrons' relationship quality has a significant effect on brand evaluation.

(3) Research Scope and Subjects

This study uses Kagoshima of Japan as the research scope. In order to achieve consistency in measurement standards, this study first selects 20 chain or well-known restaurants that are similar and have an average expenditure of about 750~3000 Japanese Yen. After discussions with the owners, 10 stores (such as Joy Full, Watami, etc.) consent to allowing questionnaire surveys of patrons after they had eaten.

(4) Questionnaire Collection Process

In order to ensure the rigorousness of the study, a pretest was conducted between March and April of 2011, which included reliability and validity testing. The official questionnaire was created after modifications were made. The official testing was conducted between July and September 2011. Sampling was conducted according to the aforementioned principles and method of sampling patrons. A total of 450 questionnaires were released, with 312 valid questionnaires returned for a retrieval rate of 69%.

(5) Questionnaire Design and Measurement

Measured variables of patron consumption actions include "socioeconomic backgrounds," "perceived quality," "relationship quality," and "brand evaluation"; other than socioeconomic background items having their own scales, the other two use the 5-point Likert scale, in which 1 point = highly disagree; 2 points = disagree; 3 points = neutral; 4 points = agree; 5 points = highly agree.

① Development of the questionnaire on patrons' socioeconomic backgrounds

This part primarily refers to Gracea and O'Cass (2004) and Wu Jiahua (2010) for the content on the socioeconomic background of patrons, including gender, marital status, age, education, and personal monthly income.

② Development of the questionnaire for perceived quality

Assessment of perceived quality primarily uses the dimensions measured by Gracea and O'Cass (2004) and is divided into three items: service scenario, core services, and personnel services.

③ Development of the questionnaire on relationship quality

This scale uses the four dimensions from the "relationship quality scale (RELQUAL scale) developed by Lages (2005). It includes "commitment," "information provision," "long-term orientation," and "satisfaction". Based on the definition by Cheng et al. (2008) of "relationship quality," the dimension of "trust" is also added, for a total of five dimensions to use in measuring the relationship quality between restaurants and customers.

④ Development of the questionnaire on brand evaluation

Wong and Merrilees (2008) believed that measurement of brand evaluation is less susceptible to using economic dimensions to measure the benefits of brands. Thus this study uses the study by Zeng Junlin (2010), combining the studies of Sweeney and Swait (2008) and Lee et al. (2008), dividing brand evaluation into the three dimensions of "buzz," "brand commitment," and "brand image."

(6) Data Analysis Methodology

Data analysis includes descriptive statistics, factor analysis, Pearson correlation analysis, and regression analysis. The analytical software used is SPSS12.0.

5. Research Results and Analysis

(1) Analysis of Socioeconomic Backgrounds of Restaurant Patrons

In Japan, the analysis of socioeconomic backgrounds of the 312 patrons shows that most are women, at 61.2% (38.8% are men); most are unmarried (52.2%); most are in the 21-30 age group (34 %), followed by those in the 31-40 age group (19.6%), and fewer than 10% are over 60 years of age (8.7%). Most have a university education (43.6%), followed by those with less than a high school education (28.2%); most are company employees, at 53%, while most have monthly incomes of less than 200,000 yen (46.5%), followed by those without regular incomes, such as housewives, at 23.7%.

(2) Analysis of Variable Factors

This study uses perceived quality, relationship quality, and brand evaluation in the scale for factor analysis. Principal axis factors are used to extract factors, keeping common factors with eigenvalues greater than 1 in accordance with the Kaiser principle. Varimax is used to conduct orthogonal rotation to produce a clear factor loading form (Kaiser, 1974; Wu Minglong, 2008).

(3) Factor Analysis of Perceived Quality, Relationship Quality and Brand Evaluation

In the factors, the KMO coefficient value of "perceived quality" reaches .907, "relationship quality" reaches .881, and "brand evaluation" reaches .795. This shows that sampling reaches an optimal level. Bartlett's test of sphericity's chi-square value of "perceived quality" is 1718.978*** (p<.001), "relationship quality" is 2105.307*** (p<.001), and "brand evaluation" is 2394.272*** (p<.001), which means that factor analysis is appropriate (Kaiser, 1974; Wu Minglong, 2008). After rotation, three factor dimensions are extracted from "perceived quality," with an accumulated explained variance of 73.842%, (Cronbach's α value at .905); five factor dimensions are extracted from "relationship quality," with an accumulated explained variance of 84.29%, (overall Cronbach's α value of .911); three factor dimensions are extracted from "brand evaluation," with an accumulated explained variance of 61.32% (overall Cronbach's α value of .814). Reliability analysis also confirms that the scale dimensions are within ideal ranges, thus they are named based on the original dimensions.

6. Correlation Analysis of Patrons' Perceived Quality and Relationship Quality

As shown in Table 1, the dimensions of perceived quality have a significant positive correlation with the dimensions of relationship quality ($p < .001$***), which means that there is a high positive correlation between patrons' perceived quality and relationship quality. Of these, perceived quality has correlation coefficients with dimensions of promised quality, satisfaction, and trust of over 0.6, which shows that if patrons' perceived quality is greater, the establishment of relationship quality between restaurants and patrons will be well.

7. Correlation Analysis of Patrons' Relationship Quality and Brand Evaluation

As shown in Table 1, the dimensions of relationship quality have a significant positive correlation with the dimensions of brand evaluation ($p < .001$***), which shows that there is a positive correlation between patrons' relationship quality and restaurants' brand evaluation (with correlation coefficients over 0.45). Therefore, the perceived quality of relationships between restaurants and patrons would result in greater patron brand evaluation toward restaurants.

Table 13-1 Correlation Analysis of Dimensions

Variables		Relationship Quality				
		Promised quality	Satisfaction	Trust	Information provision	Long-term orientation
perceived quality						
Personnel services	Pearson correlation	.621***	.658***	.612***	.393***	.483***
	significance (two-tailed)	.000	.000	.000	.000	.000
Core services	Pearson correlation	.610***	.622***	.639***	.495***	.444***
	significance (two-tailed)	.000	.000	.000	.000	.000
Service scenario	Pearson correlation	.563***	.665***	.609***	.369***	.426***
	significance (two-tailed)	.000	.000	.000	.000	.000
Brand evaluation	Pearson correlation	.460***	.536***	.492***	.447***	.486***
	significance (two-tailed)	.000	.000	.000	.000	.000

Note: *** p<.001

8. Analysis of Influence of Patrons' Perceived Quality on Relationship Quality

Model 1 of this study shows the influence of perceived quality on overall relationship quality (as in Table 2), which shows that after patrons dine at a restaurant, their perceived quality would positively affect their perception of the interactions between themselves and the restaurant. The diverse determination coefficient R^2 is 0.645, the overall test F value of the regression model is 186.612*** (p <0.001). The three predictive variables of perceived quality can effectively explain 64.5% of variance in "relationship quality." The individual factors' influence standardized regression coefficient β value shows that personnel services β value=0.324, core services β value=0.359, and service scenario β value=0.241, which shows that the quality of personnel services, core services, and service scenario positively affect the relationship quality in interaction with patrons.

9. Analysis of Influence of Patrons' Relationship Quality on Brand Evaluation

Model 2 of this study shows the influence of relationship quality on overall brand evaluation (as in Table 2). It shows that relationship quality has significant predictive ability for brand evaluation. The diverse determination coefficient R2 is 0.612, the overall test F value of the regression model is 93.001*** (p <0.001), which shows that the five predictive variables of perceived quality can effectively explain 61.2% of variance in "brand evaluation." In addition, the individual relationship quality factors' influence standardized regression coefficient β value shows that satisfaction β value is 0.283, trust β value is 0.170, information provision β value is 0.158, and long-term orientation β value is 0.211, which shows that patrons' satisfaction, trust, information provision, long-term orientation, and relationship quality with the restaurant positively affect their overall brand evaluation for the restaurant.

Table 13-2 Analysis of Influence of Observed Variables

Predictive variable	B estimation value	Standard error	Standardized regression coefficient(β)	t value	F value	R^2
Model 1 Perceived quality → Relationship quality						
(constant)	8.658	1.382		6.267		
Personnel services	.996	.148	.324***	6.736	186.612***	.645
Core services	1.037	.135	.359***	7.669		
Service scenario	.574	.114	.241***	5.035		
Model 2 Relationship quality → Brand evaluation						
(constant)	16.816	1.696		9.915		
Promised quality	-.145	.254	-.040	-.574		
Satisfaction	.775	.177	.283***	4.383	93.001***	.612
Trust	.688	.270	.170*	2.548		
Information provision	.605	.226	.158**	2.680		
Long-term orientation	.875	.257	.211***	3.399		

Note: *p<.05 **p<.01 ***p<.001

10. Conclusions and Suggestions

(1) Distribution of Patron Samples

Kagoshima's 312 patrons are mostly unmarried (52.2%), women (61.2%), between 21 and 40 years of age (34 %), usually have university educations (43.6%), company employees (as high as 53.5%), and with monthly incomes of less than 200,000 yen (46.5%).

(2) There is a significant correlation between patrons' perceived quality and relationship quality.

Pearson correlation analysis shows that the correlation between perceived quality and relationship quality is statistically significant, and that perceived quality is more related to promised quality, satisfaction, and trust. This shows that patrons' perceived quality is based on the etiquette and attitudes of service personnel, quality of food, and decoration of the restaurant, which is positively correlated with relationship quality in regard to satisfaction and trust. This result is consistent with that of Gracea and O'Cass (2004).

(3) There is a significant correlation between patrons' relationship quality and brand evaluation.

Pearson correlation analysis shows that the correlation between relationship quality and brand evaluation is also statistically significant, which is consistent with related studies (Wong & Sohal, 2006, Zeng Junlin, 2010). This shows that the quality of interaction between patrons and employees is directly related to "brand image," "brand commitment," or "buzz." This shows that if restaurants have good relationship quality with patrons, the restaurants will have a high brand evaluation.

(4) Patrons' perceived quality has a significant effect on relationship quality.

Regression analysis shows that patrons' perceived quality would indeed affect the quality of interaction between patrons and service providers, with the greatest effect on personnel services and core services, followed by service scenario. For patrons, core services of restaurants (such as food quality and service quality) are highly correlated to their trust and satisfaction (shown in Table 1), and are keys that influence overall relationship quality (as shown in Table 2). In addition, restaurants should not overlook personnel services and scenarios. Thus, this study suggests that maintenance of good relationship quality should incorporate evaluation of personnel education and training in aspects of service such as activeness of personnel, ability to recommend food to patrons, and the projection of an amiable and enthusiastic service attitude. In terms of core services, it is necessary to establish good personnel services and an effective SOP for food production and to continue to strengthen the consistency of quality in the food provided.

(5) Patrons' relationship quality has a significant effect on brand evaluation.

Regression analysis shows that the relationship quality of interaction between customers and employees would positively affect customer loyalty (Wong & Sohal, 2006). This study finds that satisfaction and long-term relationship quality have the greatest influence on brand evaluation, followed by information provision and trust. It also finds that relationship satisfaction is the sum of patrons' judgment of restaurants' food quality, professional attitudes of personnel, and smoothness of service interactions. Thus, this study suggests that if restaurants want patrons to have a positive brand evaluation, restaurants need to do their best to manage long-term relationships by taking seriously the views of patrons and understanding their inner needs. When promoting new products, they can use different channels (such as updating restaurant webpages, e-mails and Facebook, etc.) to regularly interact with patrons and provide the latest discounts. In terms of strengthening trust in the food, they can provide with production resumes for food items, so that patrons do not have to worry about what they eat. If restaurants can grasp and strengthen the feelings of consumption of patrons as they relate to perceived quality and relationship quality, create unique characteristics and increase the gap between themselves and competitors, they can create long-term brand evaluation and competitive advantages.

Table 13-3 Examination results of research hypotheses

Research hypothesis	Examination results
H1: there is a significant correlation between patrons' perceived quality and relationship quality.	Supported
H2: there is a significant correlation between patrons' perceived quality and relationship quality.	Supported
H3: there is a significant correlation between patrons' relationship quality and brand evaluation.	Supported
H4: patrons' relationship quality has a significant effect on brand evaluation.	Supported

Source: compiled by this study

【References】

[1] 岩本俊彦 (2010),「ターゲット・マーケティングにおける顧客維持戦略の階層性」『東京情報大学研究論集』Vol.13 No.2, pp.10-27.
[2] 菅野佐織 (2011),「ブランド・リレーションシップ概念の整理と課題」『駒大経営研究』第 42 巻第 3・4 号, pp.87-113.
[3] 青木幸弘 (2010),『消費行動の知識』日本経済新聞出版社。
[4] 飯島琴乃, 栗崎彩也夏, 下山雄大, 千原芳乃, 山崎洸平 (2009),「製品消費時における知覚品質を上げるための時間マーケティング」『2009 年度関東 10 ゼミ討論』, pp.1-9.
[5] 利根川孝一・白靜儀 (2008),「ブランド・パーソナリティを用いた定量的分析の提案」『政策科学』, pp.13-23。
[6] 方健頤 (2010), 婚紗旅遊之決策影響因素, 服務行動, 價值及行為意圖之相關研究－以高雄市為例, 高雄市政府研究發展考核委員會, 高雄。
[7] 吳佳華 (2010), 食客體驗滿意度與體驗行為關聯性研究－以高雄六合觀光夜市為例, 運動健康與休閒學術研討會。
[8] 吳明隆 (2008), SPSS 操作與應用問卷統計分析實務, 臺北：五南圖書出版股份有限公司, 347 頁。
[9] 李素馨, 李維貞 (2007), 外籍遊客之夜市旅遊行為與體驗關係研究, 2007 年「中華觀光管理學會」,「臺灣休閒遊憩學會」聯合學術研討會及第七屆觀光休閒暨餐旅產業永續經營學術研討會論文集, 273~288 頁。
[10] 陳宗玄 (2010), 臺灣家庭外食消費支出影響因素之研究 - 世代分析之應用, 朝陽學報, 15：45-68 頁。
[11] 曾鈞麟 (2010), 高雄地區國際觀光旅館之知識管理績效指標, 服務提供能力, 顧客關係品質與品牌績效關聯性研究, 高雄市研究發展考核委員會委託研究報告。
[12] 黃惠萱 (2007),「食饗觀光遊客動機, 體驗與體驗價值關係之研究－以台灣美食展為例」, 中國文化大學商學院觀光事業研究所碩士論文。
[13] 蔡長清, 曾鈞麟, 劉鐘珠, 侯佩瑜 (2009) ,「遊客參與動機, 體驗與體驗後行為相關研究－以高雄食品展為例」, 2009 第十屆管理學域國際學術研討會論文集, F159~174 頁。
[14] 蔡慕潔 (2009), 建構觀光夜市顧客滿意度模型, 中華大學經營管理研究所碩士論文。
[15] 薛昭義, 薛榮棠 (2007), 服務行動對關係品質影響之研究—以臺灣地區觀光飯店為例, 2007 年健康與管理學術研討會, 新竹：元培科技大學。
[16] Cheng, J. H., Chen, F. Y., & Chang, Y. H. (2008). "Airline relationship quality: An examination of Taiwanese passengers", *Tourism Management*, 29, pp. 487-499.
[17] Crosby, L. A., Evans, K. R. & Cowles, D. (1990). "Relationship Quality in Service Selling: An Interpersonal Influence Perspective", *Journal of Marketing*, 54(3), pp.

68-81.

[18] Gracea, D. & O'Cass, A. (2004), "Examining service experiences and post-consumption evaluation", *Journal of Services Marketing*, 18, pp. 450–461.

[19] Hall, C. M., Sharples, L., Mitchell, R., Macionis, N., & Combourne, B. (2003), *Food Tourism around the World: development, management and markets*, Location: Butterworth-Heinemann.

[20] Kelly, J. R. (1987), *Freedom to be: A new sociology of leisure*, NY: Practice-Hall.

[21] Lages, C., Lages, C. R., & Lages, L. F. (2005), "The RELQUAL scale: a measure of relationship quality in export market ventures.", *Journal of Business Research*, 58, pp. 1040-1048.

[22] Lee, J. S., & Back, K. J. (2008), "Attendee-based brand equity", *Tourism Management*, 29, pp. 331-344.

[23] Sweeney, J. & Swait, J. (2008), " The effects of brand credibility on customer loyalty", *Journal of Retailing and Consumer Services*, 15(3), pp. 179-193.

[24] Wong, A., & Sohal, A. (2006), "Understanding the quality of relationships in consumer services", *The International Journal of Quality & Relationships Management*, 1(23), pp. 244-264.

[25] Wong, H. Y., & Merrilees, B. (2008), "The performance benefits of being brand-orientated", *Journal of Product & Brand Management*, 17(6), pp. 372-383.

[26] Fournier, S.(1998), "Consumers and Their Brands: Developing Relationship Theory in Consumer Research", *Journal of Consumer Research*, 24, Mar., pp. 343-373.

Wu Chia Hua

Chapter 14   Business Strategies of the Taiwanese Audio Equipment Manufacturers

【Abstract】

　　Economic globalization has forced and is still forcing firms to develop new global manufacturing and distribution concepts. Through the development of economic globalization, firms in the world are proceeding to reform and redevelop in order to deal in globalization to get competitiveness. From designing products, searching customers, getting orders, inbound, operations, outbound to after service, the value chain of firms has become global. This study found the competitiveness of the Taiwanese amplifier and speaker manufacturers and questionnaires were issued to the object firms. The purpose was to find how competitive and cooperative strategies were properly for the industry. Base on M.E. Porter's competitiveness theories and value chain, a specialist questionnaire was utilized to establish a complete evaluation framework for the firms. Furthermore, cooperative strategy is important for firms to develop their manufacturing or marketing service; and the purpose is to be source of competitiveness. Firms in this industry were able to apply their core value with cooperative strategy as main tools to lower costs. They had to respond by introducing lean production and flexible organizations with a high innovation capability, and innovation in this industry was concerned about research and development capitals, quality guarantee capitals, and procurement ability in order to cost down or get added-value for customers. Cooperative strategy in the reorganization of relations to the other actors, notably, customers and suppliers are important. Therefore, interdependent relations in this industry was emphasized. The results of the research could be used as a guide for the industry to review and enhance its competitiveness in the future.

【Keywords】：Competitiveness, Amplifier, Speaker, Taiwan, Value Chain, Cooperative Strategy

1. Introduction

AMPLIFIER and speaker are two of the most important parts for audio products. Audio industry is categorized under consumer electronics. The audio industry of Taiwan established the factories in Mainland China, Vietnam or Eastern Europe. The research and development of technology of Taiwan lagged behind Europe, America and Japan. Some of them had their own brands, however, the brands were not famous and most of the main businesses were ODM/OEM for international companies, like Sony, Pioneer, Polk, Axiom, REL, etc.

In regard to technological development, globalization of the economy and competitive pressures, firms had to face more and more competitors. One of the purposes for firms was to serve their customers, thus, the regional horizontal divisions were occurred and drove the industry to develop. Moreover, in order to overcome more and more challenges as firms attempt to go global, they have to learn how to learn from the constant flow of new demands, opportunities and challenges. Recently, the new demand was energy consumption issue; firms concentrated on promoting energy efficiency in every consumer electronic devices.

Audio products are subject to safety laws which require electrical appliances must cover safety tests in accordance with standards like UL, CE, CCC, BSMI, PSE, etc., thus, while a customer approved one design, it was hard for the customer to change the same design to the other manufacturers, especially while the customer paid the

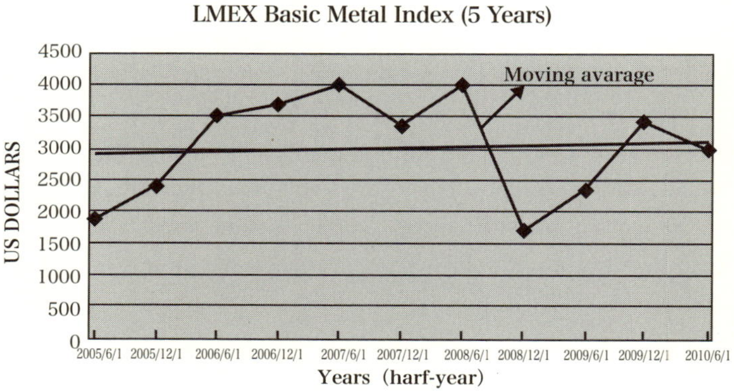

Fig.14-1 LMEX Basic Metal Index (5 Years)
Sources: London Metal Exchange www.lme.com/steel/latest_price.asp
The World Center for Non-Ferrous Metal Trading (sorted by the authors)

safety fee. The main materials for amplifiers are transformers, panels, heat-sinks, ICs, etc., and the prices up rose since 2005. Figure 14-1 showed LMEX basic metal exchange index from 2005 to 2010.

2. Literature Review

Over the last decade, many studies have been conducted on competitiveness and value chain. Organizational economics, vertical integration, organizational forms and entrepreneurial networks are important for firms. The sources of value creation in firms and what determines who will capture that value constitute a firm's competitiveness. Firms are always functioning on the maximization profit principle, and can move towards successfully achieving this goal by using innovation to create quality products and acquire services at the lowest possible prices.

Porter took a view of that the Internet will in fact have many negative effects on the nature of the competitive environment, and in particular on the ability of organizations to develop and maintain a sustainable competitive advantage. He believed that this is due to the open nature of the Internet, its accessibility, and the low cost of implementation and use .

(1) Five Force Shape Strategy

The sources of profit creation in firms and what determines who will capture this profit constitute a firm's competitiveness. Firms are always functioning on the maximization profit principle, and apply their core values as main tools in order to move towards. They are successfully achieving to create qualified products, suitable markets and acquire services at the lowest possible prices. Determining what products and services may be the most interest of customers, recognizing the needs and wants of target markets and delivering the desired satisfactions are crucial issues.

According to Porter (1998), competition is at the core to decide the success or failure of a firm. Competition determines the appropriateness of a firm's activities that can contribute to its performance, such as innovations, a cohesive culture, or good implementation. Competitive strategy for an industry is in search of a favorite position at the fundamental arena in which competition occurs. Competitive strategy aims to establish a profitable and sustainable position against the external pressure that determines the competition ability of this industry.

The first fundamental determinant of a firm's profitability is industry attractiveness. In any industry, whether it is domestic or international or produces a product or a service, the rules of competition are embodies in five competitive forces: the entry of new competitors, the threat of substitutes, the bargaining power of buyers, the bargaining power of suppliers, and the rivalry among the existing competitors.

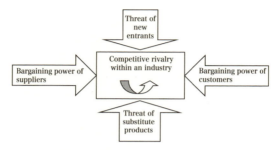

Fig.14-2　Porter's Five Forces Analysis
Source: Porter, M.E., How Competitive Forces Shape Strategy, 1979

These five competitive forces determines the ability of firms in an industry to earn, on average, rates of return on investment in excess of the cost of capital.

① The threat of substitute products: buyer propensity to substitute, relative price performance of substitutes, buyer switching costs, and perceived level of product differentiation.

② The threat of the entry of new competitors: the existence of barriers to entry, economies of product differences, brand equity, switching costs, capital requirements, and access to distribution, absolute cost advantages, expected retaliation by incumbents and government policies.

③ The intensity of competitive rivalry: number of competitors, rate of industry growth, intermittent industry overcapacity, exit barriers, diversity of competitors, informational complexity and asymmetry, fixed cost allocation per value added, level of advertising expense, and sustainable competitive advantage through improvisation.

④ The bargaining power of customers: buyer concentration to firm concentration ratio, degree of dependency upon existing channels of distribution, bargaining leverage, buyer volume, buyer switching costs relative to firm switching costs, buyers information availability, ability to backward integrate, and buyer price sensitivity.

⑤ The bargaining power of suppliers: supplier switching costs relative to firm switching cost, degree of differentiation of inputs, presence of substitute inputs, supplier concentration to firm concentration ratio, employee solidarity, threat of forward integration by suppliers relative to the threat of backward integration by firms, and cost of inputs relative to selling price of the product.

(2) Value Chain

Firms need to develop a unique set of skills that other organization do not have. This kind of abilities are supposed to be incorporated into the business's activities, but attaining them requires a detailed analysis of these very activities, which Porter groups under another fundamental notion in his thought-the value chain. Porter introduces a generic value chain in 1985. Value chain focus on cost management efforts and allows alignment of process with customers. It provides for efficient process which improves the timeliness of operations. Value chain focuses on cost management efforts and allows for an alignment owith customers. It provides for an efficient process that improves the timeliness of operations. The following drawing is of the value chain model.

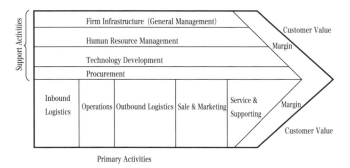

Fig.14-3　Michael E. Porter's Competitive Advantage Value Chain Model
Sources: Porter, M.E., Competitive Advantage, 1985

The primary activities of value chain are inbound logistic, operations, outbound logistics, sales and marketing, service and supporting; and the support activities are general management, human resource management, technology development and procurement. The goal of these activities is to offer customers a level of value that exceeds the cost of the activities, thereby resulting in a profit margin. Multiple infrastructures increase costs at all levels, with respect to operations, maintenance/

support, security and services. Because technology is employed to some degree in every value creating activity, changes in technology can impact competitive advantage by incrementally changing the activities themselves or by making possible new configurations of the value chain.

According to Michael E. Porter's value chain (1985), primary activities from inbound logistics to services and support activities from infrastructure, human resource to technology are the values that exceed the cost of activities, thereby resulting in a profit margin. In 2001, Michael E. Porter, Tarun Khanna and Krishna Palepu, from an empirical study of Korean, Indian and South American's industries find that most of multinational enterprises through simulating development countries' economic activities in order to create more values.

(3) Typology of Alliance

Technology alliance is defined as technological collaboration in some researches and reflects the nature that two or more partners contribute differential resources and technological know-how to jointly agreed aims of such a cooperation activity.

As Buckley, Chapman and Casson concluded, in business relationships, bounded rationality forces companies to work in the grey area where relations and trust replace the fine calculation of costs, short term profits and returns. Therefore, cooperation is a substitute for the assurance of solid quantitative evidence. While people talk about cooperation, competition must be discussed. What important is that the goals are known and that it is agreed that the different goals can be fulfilled within one and the same strategy. The primary driver of cooperative strategy is the emergence of intense global competition. By relating cooperation and conflict, Yoshino and Ragan maintained Typology of Alliance and it was showed in Table 14-1.

Table 14-1   Typology of Alliance

		Extent of Organized Interaction	
		Low	High
Conflict Potential	High	Pre-competitive Alliances	Competitive Alliances
	Low	Pro-competitive Alliances	Non-competitive Alliances

Source: Yoshino and Rangan (1995)

By relating two concepts, four types of alliances were created. A pre-competitive alliance typically bring together firms from different, unrelated industries while pro-competitive alliances are formed by firms at different industries in the vertical value chain to further the competitiveness of the chain. Non-competitive alliances are typically intra-industry alliances among non-competing firms. About pre-competitive, as an example, an amplifier manufacturer does strategy for expanding their market with customers is seemed to be a kind of pre-competitive alliance. Their extent of organized interaction is low; however, their potential conflict is high.

R. J. Liu (2008) from an empirical evidence of Taiwan's bicycle and sewing machine, etc. from his discovery, the integrating within a close supplier networks tends to provide value added integral solution to customers, called integrated co-innovative supplier networks. Firms have started to create own brands and concentrate on customer services in order to strive for competitiveness and sustainability from globalization. Innovation plays a vital role in industries. For multinational enterprises, if jobs are mainly in the skilled or high-skilled level, risks for the local economy to lose main employers are comparatively low.

Moreover, M.Y, Wu (2004) identifies that the competitiveness of a firm must be distinguished to 1) vertical integration and horizontal division, 2) upstream and downstream supply relationship and 3) competition scenario of the same industry.

3. Defining Competitive and Cooperative Strategies

The purpose of cooperative strategy is to be source of competitive advantage. Companies responded by starting to externalized activities, strategic alliances being one of the most popular means of responses. In 1993, Buckley and Chapman agreed that a property strategic alliance must be defined for a given time.

Porter took a view of that the internet will in fact have many negative effects on the nature of the competitive environment, and in particular on the ability of organizations to develop and maintain a sustainable competitive advantage. He believed that this is due to the open nature of the internet, its accessibility, and the low cost of implementation and use. This view, to some extent, negates some of the benefits promoted as accruing from the use of technology to integrate the supply chain.

Firms have taken new initiatives in managing their environmental impacts. They seek new ways to reduce their costs, increase their efficiency, lower their liabilities, and enhance their competitiveness while reducing pollution, conserving resources, and eliminating waste. Competitive strategy is the search for a favorable competitive position in an industry, the fundamental arena in which competition occurs. It aims to establish a profitable and sustainable position against the forces that determine industry competition. This research listed the previous definitions for competitiveness as below.

Table 14-2 Previous Definitions for Competitiveness

Scholar	Content
Colin Leys	The International development of financial markets, of technology and of some manufacturing and services bring firms a new set of limitations on the freedom of action of nations. To survive, nations and firms must increasingly "manage" national politics in such a way as to adapt them to the pressures of trans-national market forces.
Dennis A. Rondinelli	A competent state needs to provide for open, efficient, and competitive markets. Increasing firms' competitiveness (including social) through the implementation of sound economic policies is also crucial for good and effective governance.
John H. Dunning & Feng Zhang	The resources, capabilities and markets (RCM) which make up the physical environment in which firms and other organization create economic well-being; and second, the institutions which provide the incentive structures to make up the human environment, and which set the rules of the game for, and determine the cognition and motivation of, firms and other wealth creating entities, that produce wealth; these are the components of competitiveness.
Michael E. Porter	Competitiveness depends on the productivity with which a nation uses its human, capital, and nature resources. A nation competes to offer the most productive environment for business and thereby creates competitiveness. The public and private sectors play different but interrelated roles in creating a productive economy.

Sources: this research

According to Chandler, from 1950s to 1970s, we witnessed a dramatic growth of the multinational companies which, by means of the multi-divisional form (M-form) of organization, internalized as many activities as possible. This, on the other side, led to bureaucracy and inflexibility and form the late 1970s onwards, the companies responded by starting to externalize activities, cooperative strategies being one of the most popular means of response. This popularity has made it necessary to redefine the role of not only governments to encompass alliances but also industries to re-think as a competitive mode of organization rather than as collusion.

Assumed the partners have near complete information and thus are able to prepare a detailed plan for the strategies, in contrast as a long-term arrangement will make it difficult to foresee the end; therefore, it should also be stressed that the partners of a cooperative strategy need "not" have common goals. They may have different goals. What is important is that the goals are known and that it is agreed that the different goals can be fulfilled within one and the same strategies.

According to Wu, Se-Hwa (2000), strategies for business operation includes three factors-categories, resources and networks. Categories include markets, business activities (value chains), landforms and scales of businesses. Resources mean to create and accumulate core value of business, include tangible assets, intangible assets, and abilities of employees and power of organizations. Networks mean the series of business activities from getting materials to do marketing, include suppliers, the other manufacturers in the same industry, the other firms in different industry and strategic constituency.

4. Research Method

According to the statistics from MIC IT IS in 2004, the ratio of Taiwan international vertical integration of electronics manufacturers was around 0.26, higher than the other industry. Firms imported parts of goods and assembling, then they exported the products to the other countries. It meant Taiwan electronics industry is in the chain of international vertical integration. Moreover, IT IS showed the ratio of audio industry exporting in 2008 was higher than 2006 and 2007.

The purpose of this research was to find the competitive and cooperative strategies of the Taiwan amplifier and speaker manufacturers. And the enterprise scales were concerned in this study: large-medium enterprises, small-medium enterprises and small enterprises. According to the Executive Yuan of R.O.C., the definition of large-medium enterprise is that in the manufacturing, a paid-in capital of over NT$ 80 million or over 200 regular employees; and small-medium enterprise is identified to be a paid-in capital of less than NT$ 80 million or the number of regular employees must be less than 200; small enterprises is with the number of regular employees less than 20.

This study combined the data from Ministry of Economic Affairs, R.O.C and Bureau of Foreign Trade and there were total 145 amplifier and speaker manufacturers who also do import and export trading in Taiwan. The totals of 145 questionnaires were mailed and 81 effective returns were received in Jan. 2008. The effective return ratio was 55.86%.

(1) Model Construction and the Evaluation Framework

According to Porter's value chain, both primary activities and support activities are important for firms and value chain is seemed to be an estimation method for firms to evaluate their internal management. However, it is not limited in internal management; it must be seemed to be a kind of interaction between internal and external. In inbound logistics, firms have to search proper suppliers; in outbound logistics, firms have to find proper transportation companies; in sales and marketing, firms have to know where their target market is and how their competitors do, and in service and supporting activities, firms have to service their customers. The purpose of all the activities are service their customers to gain add-value for firms.

Combing value chain and typology alliance, this study distinguished three sections of competitive and cooperative strategies for the industry to examine who to cooperate is a proper way for the industry and how they compete with the other manufacturers in the same industry-vertical integration, horizontal division and competitive scenario of the same industry. Vertical integration is a kind of pro-competitive alliance; it focuses on the relations between suppliers and customers. Horizontal division is pre-competitive alliance, and competitive scenario of the same industry is a kind of non-competitive versus competitive relationship. The evaluation framework of this research was in Figure 14-4.

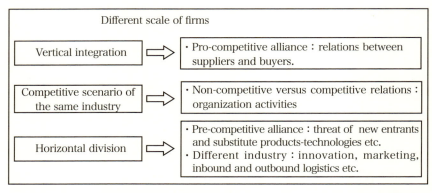

Fig.14-4 Evaluation Framework for the Taiwan Amplifier and Speaker Industry

Vertical integration meant a style of management control. It was relations between upstream and downstream which meant that suppliers and buyers made a compact of control to each other; the potential competitive was not obvious. The advantageous position for firms were different, firms must develop their strengths on the value chain to get add-value. It included support activities, primary activities, price sensitivity from suppliers and buyers, R&D and switching costs.

Horizontal division was in the sense that partners cooperate in some missions. The conflict was high but organization activities might be low. For example, an amplifier manufacturer was pre-competitive new technology development with the other manufacturer who advantaged to digital sound R&D. The two firms expect to reap profit by flexible cooperate strategies.

(2) Hypotheses

According to the framework of this research, the hypotheses were as follows.
  H1: Firms would like to vertical integration rather than horizontal division.
  H2: Different enterprise scales had different inclination toward to cooperate with customers or suppliers.
  H3: The factors to affect the competitiveness of the industry were significant.

(3) Methodology

SPSS 12.00 software was used to analyze. Descriptive statistics and factor analysis results were enclosed in estimation results.

A very readable and informative history of the development of factory analysis is provided in the beginning of Harry Harmon's (1967) classic text. Factor analysis includes exploratory factor analysis (EFA) and confirmatory factor analysis (CFA). EFA approach is presented as a method for discovering how many factors could be used to explain in the relationships among a given set of observed measures, and which variables load considerably on which factor-usually be used in pre-investigation. CFA is not concerned with discovering or disclosing factors as EFA, but instead with quantifying, testing, and confirming an a priori proposed (preconceived) or hypothetical structure of the relationships among a set of considered measures. This study used CFA to find the factors that affect the competitive and cooperative strategies for the industry.

Many scholars consider that factor analysis is one of the large-sample statistical procedures that the sample drops below an N of 100 is poor (over 200 is fair). According to Tabachnick & Fidell (2007), the correlations among the variables are high but the correlations among the factors are not high, 50-100 samples are acceptable. Kaiser-Myer-Olkin (KMO) is between 0-1, measures of sampling adequacy and Bartlett's Test of Sphericity. The KMO index can tell researchers how effectively the variables can be grouped into a smaller number of underlying factors. According to Kaiser (1974), KMO value over 0.90 is marvelous (perfect to do factor analysis), over 0.8 is meritorious (meritorious), over 0.7 is middling, over 0.6 is mediocre, Over 0.5 is miserable, and below 0.5 is unacceptable.

5. Estimation Results

Cronbach's α is a measure of how well each individual item in a scale correlates with the sum of the remaining items. Cuieford (1965) pointed out that Cronbach's α coefficient of 0.7 refers to high intensity of reliability. And the one between 0.7 and 0.35 refers to acceptable standard. Once Cronbach's α coefficient lower than 0.35, it means rejected validity.

The Cronbach's α of the vertical integration (relations with customers and suppliers) was 0.90; of the horizontal (new entrants and substitutes) was 0.68. And of perceived cooperation with the other manufacturers in the same industry was 0.75. Likert scale was used in this research, and the top ten ranking important factors that affect the activities of the industry on value chain were sorted in Table 14-3.

Table 14-3 Ranking of Factors to Affect the Activities of the Industry on Value Chain

Ranking	Section	Average scores
1	Quality demand by customers	4.12
2	Procurement ability of the firms	3.96
3	Equipment application of the firms	3.94
4	Human resources of the firms	3.82
5	Technology of supportive suppliers	3.79
6	Financial situation of the firms	3.74
7	After service demand by customers	3.74
8	Cost down demand by customers	3.73
9	R&D capitals of the firms	3.73
10	Design demand by customers	3.70

Sources: this research

(1) Descriptive Statistics

Base on Yoshino and Ragan's typology of alliance, this research sorted the average scores in Table 14-4.

Table 14-4 Average Scores on Typology Alliance in the Industry

Enterprise scales	Pre-competitive Alliances	Competitive Alliances	Pro-competitive Alliances	Noncompetitive Alliances
Large-medium	3.04	2.99	4.06	3.88
Small-medium	2.50	2.30	3.97	3.23
Small	2.92	2.56	3.63	2.88
Total	2.82	2.62	3.89	3.33

Sources: this research

The Taiwanese amplifier and speaker manufacturers would like to do procompetitive alliances which meant that firms would like to cooperate with the other industries where with lower potential conflict and lower extent of organized interaction. Most of the firms emphasized on self-development; therefore, they would like to cooperate with customers or suppliers rather than to cooperate with the other manufacturers in the same industry because this industry was high competitive. Moreover, the average score on non-competitive alliances was 3.33, it meant that firms would like to cooperate with the other manufacturers in the same industry but they were not competitors on market and their products might be differentiated. For example, firms who produce Class A/B type (analog) of amplifiers would like to cooperate with the other firms who make Class D type (digital) amplifiers while they wanted to upgrade their products. Their extent of organized interaction was high.

Table 14-5 was the average scores of the percept of the Taiwanese amplifier and speaker manufacturers to cooperate with their suppliers.

Table 14-5 the Percept of the Firms to Cooperate with their Suppliers

Enterprise scales	Case number	Percentage	Average scores
Large-medium	22	27.15%	2.93
Small-medium	37	45.70%	2.78
Small	22	27.15%	2.87
Total	81	100.00%	2.86

Sources: this research

From Table 14-5, the percept of the firms to cooperate with their suppliers was not high. And the percept of the firms to cooperate with their customers was sorted in Table 14-6 as below.

Table 14-6　the Percept of the Firms to Cooperate with their Customers

Enterprise scales	Case number	Percentage	Average scores
Large-medium	22	27.15%	3.60
Small-medium	37	45.70%	3.53
Small	22	27.15%	3.58
Total	81	100.00%	3.57

Sources: this research

Comparing with the average score in Table 14-5 and 14-6, firms trended to cooperate with their customers rather than suppliers.

About the percept of the firms to cooperate with the other manufacturers in the same industry, the average scores were showed in Table 14-7.

Table 14-7　the Percept of the Firms to Cooperate with the other Manufacturers in the Same Industry

Enterprise scales	Case number	Percentage	Average scores
Large-medium	22	27.15%	3.00
Small-medium	37	45.70%	2.56
Small	22	27.15%	3.03
Total	81	100.00%	2.86

Sources: this research

Comparing with Table 14-5 and 14-7, the total average scores on cooperating with suppliers and the other manufacturers in the same industry were the same- 2.86. Moreover, this study found that small enterprises in the industry respected on customers introduced by their suppliers or the other customers (average score 3.3) more than the large-medium and small-medium enterprises. In regard to Table 14-5 and 14-6, firms would like cooperate with customers rather than with the other manufacturers in the same industry was identified; therefore, H1 was partially significant. Furthermore, from the average scores, the percept of large-medium firms cooperating with customers and suppliers was higher than the other firms; however, by T-test, it was not significant (T-value 0.887 to cooperate with customers and 0.295 to cooperate with suppliers). H2 was not significant.

(2) Factor Analysis

In order to examine H3: The factors to affect the competitiveness of the industry were significant, factory analysis was used.

The Kaiser-Meyer-Olkin (KOM) value was between 0~1. In this case, KOM value was 0.795 and Bartlett's Test of Sphericity is approx. Chi Square 831.197 (sig. 000*). There were total 19 variables to examine the inclination of the firms toward to cooperate with customers, suppliers or the other manufacturers in the same industry, by varimax method, the factor analysis results of the Taiwanese amplifier and speaker industry was in Table 14-8.

Table 14-8   the Factor Analysis Result

Variance	Communalities	Factors Loadings			% of Variance	Cumulative %
		Factor 1	Factor 2	Factor 3		
2	0.699	0.833	0.072	0.002	22.926	22.926
1	0.553	0.769	0.082	0.049		
3	0.600	0.733	0.097	0.078		
6	0.514	0.658	0.154	0.241		
10	0.525	0.605	0.138	0.375		
4	0.414	0.596	0.217	-0.105		
5	0.342	0.557	0.145	0.102		
9	0.468	0.534	0.345	0.254		
8	0.540	0.522	0.395	0.334		
12	0.626	0.036	0.774	-0.159	18.522	41.449
11	0.596	0.230	0.733	0.082		
14	0.753	0.225	0.714	0.276		
13	0.614	0.116	0.706	0.155		
15	0.637	0.091	0.637	0.478		
7	0.580	0.497	0.574	0.057		
17	0.445	0.082	0.364	0.317		
19	0.326	0.192	0.243	0.255	9.820	51.269
18	0.547	0.175	0.196	0.929		
16	0.388	0.256	0.048	0.280		

Sources: this research

In analysis of the reliability, the coefficients of Cronbach's α were 0.692, 0.678 and 0.695. The five factors were all measured consistently. The measure of sampling adequacies (MSA) of the three factors were 0.884, 0.880 and 1.089; all of them are over 0.6 mean that they were extracted properly. And the three factors to affect the competitiveness of the Taiwanese amplifier and speaker manufacturers were identified and they were indicating good subscale reliability. Meanwhile, the present three-factor model was deemed the best solution because of its conceptual clarity and ease of interpretability. They were named as follows:

Factor 1: quality manpower and resources of the industry

Factor 2: supports from suppliers

Factor 3: cooperate with customers

Factor 1 took the percentage of variance 22.926 which meant that factor 1 was the most important factor to affect the competitiveness of the industry. Firms in order to get competitiveness were to focus on the resources of the industry and develop their manpower. H3 was verified.

(3) SWOT Analysis

There were three firms were interviewed in Shezhen, China (Taiwanese CEO lived in China) in Nov. 2007 and two firms (Taiwanese CEO) were interviewed in Kaohsiung, Taiwan in Dec. 2007. The trend and competitor analysis revealed the opportunities and threats, and organization analysis revealed the competences of the organization and also its strengths and weakness. Descriptive analysis cannot explain some detail information clearly; therefore, interview was needed in this research. In-depth interviews with CEOs, the SWOT analysis (value chain involved) were sorted in Table 14-9.

Table 14-9 SWOT Analysis for the Taiwanese Amplifier and Speaker Manufacturers

Value Chain Actibity	Strength: Opportunity & Threat	Weakness: Opportunity & Threat
Inbound Logistics According to the influence of fluctuant international material price and the upper supplier's price, to purchase different level materials and create different level's products according to customer's needs. Material warehousing was controlled by ERP systems or	S.O.: • Materials prices trended to consistency: Bulk produce might get 20% off or more, however, most suppliers did not sale for small quantity. • Clustered upper suppliers: easier to inquiry or purchase materials in one location.	W.O.: • Imitate mutually products to make new ones by self-no creating only imitate. Replacement high prices materials to cheaper to make finial products more competitive on market. • Different kinds of customized products but small quantity

others.	• No counterfeit electronic component. • Compare to Europe and USA, materials prices were inexpensive. S.T.: • High quality main parts like ICs, transistors were controlled by the Japanese and American companies (prices and lead time).	caused it was hard to reduce materials costs. W.T.: • Customers who trended to lower and cheaper products purchased in China or Vietnam domestic manufacturers directly. Firms who made low-end products must up-grade.
Operations (included R&D activities) Quality manpower and specialized equipment were needed. Divided into standard and customization production.	S.O.: • The technology was high. Not every new entrant without experiences can make amplifiers or speakers as well. • Sufficient technical staff: training from offshore foreign investors. S.T: • Less professional experience to generation • Less education trading for R&D	W.O.: • Lack of self-design ability: imitate the design and functions from developed countries. • Huge costs on R&D • Limited by laws and regulations: UL, ETL, CSA, TUV, etc.
Outbound Logistics Final product warehousing control. Customer forecast and real order control.	S.O.: • Efficient production capability and complete production line (with production know-how) S.T.: • Dispose of production line most in China where have lower labors cost or social insurances.	W.O.: • Needs to invest a huge capital on equipments. W.T.: • While firms go overseas, the transpiration (outbound logistics) and domestic government's policy was considered.
Sales & Marketing Firms did the jog as ODM/OEM for international companies. Rarely contacted with end users by own brand. Firms attracted famous factories or agencies through joining exhibits or by public praise etc.	S.O.: • Cooperation with downstream and customers could save marketing investigation costs. S.T.: • Orders were controlled by buyers. Although orders quantity normally stable but price was a main factor to attract customers.	W.O.: • Rarely contacted with end users-consumers cause lack for market trend data of consumers demands. • USA, Japan and Europe buyers required to use their own brand (patriotism). Firms can not expand their own brands on the world.

		W.T.: • Once major orders were drew out, the operation of factory would be serious (accurate plans are needed to avoid this situation)
	• New technology products, like PDA, i-phone, MP4 were substitute.	
Service & Supporting • Date of delivery • After service	S.O.: • The delivery control was important, because customers had their own produce schedule. • Immediately service (feedback customers' needs) is important. S.T.: • The service contract with customers	W.O.: • Date of delivery was influenced by material, production and transportation.

Sources: this research

In-depth interview with CEOs, amplifier and speaker industry in Taiwan is high technology industry. And firms thought that cooperate with suppliers, customers and the other manufacturers in the same industry could bring firms to be A+. Moreover, if firms were only focus on their business without collaborating with their customers, suppliers or the other manufacturers in the same industry, they might miss information and fallen on strategies. Furthermore, firms thought that they needed to face the tendencies of:

① Energy save products would be the main stream in the world, especially on consumer electronic devices.

② Environmental protection rules: firms had to do actions on WEEE (Waste Electrical and Electronic Equipment) or RoHS (Restriction of Hazardous Substances Directive), etc.

③ Material prices up and down: it made firms hardly to control their stock. Firms had to predict if the materials would be price down or price raise or their loss would be huge. Moreover, in order to face the fluctuated material prices, firms had to up-grade their products to high-end, and low-end products set free to China or Vietnam domestic manufacturers. Therefore, sharing technology in the same industry became important lessons for firms.

④ Rising wages: Many of the Taiwanese amplifier and speaker manufacturers established their factories overseas, especially in Mainland China, Vietnam or Eastern Europe. As an example of wages fluctuation in China, the labor wages had been rising. Between 1978 and 2007, the average real annual wage for staffs and workers grow more than seven fold from 3,285 to 24,943 yuan. In the period, wage growth accelerates to an astonishing 13.20%. This period of wage explosion had been coincided with China's preparation for and accession into the WTO. Figure 14-5 showed the wages comparison among China, Philippians, Thailand and Malaysia.

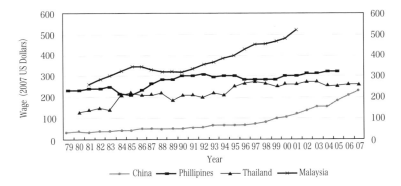

Fig. 14-5   China and Other Emerging Economies (Wages)

The Taiwanese amplifier and speaker manufacturers learnt from the Japanese and American manufacturing ways. When they went global, they were good at applying innovation to re-develop and reform the production processes by themselves to suit the domestic employees' lifestyle and the level of educations. Because amplifier and speaker manufacturers needed a large number of employees on production lines to make products, factory management was important. Human assets were one of the most valuable assets to the company. Moreover, they emphasized on production management in order to saves costs for firms. Firms focused on BOM (bill of material) and apply software like ERP systems (enterprise resource planning) to plan, revise and integrate business activities on series of production processes from inbound logistics to customer services. They were bravely to discover new management ways by their innovation. Firms thought that internal factors were much more than externals, because external factors could not be controlled but internal factors could be controlled by the managers of the firms. Firms attached importance to the learning ability of employees and thought it was important to make innovation.

6. Conclusions and Findings

The objective of this paper was to examine how the competitive and cooperative strategies of the Taiwanese amplifier and speaker manufacturers. Firms in this industry would like to cooperate with their customers rather than suppliers or the other manufacturers in the same industry; therefore, H1 was partially verified but H2 was not significant. From in-depth interview, CEOs thought to up-grade their products and technologies were important and cooperate with the other manufacturers in the same industry might help firms to get innovation on current technology and manufacturing way. The threat of substitute products was not a significant threat of the industry because the tone quality between digital devices and analog were different.

Moreover, the crucial factors that affect the competitiveness of the industry were also verified by description statistics and factor analysis. This paper demonstrated the three-factors affected the competitiveness of the industry, and they were (1) quality manpower and resources of the industry, (2) supports from suppliers and (3) cooperate with customers. By factor analysis, H3 was verified.

There were three findings of this research:

(1) Most of the firms did the jog as ODM/OEM for international companies. They did not touch final customers directly; therefore, they would like to cooperative with customers in order to know their target market and up-grade their products in order to suit for their final customers' needs.

(2) The industry was high competitive. By factor analysis, they thought that getting supports from their suppliers was important, as an example, they would like to get contract prices to maintain their quotations.

(3) Firms concentrated on up-grade their products' quality to service their customers, cost down from procurement, inbound logistics to after service in order to satisfying customer's needs, and human resources could help them get competitiveness, and the other activities in value chain were also important.

In order to grow and enhance the overall competitiveness of the Taiwanese amplifier and speaker manufacturers, the results of this paper provided views for future references.

7. The Limitations and Future Study of This Research

The object of this study was the Taiwanese amplifier and speaker manufacturers, and this study emphasized on competitive and cooperative strategies of the manufacturers. About the best way to cooperate and how to compete were not specified. Therefore, the further step of this study is to discover how to cooperate and how to compete will help firms to get competitiveness.

【References】

[1] Beamon BM. (1998), "Supply chain design and analysis: Models and Methods", *International Journal of Production Economics*, Vol. 55, pp. 281-294.

[2] Borgen, F., & Seling, M.,(1978), "Uses of discriminate analysis following MANOVA: Multivariate statistics for multivariate purposes," *Journal of Applied Psychology*, Vol.63, pp. 689-697.

[3] Buckley, P.J., and M. Casson(1996), "An Economic Model of International Joint Venture Strategy", *Journal of International Business Studies*, Vol.27, No.5.

[4] Buckley, P.J., and M. Chapman (1993),"Bounded Rationality in the International Strategic Alliance", *Paper presented at the EIBA conference*.

[5] Chandler, A.D., (1990), *Scale and Scope: the Dynamics of Industrial Capitalism*,Harvard University, Cambridge, Mass.

[6] Colin Ley, (2001), *Market-Driven Politics, Neo-liberal democracy and the public interest*, London, Verso Books 280.

[7] Cuieford, J.P. (1965), *Fundamental Statistics in Psychology and Education*, 4th ed., McGraw Hill, N.Y..

[8] Fitzsimmons, J.A. and Fitzsimmons, M.J., (2006), *Service Management* 5th ed., McGraw-Hill, New York.

[9] Harmon, H.H., (1967), *Modern factor analysis* 2nd ed., Chicago: University of Chicago Press.

[10] J. Dunning & Feng Zhang(2007), "Meeting of Experts on FDI",*Technology and Competitiveness*, U.S.A.

[11] Kaiser, H.F., Little Jiffy, Mark IV(1974), *Educational and Psychological Measurement*, 34, pp.111-117.

[12] Lancioni. R., Smith. M., & Oliva, T.(2000), "The Role of the Internet in Supply Chain Management", *Industrial Marketing Management*, Vol.29, No.1, pp. 45-56.

[13] Lawrence S. Meyers, Glenn Gamst and A.J. Guarino (2006), *Applied Multivariate*

Research, Sage Publications, Inc., UK. pp. 467-468.

[14] M.L. Wu(2007), *SPSS Operation and Application-the Practice of Quantitative Analysis of Questionnaire Data*, Wunan Publication, Taiwan, pp. 296-299.

[15] Patricia Mayer Milligan, Donna Hutcheson (2007), "Business Risks and Security Assessment for Mobile Devices", *Proceedings of the 8th WSEAS International Conference on Mathematics and Computers in Business and Economics*.

[16] Porter, M.E., (1979), "*How Competitive Forces Shape Strategy*," *Harvard Business Review*.

[17] Porter, M.E., (1985), *Competitive Advantage*, N.Y.: The Free Press.

[18] Porter, M. E. & Fuller, R. (1986), *Competition Global Industries*, Harvard Business Press, Boston.

[19] Porter, M. E.(1990), *the Competitive Advantage of Nations*, the Free Press, New York, pp. 179-238.

[20] Porter, M. E., (1998), *Competitive Advantage-Creating and sustaining superior performance*, The free press, A division of Simon & Schuster Inc., N.Y.

[21] Porter, M. E., (2001), "Strategy and the Internet", *Harvard Business Review*, Vol.79, No.3, pp. 63-78.

[22] Porter, M. E.(2010), *Regions and Competitiveness: Implications for Saudi Arabia*, January 2010, Global Competitiveness Forum Riyadh, Saudi Arabia conference.

[23] Ren-Jye Liu (2008), *Co-innovation: A New Competitive Model of Taiwan Industry*, Yuan-Liou Publishing Co., Ltd., Taipei, Taiwan, pp.8-55.

[24] Rondinelli, D.A., (2005), *Assessing government policies for business competitiveness in Grosse, International Business and Government Relations in Emerging Economics: An Institutional Approach in the 21st Century*,Cambridge, Cambridge University Press, pp. 395-420.

[25] Tabachnick, B.G., & Fidell, L.S.,(2007), *Using multivariate statistics*, 5th ed., Needham Heights, MA: Allyn and Bacon.

[26] Yoshino and Rangan, Michael Y. and U. Sriniovasa.(1995), *Strategic Alliance-An Entrepreneurial Approach to Globalization*, 1st ed., Boston.

[27] Wu, Min-Yu(2008), "An Index for Industry Competitive-Vertical Integration and Up-down-stream Supply Chain Relationship", *Macroeconomic IT IS*.

[28] Wu, Se-Hwa (2000), *The Nature of the Strategy*, 3rd Ed., Taipei, Taiwan, Faces Publishing LTD.

[29] Yamata Tarou.(2007), *The Sub-generation Strategies in the Japanese*

Manufacturing, Toyo-Keizi.

[30] London Metal Exchange, the World Center for Non-Ferrous Metal Trading www.lme.com

[31] Industry & Technology Intelligence Services www.itis.org.tw

[32] Small and Medium Enterprise Administration, Ministry of Economic Affairs under the Executive Yuan of R.O.C. www.moeasmea.gov.tw (identify small-medium enterprise)

[33] Ministry of Economic Affairs, R.O.C. contact to http://gcis.nat.gov.tw/open_system_1.htm to search for the object (amplifier and speaker manufacturers)

[34] Bureau of Foreign Trade contact to http://cweb.trade.gov.tw contact to search for registered manufacturers

Chunwei, Lu

Chapter15 Research of the Consumer's preference behavior for Japanese healthy food

【Abstract】

According to the indicators of WTO (World Health Organization, WHO), it is an aging society if the elderly population is 7% more than the country's total population. However, Japan has become to an aging country in early years ago. And now, Japan is in the needs for longevity, health, health's care spending reducing, so that the demand for healthy food is keeping increased. On the other hand, the uplift of Japan's domestic consumer awareness of health, the increase in chronic diseases of civilization, and social demographic structure tend to be aging because of low birth rate, which cause Japanese demand for healthy food, nutrition and dietary supplements by a high importance that prompting a new wave of healthy food and fast boomed in recent years.

What kind of preference will be arose for the consumers in such a huge business opportunity? In this study, the main objects are the Japanese healthy food consumers, and in order to explore how the preferences behavior of them which affect the purchase intention, many analysis methods are applied to find out the affect factors.

According to the theme study above, the Japanese healthy food consumers and consumer preference are investigated, in order to understand the region characteristic in the consumer preference of Japanese healthy food consumers. From the data analysis results, the consumer preferences for healthy food are respected to the high importance on product safety, quality, ingredients and professional consulting.

Consumers respect more importance on the awareness of the enterprise image and brand equity. Brand and its reputation have a certain degree of impacts for the healthy food purchasing behavior. Price and quality variables play an indicative role for healthy food purchasing behavior of consumers.

【Key-Words】:Healthy Food, Purchase Intention, Consumer Preference

1. Introduction

The modern people are under the needs on longevity, health and reducing health care spending, and the demand for the related market of healthy food is increasing. The current stages of the global health food market are expanding and becoming a highly competitive situation among the brands. Enterprises have continuing to think about how to establish good relationships with consumers in order to encourage consumer purchase intention. The market has launched numerous healthy foods. It caused not only the formation of various manufacturers' competition but also let consumers faced with the choice issue.

However, along with different social backgrounds, consumers might have different buying behaviors when buying healthy products. Consumers' demand and resulting behavior are also different from the past. Therefore, consumer behavior will have different factors in different regions. In other words, what will be the different for the healthy food consumer behaviors in the different circumstance of regions and cultural background?

In this study, Japanese healthy food consumers as the main target and explore the following topics:

(1) In the consumer behavior for Japanese local healthy food consumer preferences, what regions characteristics will affect the purchase intention of healthy food?

(2) In the influence on purchase intention relationship for Japanese healthy food consumers, what factors with what roles will be in decision-making?

Research by the above mentioned topics, healthy food consumers and consumer preference in Japan. Make the order to understand the region characteristic for Japanese healthy food consumers' preference, and trying to sort out a worthy part for reference.

2. Literature Review

According to statistics, the annual rate growth of healthy food sales in developed countries is 13%. Global healthy food sales have nearly $ 230 billion on 2007. The healthy food sales amount in United States as a kingdom of healthy foods has been grown 36 times nearly 20 years, and sales reached $ 85 billion. Japan is an ethnic who the most emphasis on health care, which 90% of the population is long-term use of healthy food, for 20 years Japanese healthy food grew 32 times. The Japanese healthy food sales reached $ 1.65 trillion yen in 2006. And the market scale will approach $ 2 trillion yen if coupled with a specific healthy food (functional foods legal name) and the healthy foods which the annual output is over more 3000 kinds. In China, due to the vast land, densely population and economic progress, the sales amount for healthy food reached $ 30 billion yen in 2003, and rushed to $ 50 billion yen in 2007 which make a great enhancement for the healthy food sales by 66%. The external trade in 2007, record raised and reached to $38.59 billion. An increase of 25.6% compared with 2006. As regards European, the healthy food market scale is $ 35 billion US dollars. An annual output is more than 2000 kinds, annual sales of high-speed growth at 17%. (Qian Wei, Fan 2008).

Argued the trilogy for modern marketing strategy - segmentation, targeting and positioning, has always been the core concepts for the marketing management. Although the accuracy and validity of this concept are unquestionable, the complexity and heterogeneity of consumer behavior are a grim ordeal for this practice which if can truly be implemented effectively. Therefore, how consumer preference structure can be estimated with the most accurate will be a primary marketing challenge and difficulty which must be overcome (Wen Wei, Xie 2005). According to the above-described statistics, we can clearly understand that this will be a huge market, and in such a huge market, what kind of the consumer preferences will exist in Japan to the end?

This research also refers RAVI DHAR and ITAMAR SIMONSON (2003)'s theories. Research indicates in some cases that when consumers under an uncertain situation but still have to choose from the available options to make a choice, he (she) would prefer to make an easy relative assessment for the errors and low regrets probability. But the decision may not be the best prefer option for reducing the ambivalence and discomfort.

(1) Definition of Consumer Preferences

Consumer preference is a degree of preference for commodities and commodity combination. Consumers will sort according to their own intensions. The sort ordering reflects consumers' individual needs, interests and hobbies. Demands for a commodity and consumer preference are the positive correlation. If other factors constant, degree of preference for certain commodity is higher, then the consumer's demand is getting more for that commodity.

Different personal characteristics will generate different consumer preferences, and also have an impact on purchasing behavior. Japanese well-known trend master Kenichi Ohmae has mentioned in his book <China Federation>: The success of marching towards the 21st century is "four C's": Communication, Capital, Corporation and Consumer. And if convert into action, it becomes "Four I", Information, Investment, Industry and Individual. However, such successful enterprises like 7-ELEVEN, Kunimoto Ryuichi a Japanese writer was mentioned in his book <Japanese 7-ELEVEN Consumer Psychology>: The low popularity of buying on the market today is not because consumers do not have purchasing ability, but is because the consumers' purchasing mindset becomes cold. And how to get consumers mindset heated again? This is not a question for economics but for psychology; therefore, only conscientiously deliberate the consumer psychology can generate the business opportunity. And can really grasp the key to engage the business. Like those enterprises that still retain viability in the economic depression, the major premise for management is the sake of consumers. Like Isetan Department Store calls the store "Buying Market", that is exactly considering for customer position. (Yi Wan, Huang 2003).

(2) Consumer Preferences (Personal characteristics)

There is a very important part in consumer behavior study that is the personal characteristics. McAdams (2001) Study the individual behavior by the three-dimensional structure through a psychological point of personal characteristics. Those are the personal characteristics, personal attention and life experiences. In terms of life experiences, Escalas and Bettman (2000) thinks that past experience of the brand brings a pleasant feeling, and this often results into personal consumption preferences. In other words, the consumers experience of self-creation will be linked together strongly with the self-awareness of brand. Baumgartner (2002) illustrates the consumer applications by the three-dimensional structure. The first dimension is the thinking type of purchase and feeling type of purchase. The second dimension is the high involvement type and low involvement type of purchase. The third dimension is careful purchase type and involuntary purchase type. From the above, we understood that personal characteristics have potential impacts on consumer behaviors. And the consumers for healthy foods will have regional characteristics of the consumer preferences.

3. Research Methods

(1) Secondary Data Method:

Data includes different sources and the collection data by other researchers or by different forms of files. These data sources include government reports, business and industry research, documentation databases, organizations data, books and periodicals from libraries. Secondary data can provide a very convenient and economical path to answer different questions. Secondary data comprises a more important meaning, that is, to make a new direction of analysis for the raw data originally collected.

Secondary Data Analysis is to use the existing data (e.g. census) or large academic database to study, which is an empirical research method to explore the theme for study.

The main superiority of using secondary data is that:

① The researchers do not need to spend a lot of money. It means the research funding can be saved more efficiently.
② The researchers can save a lot of time, so that they can aim to analyze the data provided by large samples.
③ Have the effect of stacking knowledge; keep continuing the research of others can therefore stack the function of research results.
④ Databases usually contain few phases of researches which can search and survey the changes of research topics by crossed times. With the improvement of statistics software and the developed internet interface, it becomes more convenient to publish the application of secondary database.

(2) Research Process

Research Process: The study was carried out using the steps in the following

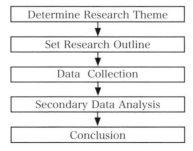

Fig. 15-1 Research Flowchart

4. Data Analysis

Since the financial tsunami in 2008, the economy state of Japan has been in a depressed state. But it shows a sign of recovery in 2011. It is also started significant changed in consumer trends at the same period. The trend did not stop even after the earthquake and even has a more accelerated pace of change tendency. Now supporting the Japanese national consumption are the middle-aged and the elderly who are the majority proportion of the population and have a higher average propensity to consume. (Proportion of income is used for consumption.) The age for consumption patterns has been changing after 311 earthquakes. Each age bracket has expanded and mastered the leadership of consumer trends.

The concept of Japanese changed, which would rather to enjoy life everyday better than sacrifice daily life for paying the long term loans responsibility. And the opinion of money values has been changed to not to hesitate to pay for money. Especially the requirements for safety and confidence are enhanced because of the earthquake and the Fukushima nuclear power plant accident. Many consumers seek the "confidence and safety" especially put emphasis on foods. After the earthquake, people is anxious about the radiation contamination of drinking water and food, this caused people in a panic buying and hoard temporary. But most of all imported foreign drinking water is "hard water" and not suitable for infants, so no matter how plentiful commodities at storefront stacked still no avail at all. In addition, the nuclear power plant accident also changes the consumption propensity in the metropolitan area. The metropolitan area is very sensitive to radiation pollution, so consumers buy the fresh fruits and vegetables from West Japan that far distance away from Fukushima Daiichi nuclear power plant through the internet. No matter it is in department store or supermarket, all consumers want to buy is the food from West Japan.

After the 311 earthquake, although the environment is still depression, but the self-controlled mentality of spending in the past has gradually begun to rebound. The customer hold the thought is increased, that is "buy the commodity genuine desire to satisfy themselves." And in fact the premium brands or senior New Year dishes selling became hot. Consumers tend to buy the goods really needed, or the special scarcity of merchandise. For example, the price is very expensive but can be used for a long time, like the mink fur and other advanced materials, or the exclusive products are very popular. That is to say the current consumption trends in Japan are "meaningful consumption." According to METI conducted a market survey on e-commerce transactions, while buying healthy food, the Japanese impressions for the healthy food using domestic raw materials are: "expensive" 69%, "Safe" 63%, "Delicious" 55%, which are good reviews. Conversely, for reviews of imported food is "Inexpensive" 68%, "Safe" 1.5%, "Delicious" 3.2%, which shows exactly opposite result from the using domestics row.

On the other hand this study compiled past scholars theory, making analysis and sorts for consumer preference as below:

Table 15-1 Comparison table

Author	Introduction	Summarize the factors
Assael,1998	Although in the past behavior of the purchase study, demographic variables has been regarded as an important market segment variables. This study differs from previous research on the purchasing decision behavior, not only resolve from the gender, age, and income, while incorporating other family members, relatives and other variables. Thoroughly investigate that in a different social structure and economic patterns change, the impacts of demographic statistics variables on health food purchasing behavior.	To resolve the demographic variables, gender, age, income, this in a different social structure and economic patterns changes, the impacts of demographic statistics variables on health food purchasing behavior.
Babin and Boles,1999	Pointed out that the power of products has a direct impact on purchase intention. While the sales staff response has indirect impact on consumer purchase intention. Theoretically in the study for car sales found the similar results. Professional consultants have a significant impact on consumer purchase intention for health food purchasing behavior.	Pointed out that the power of products has a direct impact on purchase intention. While the sales staff response has indirect impact on consumer purchase intention. Theoretically in the study for car sales found the similar results. Professional consultants have a significant impact on consumer purchase intention for health food purchasing behavior.
Childs and Poryzees, 1998	In the study for the prevention of diseases in food consumption attitudes, also believes the importance to understand the potential inner demand and the attitude shaped outside. While emphasizing the importance of	Emphasizing the importance of past factor is the personal food consumption habits and flavors. But in the future, it will contain other complex factors such as consideration of the function of preventing disease

	past factor is the personal food consumption habits and flavors. But in the future, it will contain other complex factors such as consideration of the function of preventing disease.	
Elaine,1999	Summarized that the factors influence consumer choice of food including social factors, psychological factors, lifestyles and food trends.	Social factors, psychological factors, lifestyle and food trends.
Jose Cuellar,2004	The objective of this thesis is to better understand Mexican consumer preferences for biotechnology and retail food outlets	The objective of this thesis is to better understand Mexican consumer preferences for biotechnology and retail food outlets
Lee and Collins,2000	Research indicates that he core has two children in the family. The children have an important influence on purchasing behavior. Especially daughter in the family has more influential purchase decision-making than boys.	Research indicates that he core has two children in the family. The children have an important influence on purchasing behavior. Especially daughter in the family has more influential purchase decision-making than boys.
Macdonald and sharp, 1995	Under a test in a series of very different brand of products, found that in addition to the quality and price of different things, greater popularity of the brand is clearly subject to more preferences. For a long time, in marketing goal is how to improve and maintain brand awareness.	The quality and price, greater popularity of the brand are clearly subject to more preferences. For a long time, in marketing goal is how to improve and maintain brand awareness.
Ophuis,1989	The concept of health-conscious assess individuals to believe they can control their own healthy personality performance, and by external lifestyle variables. From a psychological dimension to explore the impact on consumers to buy health food.	From a psychological dimension to explore its impact on consumers to buy health food.

Ravi Dhar and Itamar Simonson ,2003	The authors propose that consumer choices are often systematically influenced by preference fluency (i.e., the subjective feeling that forming a preference for a specific option is easy or difficult).	In some cases, when consumers prefer uncertain, but must choose from the options available and making a choice, would prefer relatively easy to assess, errors and estoppel low probability, but maybe not their most preferred option in order to reduce ambivalence and discomfort.
Schifferstein and Ophuis,1997	Pointed out that the purchase of health food mostly depends on their personal attitudes and characteristics.	Personal attitudes and characteristics
Shewfelt,1999	Broad definition of quality, from product tendency and consumers' tendency to illustrate, considered the quality for health food is the functional ingredients, nutrients, safety which can be analyzed by the instrument, and to meet consumer sensory perception characteristics. That is saying that products characteristics are able to meet consumers' needs and expectations, and also an important consideration that willing to buy. Price, quality variables on consumer play an indicative role for healthy food purchasing behavior.	Price, quality variables on consumer plays a indicative role for health food purchasing behavior.
Shohei Hasegawa and Nobuhiko Terui, 2012	In this paper, we explore dynamics of consumer preference induced by the experience of consuming purchased brands.	The dynamics of consumer preference induced by the experience of consuming purchased brands.
Yuki Tamari and Kazuhisa Takemura, 2012	The purpose of this study is to propose a quantitative method for consumers' preference analysis using picture drawings.	The purpose of this study is to propose a quantitative method for consumers' preference analysis using picture drawings.

Zhong Shan-Mei, 1999	For situational factors impact on consumer behavior, pointed out that consumers in the gift-giving situations, the more emphasis are on packaging and label. If for their own use situation, then more emphasis are on price and consumption of convenience. So personally believe that the price of this variable should have its impact on the purchase behavior, but the potential psychological thinking is the study want to explore. Like the response of price to the purchaser will be reduced or not if the sensitivity motive object is different. Such research. The quality has always been a broad interpretation of the wording of product strength.	The price of this variable should have its impact on the purchase behavior. The quality has always been a broad interpretation of the wording of product strength.

Source: This research

In this study, compiled past academic theory, to analyze and sort to consumer preference, understood from the information collected, that consumer market today has been changed from the past which is from the focus on production, marketing to consumer-oriented. And the marketing activities are emphasized the focus on more consumers. Elaine (1999) summarized that the influence factors of consumers' choice of food are including social factors, psychological factors, lifestyles and foods trends and so on.

5. Conclusions and Suggestions

(1) From the data analysis, we found the consumer preference of healthy food is attached to a great importance on product safety, quality, professional consulting and ingredients.

(2) Consumers attach more importance on the enterprise image and brand equity awareness. Brand and reputation have a certain extend of impacts to the healthy food purchasing behavior. Price and quality variables play an indicative role for healthy food purchasing behavior.

(3) In recent years, biotechnology has been advanced in technology. Many firms keen

to extend the application of biotechnology in food industry, and offer a variety of healthy foods. Besides, to improve added value for products and to avoid the competition of market price. Although the point of view of technology shows gene technology gradually matured, and undoubted for component safety. But from the consumer psychological aspects, whether there still exists doubts as GM foods.

(4) In the area of the consumer preference, the safety of consumer behavior is also a topic worth exploring, and maybe the researchers can focus on this issue to study in the future. To circulation the safety knowledge of healthy food and to enhance the acceptance of healthy food for consumers, thereby to promote the development and make popular for healthy foods.

(5) As this study attributes the secondary data analysis, and because of the lack of information in Japan, there are still many spaces we have to work hard. Therefore it is recommended that in the future studies can compare and research the difference overall for the other regions within the permitting for human power, material and time.

【References】

[1] Englewood Cliffs(2000), *Strategic marketing management point of view*, Huatai cultural undertakings of the Company.

[2] Peng Feng-mei(2001), "People lifestyle medical resource utilization and health status of the study - to Hsinchu Science Park staff, for example", National Yang-Ming University, Institute of Community Nursing, Thesis.

[3] Qian Wei, Fan(2008), "Downturn alchemy: popular health food", Industry close up - Global Market ultra-ram, *Healthy food Analysis and Outlook*.

[4] San Mei ,Chung(1999), "*The Analysis of Situational Influence on Consumer Behavior - a Case Study on the Agricultural*", Display Center of National Chung-Hsing University.

[5] Shyh-Rong Fang translation(1999),Philip Kotler & Gary Armstrong with, *Principles of Marketing*, Eighth Edition, New York, Prentice Hall.

[6] Wann-Yih Wu, Lin Ching(2000), *Business Research Methods*, first edition, Tainan, Huatai Publishing Company.

[7] Wen Wei, Xie(2005), "*Integration of conjoint analysis and prediction of response time in customer preferences*", National Taiwan University / School of Management / International Institute of enterprises. 2005. pp. 106-107.

[8] Wu Yudong(1999), *"Multivariate statistical methods used in mobile phones and consumer buying behavior Satisfaction"*, National Cheng Kung University Institute of Statistics, Thesis.

[9] Zhang Yimin(1999), *Marketing Science*, Prentice Hall utility companies, the first edition.

[10] Aaker, David(1991), *Managing Brand Equity : Capitalizing on the Value of Brand Name*, New York : The Free Press.

[11] Assael, H.(1998), *Household Decision Making in Consumer Behavior and Marketing Action*, Cincinatti : South-Western College Publishing, Cincinatti, OH, pp.565-601.

[12] Babin, Barry J. and Darden, W.R.(1996), "Good and Bad Shopping Vibes: Spending and Patronage Satisfaction, "*Journal of Business Research*, V.35, January, pp. 201-207.

[13] Babin, Laurie A., Barry J. Babin, James S. Boles(1999), "The Effects of Consumer Perceptions of The Salesperson, Product and Dealer on Purchase Intentions", *Journal of Retailing and Consumer Services*, v.6, December, pp.91-97.

[14] Baumgartner, Hans(2002), "Toward a Personology of The Consumer", *Journal of Consumer Research*, v. 29, September, pp.286-291.

[15] Brunso, Karen and Klaus G., Grunert(1998), " Cross-Cultural Similarities and Differences in Shopping for Food", *Journal of Business*, v.42, July, pp.145-150.

[16] Chandon, P., & Wansink, B.(2002), "Dose Stockpiling Accelerate Consumption? A Convenience Salience Framework of Consumption Stockpiling", *Journal of Marketing Research*,v . 38(3), pp. 37-55.

[17] Childs, Nancy M. and Gregg H.Poryzees(1998), "Food That Help Prevent Disease: Consumer Attitudes and Public Policy Implications", *British Food Journal*, 100/9, pp.419-426.

[18] Dryden. 3. Hill, C.W. and Jones, G. R.(1998), *Strategic Management Theory*, pp.48.

[19] Elaine, H. Asp(1999), "Factors Affecting Food Decision Made by Individual Consumers", *Food Policy*, v. 24, October, pp. 287-294.

[20] Erdem, Tulin, Joffre Swait and Jordan Louviere(2002), "The Impact of Brand Credibility on Consumer Price Sensitivity", *Inter-nation Journal of Research in Marketing*, v.19, September, pp. 1-19.

[21] Escalas. Jennifer E.and James R. Bettman(2000), "*Using Narratives to Discern*

Self-Identity Related Consumer Goals and Motivation", in Ratneshwar et al.pp. 237-258.

[22] Gelperowic Roseline and Brain Beharrell(1996), "Healthy Food Products for Children: Packaging and Mothers' Purchase Decisions", *British Food Journal*, v.96(11),pp. 4-8.

[23] Hoyer, W.D., and Brown, S.P.(1990), "Effects of Brand Awarenes on Choice for a Common, Repeat purchase product", *Journal of Consumer Research*, v.17, pp. 141-148.

[24] Kotler P.(1994), *Marketing Management-analysis, planning, implementation and control*. 8 Ed., Prentice-Hall, New Jersey.

[25] Kotler P.(1998), *Marketing Management: Analysis Planning Implementation and Control*, 9th Edition, Prentice-Hall.

[26] Lee, Christina Kwai-Choi, Brett A.Collins(2000), "Family Decision Making and Coalition Patterns, " *European Journal of Marketing* ,v.34, (9/10), pp. 1181-1198.

[27] Lynch, J.w., Kaplan, G. A. & Salonen, J.T.(1997), "Why do Poor People Behave Poorly? Variation in Adult Health Behaviours and Psychosocial Characteristics by Stages of the Socioeconomic Life-course", *Soc. Sci*. Med.44, pp. 809-819.

[28] Macdonald, Emma K. and Byron M. Sharp(1995), "Brand Awareness Effects on Consumer Decision Making for a Common, Repeat Purchase Product : A Replication", *Journal of Business Research*, v.48, July, pp. 5-15.

[29] McAdams, D.(2001), "The psychology of life stories." *Review of General Psychology*,5(2), pp. 100-122.

[30] McAdams, Dan P.(1996), "Personality, Modernity, and the Storied Self : A contemporary Framework for Studying Persons," *Psychological Inquiry*, 7(4), pp. 295-321.

[31] McAdams, Dan P.(2001), *The Person : An Integrated Introduction to Personality Psychology*, 3rd Ed., Fort Worth, TX : Harcourt College Publishers.

[32] Oliver, John, P. and Sanjay Srivastava(1999), "The Big Five Trait Taxonomy : History, Measurement, and Theoretical Perspective, " in *Handbook of Personality : Theory and Research*, 2nd Ed.", Lawrence A.Pervin and Oliver P.John, New York : Guilford, pp.102-138.

[33] Oude Ophuis, P. A. M.(1989), "Measuring health orientation and health consciousness as determinants of food choice behavior: Development and implementation of various attitudinal scales", In G. J. Avlonitis,A.C. Hoek et al. /

Appetite 42 (2004) 265–272 271 N. K. Papavasiliou, & A. G. Kouremenos (Eds.) *Marketing thought and practice in the 1990's EMAC XVIII* (pp.1723-1725). Athens: Athens School of Economics and Business.

[34] Prescott, J. and R Stevens(2002),"Motives for Food Choice: A Comparison of Consumers from Japan, Taiwan, Malaysia and New Zealand", *Food and Quality and Preference*, v.13, December, pp. 489-495.

[35] Ravi Dhar and Itamar Simonson(2003), "The Effect of Forced Choice on Choice", *Journal of Marketing Research*, 40, May, pp.146-160.

[36] Reid David A., Ellen Bolman Pullins, Richard E. Plank(2002), "The Impact of Purchase Situation on Salesperson Communication Behaviors in Business markets", *Industrial Marketing Management*, v.31, November, pp. 205-213.

[37] Schifferstein, Hendrik N.J. and Peter A.M.Oude Ophuis(1997),"Health-Related Determinants of Organic Food Consumption in The Netherlands", *Food and Quality and Preference*, v.9(3), pp. 119-133.

[38] Schindler, M. Robert and Thomas M. Kibarian(1996),"Increased Consumer Sales Response Though Use of 99-Ending Prices", *Journal of Retailing*, v.72(2), pp. 187-199.

[39] Shahar, D. R. Kristal-Boneh, E., Froom, P., Harari, G., & Ribank, J.(1995), "Smoking, Diet and Health Behaviors Among Lead-exposed ", *International Journal of Occupational and Environmental Health*, v.5(2), pp. 101-106.

[40] Shewfelt R. L.(1999),"What is Quality?" *Journal of Postharvest Biology and Technology*, v. 15, November, pp. 197-200.

[41] Shohei Hasegawa, Nobuhiko Terui and Greg Allenby(2012),"Dynamic Brand Satiation", *Journal of Marketing Research*, v. XLIX, pp. 842-853.

[42] Shuitz, C.M.S. (1984),"Lifestyle assessment : A Tool for Practice," *Nursing Clinics of North America*, v.19(2), pp. 271-281.

[43] Yuki Tamari; Kazuhisa Takemura(2012),"Analyzing Consumer Preference by Using The Latent Semantic Model for Picture Drawing", *Transactions of Japan Society of Kansei Engineering*, v.11(1), pp. 89-95.

LIAO, Li-Hsien

Chapter 16 The Application of Game Theory in the Investment Strategy

【Abstract】

Game theory is a set of ideas and methods specially analyzed for model of gaming situation and exploration of the optimal strategy. Its researching object is the events where in each decision-maker acts according to certain rules and chooses his strategy on the basis of the other's strategies. Game theory can help us to analyze the mutual reactions of each other's various strategies. In this paper, in stead of putting emphasis on the history of game theory and many unique opinions raised by specialists who have done great contribution in this area, the authors just want through our study and working experiences to present some valuable suggestions and exploration about game theory's applications in the strategies of transnational direct investment on the basis of predecessors' researches. The application of game-theoretic model in investment strategy illustrates the process of translating an informal description of a multi-person decision situation into a formal game-theoretic problem to be analyzed.

【Keywords】: The doctrinal model of game theory; the application of game theory; gain; the chooses of the investment strategies

1. Introduction

"Bo Yi" got the name first time from The Collection of Ancient Philosophers' Books *"The Analects of Confucian volume twenty -Yang Huo the seventeen"* "Isn't there games, gaming would rather be better than idling away one's time." At that time, "Bo means a game with six sticks and 12 pieces for several players; Yi means weiqi [1] (go)." [2] With the advance of human society and the development of science and technology, the content of game (Bo Yi) has no longer been limited in the form of game and gambling. In the book *Games, Theory and Application*, the English scholar L.C.Thomas presented

---

(1) A game played with black and white pieces on a board of 361 crosses.
(2) The Collection of Ancient Philosophers' Books (1935), *The Analects of Confucian volume twenty -Yang Huo the seventeen*(Chinese), World Publishing House, pp. 383-384.

the definition of gaming as following: "Gaming is the playing of a situation involving two or more decision-makers, which can be modeled as a game." [3]

Game theory, the formalized study of strategy, began in the 1940s by asking how emotionless geniuses should play games, but ignored until recently how average people with emotions and limited foresight actually play games. It is a theory of how people learn from experience to make better strategic decisions. Strategic interactions that can be explained by behavioral game theory. Game theory is a set of ideas and methods specially analyzed for model of gaming situation and exploration of the optimal strategy. Its researching object is the events where in each decision-maker acts according to certain rules and chooses his strategy on the basis of the other's strategies.

In this paper, in stead of putting emphasis on the history of game theory and many unique opinions raised by specialists who have done great contribution in this area, the authors just want through our study and working experiences to present some valuable suggestions and exploration about game theory's applications in the strategies of transnational direct investment on the basis of predecessors' researches.

2. Theoretic Model of Game Theory

Mathematical method of researching is to abstract the essential elements from plentiful phenomena of the same type and further to build a model that it can describe the phenomena. With the help of mathematics concepts such as matrix, maximum and minimum in probability, probability distribution and expected value, and combined with western economic concepts such as utility, expectation, margin and balance, game theory can be used to scientifically analyze and judge people's behavioral decision.

In 1944, John Von Neumann collaborated with Osker Morgenstern on *Theory of Game and Economic Behavior*, which they summed up the results of some early researches; lay the foundation of game theory. Since then, a large number of scholars started working in this area. Their researching primarily developed in two directions: the doctrinal model and the strategic model of game theory.

---

(3) Thomas, L.C. (1984) *Games, Theory and Application*, Ellis Horwood Limited, p. 233.

(1) The Doctrinal Model of Game Theory

In any game the participants' behaviors are various, so the results of the game are not certain in some degree. The doctrinal model of game theory makes assumption about the game-players' behaviors so as to eliminate the uncertainty of the results. These assumptions are included in the doctrinal system of game solving function, so the only certain game solution can get solution under the constraint of the doctrinal system. J.F. Nash was the founder in this aspect of game theory. Those doctrine rose by him such as Pareto' optimality principle, symmetric doctrine, invariance principle of natural mapping transformation and independent doctrine of irrelevant alternatives have still been used as the basic theoretical tools to research game-players' behaviors by now. Therefore, it must be taken by the specialists who work in this area as their necessary job to look for the doctrinal game solution—Nash solution [4].

But Nash solution—the game equilibrium point establishes itself on the condition that both players will not make the unilateral change of strategy and both of them will neglect the probability that their opponents make change in the strategy. Obviously the assumption is not in accordance with the real life conflict situation so that it is not so convincing. However, with the raising of this concept many researchers have an important method to look for the practical solution in the game-theoretic framework.

After Nash, many scholars have reconsidered the Nash equilibrium point and modified it on the basis:

① In the process of game, the first player make the advantage of playing in advance and the fact that the other players must react rationally to find out the most privileged Nash equilibrium point for himself.

② Each player may make a mistake occasionally when he plays according to the strategy of Nash equilibrium point not choose correctly the optimal strategy.

Nash equilibrium point concepts mentioned above are all under the assumption that the player has complete information. Although it is not realistic or in other words it is very harsh to realize, complete information is still much importance in the analysis of economic activities, for the reason that only when the ideal equilibrium point has been made as the reference point, can the researchers judge and analyze the basic state of the economic activities in the real world, in which direction, in what degree

---

(4) Nash, John F. (1951) "Non-Cooperative Games", *Annals of Maths*, 54, pp. 286-295.

and in what way the economic activities deviate from the ideal economic equilibrium point. That is why the doctrine model of game theory still has a methodological significance.

(2) The Strategic Model of Game Theory

The strategic model of game theory is a model, which mathematical theories are applied to research the situation of game, to find out the optimal game strategy. It mainly centers on: Assume there are N players in a game C, what a strategy will be chose by the player Pi to get his optimum results? Assume at the end of each game, Pi will receive the amount of Mi as a payoff. We consider Mi > 0 as a gain and Mi < 0 as a loss. Each player will make the optimal strategy rationally to maximize his own payoff M. The optimum is an economic sense no matter of politics or morality. Strategic model of game theory is generally divided into two types: the matrix form is called the normal form and the tree form also is called the extensive form in game theory.

① Simple Example of Matrix Form in Game Theory

P1, P2 are the two players in a game. They respectively make three strategies as (X_1, X_2, X_3) and (Y_1, Y_2, Y_3), which can be arranged in matrix form (shown in Fig 16-1).

The row in matrix indicates the possible strategies of P1 and the column in matrix

		P1		
		Y_1	Y_2	Y_3
	X_1	3	−1	−5
P2	X_2	2	1	2
	X_3	−1	0	7

Fig. 16-1 Simple Example of Matrix Form

indicates the possible strategies of P2. The number at the cross of the row and the column is the payoff value (also called one player's gain). The matrix form in game is distinguished for its simplicity and clarity, which makes the analysis and the solution easy to the game-player by listing the possible strategies and the corresponding payoff clearly in the matrix. But it can only represent the static gaming because it cannot show the order of the player's strategies. When the number of available strategies increases, so long as the number is still finite, we can accordingly increase the rank of the matrix; but when the number of game-player increases, it will be inconvenient to increase the number of the matrix.

② Simple Example of Tree Form in Game Theory

In this model, A represents one planning to enter a market while B represents one originally monopolizing the market. If A do not enter the market M_{11}, he has no gain or loss while B remains his 100 unit value gain. If A enters the market M_{12}, B will have two reactions: one is that B chooses the low price strategy to make A has 10 unit value loss and himself remains 30 unit value gain; the other is that B chooses the high price strategy to share the market with A, in which situation B will have 60 unit value gain while A will have 30 unit value gain. A tree form can represent this example as the following:

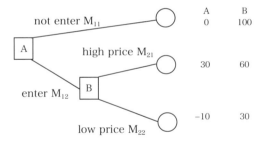

Fig.16-2　Simple Example of Tree Form

In Fig.16-2, □ represents game start point (also called as decision point) and ○ represents game strategy (also called as state point).

There are two sets of Nash equilibrium point (M_{12},M_{21}) and (M_{12},M_{22}), that is to say, B may have two strategies: ① taking the high price strategy to share the market with A;　② taking the low price strategy to drive A away by making A has 10 unit value loss. But to B taking ② is not the best strategy and is not the rational strategy too. Because B can only get 30 unit value gain in the low price strategy while the high price strategy will bring him 60 unit value gain.

If A knows this, he must choose to enter the market, so in this game process the best and rational choice is (M_{12}, M_{21}), that is A taking the entering strategy and

B taking the high price strategy. In the real life, B is most likely to give up the best strategy (high price strategy) to remain his long-term monopolistic position in the market so that he can get the high profit (100 unit value gain) as a monopolist by sacrificing the short-term low profit (30 unit value gain). In this situation, the best strategy to A is not entering the market.

The tree form in game theory can clearly record all the order in a gaming process so it is special fit for representing the dynamic gaming. Its primary thinking is that: one game-player will make a proper decision according to any strategy of the other game player, i.e. the other player's the last strategy shall furnish the basis for one's own next step strategy. This extensive form of gaming model can be extended to other more stages and more complicated dynamic gaming. However, this model should be appropriately improved with the change of the situation.

(3) The Application of Game-Theoretic Model in Investment Strategy

Game theory is a theory that it reflects some rational behaviors, which can help us to analyze the mutual reactions of each other's various strategies. In the international market was full of sharp competition, every multinational corporation (M.N.C.) can be considered as a game-player under some conditions and will change its own strategy according to the actions that it thinks its opponents might take. The strategy choice of those competitors entering the international market can be considered as an application of game theory in these relative areas.

A multinational corporation wants to determine the degree of investment involvement in Chinese market next year, so it entrusts a Chinese investment consulting company to make a marketing investigation. The investment involvement of this multinational corporation depends on Chinese investment conditions, which are determined by many internal and external factors. We cannot influence any of these factors.

We assume the degree of the M.N.C.'s investment involvement can be divided into three kinds: low, moderate and high, which are reflected by the amount of capital in the M.N.C.'s investment. Also we assume Chinese investment conditions have three kinds: suitable, moderate and unsuitable. According to this Chinese investment consulting company's collection and analysis on a large quantities of data from some marketing investigations, the M.N.C.'s investment involvement and the corresponding results (e.g. gain) in the various investment conditions are as follows (see in Fig.16-3):

Investment condition

		suitable	moderate	unsuitable
investment involvement	low	6	4	1
	moderate	15	8	0
	high	30	5	−5

Fig.16-3　The Degree of Investment Involvement

The gain shown in the Fig. 16-3 is the result of strategies in the different investment conditions. For example, high investment involvement but unsuitable investment condition will lead to a loss of 5 unit value gain (-5). Here the data are derived from the collection and analysis of the Chinese investment consulting company. How to choose the strategy to maximize the gain is up to the M.N.C.'s decision-maker. There are many ways to solve this problem. Here we will take a conservative one—the mini-max theorem in game theory (i.e. get maximum available gain in his minimum payoff) — to choose the investment strategies (see in Fig. 16-4).

Investment condition

		suitable	moderate	unsuitable	Minimum
investment involvement	low	6	4	1	1
	moderate	15	8	0	0
	high	30	5	−5	−5
	Maxmum	30	8	1	

Fig.16-4　The Chooses of the Investment Strategies

The solution under the mini-max theorem in game theory is that the M.N.C. takes lower involvement to invest in China and gets less. If the decision-maker of this M.N.C. holds optimistic view of the investment in China and the M.N.C itself has a powerful economic strength, it can also take the investment strategy in high involvement in accordance with the maxi-max theorem in game theory. This strategy will lead to 30 unit value gain if the investment condition in China is suitable. However this decision-making behavior usually involves the risk of a large loss. We will put the application of expected mean value theorem (Bayes' Decision Rule) in the next example.

A M.N.C., M plans to invest in the production of communication cable in China. There are three Chinese corporations C_1, C_2, C_3 in the different area interested in cooperating with M. Every corporation has his superiority and inferiority. If we assume Si is the situation may be occurring after M cooperates with the three corporations. (e.g. S_1: convenience of traffic while high land price; S_2: differ in opinions about cooperation among the administration but support from the involved government authority; S_3: strong determination of the administration but low initiative of workers etc.). M does not know with certainty which situation would occur. What he wants to know is the amount of value gain under a certain situation after cooperating with a Chinese corporation.

So it is necessary for M to get some reference data and records from an investment consulting company. For the convenience of explanation we can assume there are only 4 situations may occur, S_1, S_2, S_3, S_4 (although there are always much more situations in the real life). According to the 4 possible situations, the results of investigation are as follows: (see in Fig 16-5)

	S_1	S_2	S_3	S_4
C_1	8	8	6	2
C_2	6	4	4	6
C_3	10	4	0	4
$P(S_i)$	0.2	0.1	0.5	0.2

Fig.16-5 The Results of Investigation

When M chooses C_1 as his cooperative partner, M will have 8 unit value gain under condition S_1 and when C_3 is the cooperative partner, M's gain is zero under condition S_3. In addition we get the probability of each situation:

$P(S_1)=0.2$; $P(S_2)=0.1$; $P(S_3)=0.5$; $P(S_4)=0.2$

Hence, the M.N.C., M cannot exactly know the development of the environment in the days to come. For example: M cannot know whether the economic development in the area where the cooperative partner is located is faster or slower than that of the whole country, or the development of the traffic in this area from now on; or the development policy of Chinese government will take in the industry of communication cable etc.. M can only estimate the possible situation. Here we take the Bayes' decision rule- expected mean value theorem to find out the solution.

Expected Mean Value $(C_1) = 8*0.2+8*0.1+6*0.5+2*0.2=5.8$

Expected Mean Value $(C_2) = 6*0.2+4*0.1+4*0.5+6*0.2=4.8$

Expected Mean Value $(C_3) = 10*0.2+4*0.1+0*0.5+4*0.2=3.2$

The above results show the expected mean value of C_1 is maximal, so choosing C_1 as the cooperative partner is the optimal strategy in the light of the long-term interests, but cannot lead to the maximum available gain in the first period. C_3 is the optimal partner when we apply the maxi-max theorem in game theory and C_2 is the best one when we apply the mini-max theorem in game theory.

3. Conclusions

Game theory is a set of ideas and methods specially analyzed for models of gaming situation and exploration of the optimal strategy. Its researching object is the events where in each decision-maker acts according to certain rules and chooses his strategy on the basis of the other's strategies. The authors think the economic applications of game theory at least as much as the pure theory itself. The application of game-theoretic model in investment strategy illustrates the process of translating an informal description of a multi-person decision situation into a formal game-theoretic problem to be analyzed. Also, the variety of applications shows that similar issues arise in different areas of economics, and that the same game-theoretic tools can be applied in each setting. Strategic decision-making is a great and growing importance and decision-making in general that is indeed the central issue in every company's management and operations. It determines external as well as internal action and reaction. Managers have to make decisions and act so as to avoid bankruptcy but instead ensure the company's livelihood and enhance the company's value. These represent two of the major managerial goals. It is, however, an art to appropriately assess situations of decision-making. Companies and their environment are typically dynamic and strategy cannot be viewed isolated, as its success will depend on the decisions of others also. Game Theory as a theory of interaction provides appealing formal concepts and tools for examining such interdependent strategic behavior in business and economic settings.

【References】

[1] Camerer, Colin F. (2003), *Behavioral Game Theory: Experiments in Strategic Interaction*, Princeton University Press.

[2] The Collection of Ancient Philosophers' Books (1935), *The Analects of Confucian volume twenty -Yang Huo the seventeen*(Chinese), World Publishing House.

[3] Fudenberg, Drew & Tirole, Jean (1991), *Game Theory*, The MIT Press.

[4] Gibbons, Robert (1992), *Game Theory for Applied Economists*, Princeton University Press.

[5] Kreps, David M. (1990), *Game Theory and Economic Modelling*, Oxford University Press.

[6] Myerson, Roger B. (1997), *Game Theory: Analysis of Conflict*, Harvard University Press.

[7] Nash, John F. (1951), "Non-Cooperative Games", *Annals of Maths*, 54.

[8] Neumann John V. & Morgenstern, Osker (1944), *Theory of Game and Economic Behavior*, Princeton University Press.

[9] Thomas, L.C. (1984), *Games, Theory and Application*, Ellis Horwood Limited.

Toshimichi Haraguchi

Jin Yu

亜東経済国際学会の概要

設立　1989年に東アジアの経済・経営に関心のある研究者・実務家によって結成される。現在，日本，中国，台湾地区，韓国などの会員から構成される。

活動　毎年海外の学会や大学と共催で国際学術会議を開催し，その研究成果は国内外の著名な出版社から亜東経済国際学会研究叢書として出版している。

第1回　1989年　亜東経済国際学会（於台湾中華工商研究所，台湾東海大学）

第2回　1990年　亜東経済国際学会（於日本大牟田ガーデンホテル，九州帝京短大）

第3回　1990年　亜東経済国際学会（於中国東北財経大学，中国人民大学）

第4回　1991年　The Eastern Economies International Academy IV
（於 CHINESE UNIVERSITY OF HONG KONG）

第5回　1992年　国際財経学術研討会（中国上海財経大学と共催）（於中国上海財経大学）

第6回　1993年　中外合資企業経営国際学術研討会（中国復旦大学・上海管理教育学会と共催）（於中国復旦大学）

第7回　1993年　国際工商管理学術研討会（中国杭州大学と共催）（於中国杭州大学）

第8回　1995年　中日工商管理学術研討会（中国地質大学武漢人文管理学院と共催）（於中国地質大学武漢人文管理学院）

第9回　1995年　中国三資企業発展與管理問題国際討論会（中国復旦大学と共催）（於中国復旦大学）

第10回　1996年　亜東経済学術研討会（中国華東師範大学国際金融系と共催）（於中国華東師範大学国際金融系）

第11回　1997年「中国対外開放與中日経済関係」学術研討会（中国上海対外貿易学院と共催）（於中国上海対外貿易学院）

第12回　1998年　亜洲経済問題研討会（中国華東師範大学経済系と共催）（於中国華東師範大学経済系）

第13回　1998年　亜東経済国際学会'98年会（中国青島大学国際商学院と共催）（於中国青島大学国際商学院）

第14回　1999年　亜洲経済研討会（中国上海財経大学国際工商管理学院と共催）（於中国上海財経大学国際工商管理学院）

第15回　2000年　中日経済，社会，文化学術研討会（中国上海財経大学国際工商

管理学院と共催）（於中国上海財経大学国際工商管理学院）
第16回　2000年　社会與経済学術研討会（中国厦門大学社会科学部と共催）（於中国厦門大学社会科学部）
第17回　2001年　亜東経済與社会学術研討会（中国厦門大学社会科学部と共催）（於中国厦門大学社会科学部）
第18回　2001年　東亜経済與社会学術研討会（中国青島大学国際商学院と共催）（於中国青島大学国際商学院）
第19回　2001年　21世紀産業経営管理国際学術研討会（台湾国立高雄応用科技大学と共催）（於台湾国立高雄応用科技大学）
第20回　2002年　韓日国際経済・社会学術研討会（韓国高神大学校と共催）（於韓国高神大学校）
第21回　2002年　国際化與現代企業学術研討会（中国華東師範大学商学院と共催）（於中国華東師範大学商学院）
第22回　2003年　企業的国際化経営和管理策略国際学術研討会（中国復旦大学管理学院企業管理系と共催）（於中国復旦大学管理学院企業管理系）
第23回　2004年　中日社会與管理国際学術研討会（中国広西大学社会科学興管理学院と共催）（於中国広西大学社会科学興管理学院）
第24回　2005年　経済全球化與企業戦略国際学術研討会（中国上海立信会計学院・台湾中華工商研究院と共催）（於中国上海立信会計学院）
第25回　2006年　全球化時代的経済與社会国際学術研討会（台湾国立雲林科技大学管理学院・中国上海立信会計学院と共催）（於台湾国立雲林科技大学管理学院）
第26回　2007年　亜洲産業発展與企業戦略国際学術研討会（中国復旦大学管理学院産業経済学系・鹿児島国際大学・台湾高雄応用科技大学と共催）（於中国復旦大学管理学院産業経済学系）
第27回　2008年　東亜経済管理與社会保障国際学術研討会（中国南昌大学と共催）（於中国南昌大学）
第28回　2009年　東アジア産業経済・企業管理国際学術会議（中国復旦大学管理学院産業経済学系・台湾高雄応用科技大学と共催）（於鹿児島国際大学）
第29回　2009年　亜洲産業競争力與企業経営管理国際学術研討会（台湾南開技術学院・中国復旦大学管理学院産業経済学系と共催）（於台湾台中市）
第30回　2010年　学会創立20周年記念大会・東亜企業管理発展戦略国際学術会議（台湾高雄応用科技大学と共催）（於鹿児島国際大学）
第31回　2010年　21世紀産業経営管理国際学術研討会（台湾国立高雄応用科技大学管理学院と共催）（於台湾国立高雄応用科技大学管理学院）

第 32 回　2010 年　東アジアの産業発展・企業管理国際学術会議（中国復旦大学管理学院産業経済学系・台湾高雄応用科技大学管理学院と共催）（於鹿児島国際大学）

第 33 回　2011 年　東北亜福祉経済共同體国際学術研討会（韓国釜山長善綜合福祉共同體・東北亜福祉経済共同體フォーラム・日本中国社会福祉研究会と共催）（於韓国釜山市長善綜合福祉共同體大講堂）

第 34 回　2011 年　劉成基博士傘寿記念大会・東アジアの産業・企業国際学術会議（台湾高雄応用科技大学管理学院・東北亜福祉経済共同體フォーラムと共催）（於鹿児島国際大学）

第 35 回　2012 年　東アジアの産業経営管理国際学術会議（台湾産業競争力暨学術研究交流協会と共催）（於鹿児島国際大学）

第 36 回　2012 年　亜洲産業発展與企業管理国際学術研討会（台湾国立屏東科技大学・東北亜福祉経済共同體フォーラムと共催）（於台湾国立屏東科技大学）

第 37 回　2013 年　亞洲的社會現狀與未來国際学術研討会（「アジア社会の現状と未来」国際学術研討会）（台湾南台科技大学応用日本語学科・台湾産業競争力暨学術研究交流協会 (TISIA) と共催）（於台湾南台科技大学）

第 38 回　2013 年　東アジアの社会・産業・企業発展国際学術会議（東北亜福祉経済共同體フォーラム・台湾國立高雄應用科技大學観光管理系・台湾産業競争力暨学術研究交流協会 (TISIA) と共催）（於鹿児島国際大学）

第 39 回　2014 年　東亜の福祉ビジネス・産業経営国際学術研討会（東北亜福祉経済共同體フォーラム・韓国長善綜合福祉共同體等・韓国富者学研究学会と共催）（於韓国済州ベネキア・マリンホテル）

第 40 回　2014 年　アジアの社会・産業・企業国際学術会議（長崎県立大学東アジア研究所・東北亜福祉経済共同體フォーラム・中国復旦大学東水同学會と共催）（於長崎県立大学佐世保キャンパス）

亜東経済国際学会研究叢書の出版

第 1 冊　1992 年　『企業経営の国際化』（日本・ぎょうせい）
第 2 冊　1994 年　『東亜企業経営（中文）』（中国・復旦大学出版社）
　　　　　1995 年　『東アジアの企業経営（上）』（中国・上海訳文出版社）
　　　　　1995 年　『東アジアの企業経営（下）』（中国・上海訳文出版社）
第 3 冊　1997 年　『中国三資企業研究（中文）』（中国・復旦大学出版社）
第 4 冊　1999 年　『中国対外開放與中日経済関係（中文）』（中国・上海人民出版社）
第 5 冊　2002 年　『国際化與現代企業（中文）』（中国・立信会計出版社）
第 6 冊　2004 年　『企業国際経営策略（中文）』（中国・復旦大学出版社）

第 7 冊　2006 年『中日対照　経済全球化與企業戦略』(中国・立信会計出版社)
第 8 冊　2008 年『亜洲産業発展與企業発展戦略（中文)』(中国・復旦大学出版社)
第 9 冊　2010 年『東亜経済発展與社会保障問題研究（中文)』(中国・江西人民出版社)
第 10 冊　2009 年『東亜産業発展與企業管理（中文・繁体字)』(台湾・暉翔興業出版)
第 11 冊　2010 年『亜洲産業経営管理（中文・繁体字)』(台湾・暉翔興業出版)
第 12 冊　2011 年 亜東経済国際学会創立２０周年記念論文集『アジアの産業発展と企業経営戦略』(日本・五絃舎)
第 13 冊　2011 年『東亜産業與管理問題研究（中文・日文・英文)』(台湾・暉翔興業出版)
第 14 冊　2012 年 劉成基博士傘寿記念論文集『東アジアの産業と企業』(日本・五絃舎)
第 15 冊　2012 年『東亜産業経営管理（中文・英文・日文)』(台湾・暉翔興業出版)
第 16 刷　2014 年『東亜社会発展與産業経営（中文・日文)』(台湾・暉翔興業出版)
第 17 冊　2014 年『東アジアの社会・観光・企業（日文・英文)』(日本・五絃舎)
第 18 冊　2015 年『亜洲産業発展與企業管理（中文・英文・日文)』(台湾・高雄出版社)

学会役員・理事

会　長　原口俊道（日本・鹿児島国際大学大学院経済学研究科博士後期課程教授・中国華東師範大学顧問教授，商学博士）
副会長　劉成基（台湾・台湾支部長・首席研究員・鹿児島国際大学大学院経済学研究科ワークショップ特別講師・経済学博士）
副会長　兪　進（中国・上海支部長・首席研究員・鹿児島国際大学大学院経済学研究科ワークショップ特別講師・経済学博士）
理　事　蘇　勇（中国・復旦大学博士生導師・教授・経済学博士）
理　事　王明元（台湾・国立高雄応用科技大学副教授・経済学博士）
理　事　許雲鷹（中国・上海財経大学副研究員）
理　事　羅　敏（中国・広西大学専任講師・経済学博士）
理　事　黄一修（台湾・中華工商研究院総院長・経済学博士）
理　事　黄惇勝（台湾・台北城市科技大学副教授・経済学博士）
理　事　太田能史（日本・太田総合経営研究所所長・鹿児島国際大学大学院経済学研究科非常勤講師・経済学博士）
理　事　三好慎一郎（日本・宮崎大学非常勤講師・経済学博士）
理　事　黒川和夫（日本・鹿児島国際大学大学院経済学研究科非常勤講師・経済学博士）
理　事　劉水生（台湾・滋和堂企業股份有限公司董事長・鹿児島国際大学大学院経済学研究科ワークショップ特別講師・経済学博士）
理　事　林雅文（台湾・弘光科技大学助理教授・経済学博士）

| 理　事 | 藤田紀美枝（日本・人材育成研究所所長・日本橋学館大学客員教授）
| 理　事 | 中山賢一（日本・中山賢一経営士事務所所長）
| 理　事 | 張慧珍（台湾・国立屏東科技大学副教授・経済学博士）
| 理　事 | 盧駿葳（台湾・南臺科技大學助理教授・経済学博士）
| 理　事 | 李建霖（台湾・台湾支部研究員・経済学博士）
| 理　事 | 呉佳華（台湾・和春技術学院助理教授・経済学博士）
| 理　事 | 國崎　歩（日本・日本薬科大学非常勤講師・福岡支部研究員）
| 理　事 | 廖筱亦林（中国・上海支部研究員・経済学博士）
| 理　事 | 祖恩厚（中国・河南科技大学講師・経済学博士）
| 理　事 | 原口俊彦（日本・福岡支部研究員）
| 理　事 | 廖力賢（台湾・台湾支部研究員）

亜東経済国際学会

日本事務局　〒891－0197　鹿児島市坂之上8丁目34番1号
　　　　　　鹿児島国際大学大学院経済学研究科　原口俊道研究室内
　　　　　　E mail:haraguchi@eco.iuk.ac.jp
　　　　　　電話・FAX　099－263－0668
上海支部　　電話・FAX　86－21－64011549, 86－21－64012164
台湾支部　　電話・FAX　886－2－2633－7986

東北亜福祉経済共同體フォーラムの概要

　昨今の世界は，すでに20世紀の「国民主義」を超えて同一地域の国々がさまざまな方法に基づいて相互協力し，また相互依存することで，一国レベルでは不可能な「関係性」に基づく福祉と経済の交流を志向する「地域主義」と「共同體主義」の時代に直面していることに注目する必要がある。かつてEUが構築されたヨーロッパの地域はもちろんのこと，朝鮮半島を取り巻く地域でも，「東北アジア地域共同體」の概念が台頭するなど，無限のグローバル競争体制の下で，地域の競争力を確保し，また排他的な一国主義を超えて共生の価値を実現する地域共同體の必要性が提起されていることも周知の事実である。新保守主義の時代の流れでは，経済を通じた福祉の量的・質的な向上が不可欠である。福祉は経済の活性化に反するという認識が広がって来ているが，本東北亜福祉経済共同體フォーラムは，福祉事業の展開を通じて経済の活性化を達成することができると認識し，また国民の福祉を通じて東北アジア地域経済の活性化を誘導することができると認識し，さらに民主主義が持続可能な経済成長の必須条件であると認識している。

　本東北亜福祉経済共同體フォーラムは，「共同體主義」の必要性を早くから認識し，1952年創立以来，児童・高齢者・障害者など多様な階層を対象に，幅広い形態の福祉サービスを提供してきた韓国長善総合福祉共同體の理念と経営哲学を生かし，「地域主義」と「共同體主義」というこの時代のキーワードを積極的に認識し，またこれを具體的に実践しながら，なおかつこれと関連する従来の論議とのネットワークを強化し，同一の漢字文化圏域内のいくつかの多国家間の福祉経済交流および開発協力の共同體を達成することを目指している。これは正に"地域や国境を越えて公益価値の生産拡大を目指していくための国際的ネットワークの展開"を実現することである。

　本東北亜福祉経済共同體フォーラムは，2014年現在，韓国・日本・中国・台湾などからの福祉経済分野の各専門家たち約50人程度が参加して，毎年定期的に集会や会議を開催している。

索　引

(あ行)

アイシン精機　146
生きがい　156, 164
インターネット販売　61
ウィリアム・ペティ　47
影響力分析　120
エコマネー　30
MB政府　31
岡本康雄　90

(か行)

海外子会社の社長　133
回帰分析　120
外資流通業　128
買い手の交渉力　102
外部環境　114, 117, 118, 120, 122
環境保護　45, 46, 51
関係経済　52
関係性　41
関係的信頼　142, 144, 145, 150
観光　45
観光イメージ　75, 77, 81, 85
観光基本法　60
観光客のライフ・スタイル　87
観光行動欲求　75, 77, 82, 85
観光行動理論　76
観光行動論　75
観光行動論の体系　76
観光産業　45, 49, 57
観光産業の発展　58
観光重視程度　75, 77, 85
観光消費者　68
観光消費者行動　57, 65
観光消費者行動の特性　72
観光消費者の属性　66
観光消費者の旅行行動　66
観光消費者の旅行への認識　66
観光の定義　76
観光発展　53
観光マーケティング　58, 62, 71
観光マーケティング戦略　72
観光目的地選択　75, 78, 85
観光立国推進基本法　62
幹部の現地化が困難な理由　134
企業間信頼　142, 143, 144, 150, 151
企業属性　126
基本属性　156
業者間の敵対関係　102
業種　127, 138
喬晋建　130
競争状況の認識　100
競争戦略　89, 90, 94, 108
競争優位　94, 90, 108
競争優位の水準　105
競争優位の内容　103, 104

共同體主義　　21, 22
グリーン産業　　53
グローバル市場志向戦略　　91, 97, 128
経営幹部の現地化　　134
経営現地化　　127
経営現地化の重視度　　137
経営現地化の重視度に影響を及ぼす要因　　138
経営資源の内製化と外注化　　149
経営成果　114, 118, 119, 121, 122, 123, 124
経営戦略　　97, 98, 127, 137
経済共同體　　23
系列経済　　52
健康　　37
健康いきいき職場環境　　162
健康いきいき職場モデル　　163
健康管理　　37
現地事業戦略　　99
現地市場＋海外市場志向戦略　　91, 97, 128
現地市場志向戦略　　91, 97, 128
現地人幹部登用の成功に必要な準備　　136
現地人幹部の問題点　　136
現地人幹部の要件　　136
現地人社長の短所　　133
現地人社長の長所　　133
公益価値　　29
孔子　　39, 40
交通誘導警備　　153
交通誘導警備員　　153
合理的信頼　　142, 144, 145, 150
高齢化社会　　36

五経　　39
国内観光　　60
国民福祉教育　　27
心の健康　　163, 166
コミュニティ　　28, 30
コミュニティ・トータル・ケアシステム　　29
コーリン・クラーク　　47
ゴールデン・エージ　　35, 42

(さ行)

サービス経済化　　47
サービス産業　　45, 48
サービス産業の経済化　　47
サービス社会　　46, 54
在中・台の日系サービス企業　　114
サイモン・クズネッツ　　47
三教帰儒　　41
産業内の同業者間での競争の激しさ　　102, 103
CVNB　　31
CVNB コーディバンク　　31
事業継続マネジメント　　148
事業継続計画　　148
四書　　39
四書五経　　40
司馬遷　　47
社会的価値　　30
社会的企業　　30
社会的不確実性　　141
社会福祉思想の源流　　35
社会福祉　　37
社会福祉問題　　43
社長の現地化　　133

収益率を規定する5つの競争要因　103
主観的評価法　155
儒教　35, 40
儒教の中心思想　39
儒教文化圏　43
主要な競争相手　101
循環型経済社会　45, 46
少子高齢化　36
消費者行動論　75
職務満足　153
職務満足度　162, 163, 165, 166
シルバー　35
仁　39, 40
進出形態　127, 137
新職業性ストレス簡易調査票　156
信頼　141, 142, 149
信頼概念　142
信頼性分析　117
ストレス　155
ストレス差　162
スモールワールド・ネットワーク　150
生産ネットワーク　145, 148
生理指標　154, 155
生理的ストレス　160, 164
生理的ストレス反応　154
関満博　129
相関分析　117

(た行)

大衆儒教文化　41
唾液アミラーゼ　153
唾液アミラーゼ活性　155, 159
唾液アミラーゼモニタ　154, 155
ダブルバインド　153
地域共同體意識　28
地域主義　21, 22
中国日系小売企業　127, 131
中国日系自動車部品製造企業　131
中国日系自動車部品製造企業の経営現地化　130
中国日系繊維製造企業　89
中国日系電機製造企業の競争優位の内容　94
中国日系電機製造企業の経営戦略　93
動機づけ-衛生理論　165
東北亜幸福共同體　25, 26
東北アジア　21, 24
東北亜福祉経済共同體　21
東北亜福祉経済共同體構想　22, 24
東北亜福祉経済共同體フォーラム　27

(な行)

内部環境　114, 117, 118, 120, 121
日系企業の経営現地化　130
日系企業の現地化　129
日系サービス企業　113
日本の対中国直接投資　89
ネットワーク　143
ネットワークの関係性　150

(は行)

場の転換　141
ピアソンの相関分析　117
東アジア日系企業の競争優位　92
東アジア日系企業の競争優位の水準　92
東アジア日系企業の経営戦略　91
非常時　141, 142

フィリップ・コトラー　62
福祉教育共同體　27
福祉経済共同體　23
普遍的福祉社会　27
古田秋太郎　129
平常時　141, 142
ペティの法則　47
保健福祉事務所　32
ホスピタリティ　45, 50
ホスピタリティ産業　46, 49, 50
ホスピタリティ社会　46, 54
ホスピタリティ・マインド　45, 50

(ま行)
マイケル・ポーター　89
マーケティング戦略への影響要因　114

マーケティング戦略　113, 114, 119, 123, 124
孟子　39, 40
最も進めている経営現地化の側面　132
モデレーター要因　155, 156, 163
モラル・ルネサンス　52

(ら行)
楽齢　35
楽齢大学　38
リケン　147
倫理道徳　45, 46
ルネサス　148
労働実態　153
論語　39

欧文索引

(a)
amplifier and speaker industry　236
audio industry　220

(b)
brand evaluation　205, 208, 211, 213
business professionals　201

(c)
Carol R. Ember and Melvin Ember　178
Chinese culture　179
Competition　188

competitive and cooperative strategies of the manufacturers　239
competitiveness　185, 187, 188, 189, 191, 219, 221,
Confucianism　178
consumer behavior　244
consumer preferences　243, 244, 246
cooperate with customers　234
cooperative strategy　219, 225
corporate culture　192, 197
cross-cultural conflicts　171, 174, 182
Cultural Differences　174

cultural diversity 175

(d)
direct investment 258
domestic travel 187

(e)
enterprise business strategy 189
external factors 237

(f)
five competitive forces 222
foods trends 252

(g)
game theory 257, 258
Geert Hofstede 175

(h)
healthy food 243
Hedlund Gunner 180
horizontal division 229

(i)
Illusions of the Chinese Staffs 173
Illusions of the Foreign Staffs 172
industry attractiveness 221
interdependent strategic behavior 265
internal factors 237
international travel 187
investment condition 263
investment involvement 262, 263
investment strategy 257, 263, 265

(l,m)
lifestyles 252
M.E. Porter 189, 219
mainland tourists 186, 201
marketing strategy 245

(n)
Nash equilibrium 259
Neil Bohr 179

(p)
perceived quality 205, 207, 211, 212
personal characteristics 246
Peter F. Drucker 176
positioning 245
profit creation 221
psychological factors 252
purchase intention 243, 244

(q,r)
quality manpower and resources of the industry 234
relationship quality 205, 207, 211, 212, 213
restaurant patrons 205

(s)
segmentation 245
service awareness 199, 201, 202
Sino-foreign enterprises 171, 182
Sino-foreign joint ventures 171
social factors 252

Stephen P. Robbins 177
strategic alliance (s) 189, 190, 191
Strategic model 260
supports from suppliers 234
SWOT Analysis 234

(t)

Taiwan travel agencies 192
Taiwan travel industry's competitiveness 202
Taiwan's tourism industry 185
targeting 245
Technology alliance 224

The Illusions of Both Sides 174
The matrix form 260
The tree form 262
Tourism 185
travel agencies 186
typology alliance 228

(v,w,z)

value chain 219, 221, 223, 228
vertical integration 229
William Ouchi 179
Z Theory 179
Z-Type Culture 179

執筆者一覧

（※※印は監修者，※印は編著者を示す）

※朴峰寛（韓国・日本経済大学経営学部教授，東北亜福祉経済共同體フォーラム共同代表，韓国長善綜合福祉共同體代表理事，博士(社会福祉学)）第 1 章担当

劉成基（台湾・亜東経済国際学会副会長・同台湾支部長，鹿児島国際大学大学院経済学研究科ワークショップ特別講師，博士（経済学））第 2 章担当

※劉水生（台湾・滋和堂企業股份有限公司董事長，鹿児島国際大学大学院経済学研究科ワークショップ特別講師，博士（経済学））第 3 章担当

祖恩厚（中国・河南科技大学管理学院講師，博士（経済学））第 4 章担当

原田倫妙（日本・亜東経済国際学会台湾支部研究員）第 5 章担当

※※原口俊道（日本・鹿児島国際大学大学院経済学研究科博士後期課程教授，亜東経済国際学会会長，中国華東師範大学顧問教授，博士(商学)）第 5 章，第 6 章(翻訳)，第 8 章，第 11 章，第 16 章担当

國﨑 歩（日本・日本薬科大学非常勤講師）第 7 章担当

石田幸男（日本・明治大学大学院経営学研究科博士後期課程）第 9 章担当

岩崎龍太郎（日本・株式会社サンプラスワン副代表）第 10 章担当

難波礼治（日本・第一工業大学講師）第 10 章担当

俞 進（中国・独立研究員，亜東経済国際学会副会長・同上海支部長，鹿児島国際大学大学院経済学研究科ワークショップ特別講師，経済学博士）第 11 章，第 16 章担当

李建霖（台湾・亜東経済国際学会台湾支部研究員，博士（経済学））第 12 章担当

呉佳華（台湾・和春技術学院助理教授兼学務長，博士（経済学））第 13 章担当

※盧駿葳（台湾・南臺科技大學応用日語系助理教授，鹿児島国際大学大学院経済学研究科ワークショップ特別講師，博士（経済学））第 14 章担当

廖力賢（台湾・亜東経済国際学会台湾支部研究員）第 15 章担当

監修者紹介
原口俊道（はらぐち・としみち）
 現在 鹿児島国際大学大学院経済学研究科博士後期課程教授, 亜東経済国際学会会長,
    中国華東師範大学顧問教授, 博士（商学）
著書
 『動機づけ-衛生理論の国際比較――東アジアにおける実証的研究を中心として――』
  同文舘出版, 1995年。
 『経営管理と国際経営』同文舘出版, 1999年。
 『東亜地区的経営管理（中文）』中国・上海人民出版社, 2000年。
 『アジアの経営戦略と日系企業』学文社, 2007年。
 『東アジアの産業と企業』（編著）五絃舎, 2012年。

編者紹介
朴峰寛（ぼく・ぼんかん）
 現在 日本経済大学経営学部教授, 東北亜福祉経済共同體フォーラム共同代表,
    韓国長善総合福祉共同體代表理事, 博士(社会福祉学)
著書
 『認知症ケアの国際的共同研究』（共著）釜山女子大学出版部, 2008年。
 『ケアのためのユニバーサルデザインの観点』釜山福祉開発院, 2009年。
 『福祉ビジネスの発展と限界』東北亜福祉経済共同體フォーラム出版, 2010年。
 『Community Total Care System の構築』（編著）, 図書出版正印, 2012年。

劉水生（りゅう・すいせい）
 現在 台湾・滋和堂企業股份有限公司董事長, 鹿児島国際大学大学院経済学研究科ワー
    クショップ特別講師, 博士（経済学）
著書
 『東亜産業発展與企業管理（中文・繁体字）』（副主編）台湾・暉翔興業, 2009年。
 『東亜経済発展與社会保障問題研究（中文）』（副主編）中国・江西人民出版社, 2010年。
 『東亜産業與管理問題研究（中文・繁体字）』（主編）台湾・暉翔興業, 2011年。
 『東アジアの産業と企業』（編著）五絃舎, 2012年。

盧駿葳（るー・ちんうえい）
 現在 台湾・南臺科技大學応用日語系助理教授, 鹿児島国際大学大学院経済学研究科
    ワークショップ特別講師, 博士（経済学）
著書
 『東亜産業発展與企業管理（中文・繁体字）』（共著）台湾・暉翔興業, 2009年。
 『アジアの産業発展と企業経営戦略』（共著）五絃舎, 2011年。
 『東亜産業與管理問題研究（中文・繁体字）』（副主編）台湾・暉翔興業, 2011年。
 『東アジアの産業と企業』（共著）五絃舎, 2012年。

東アジアの社会・観光・企業
亜東経済国際学会研究叢書⑰
東北亜福祉経済共同體フォーラム①

2015年3月25日　第1版第1刷発行

監修者：原口俊道
編　者：朴峰寛・劉水生・盧駿葳
発行者：長谷雅春
発行所：株式会社五絃舎
　　　　〒173-0025　東京都板橋区熊野町46-7-402
　　　　電話・ファックス：03-3957-5587
組版：Office Five Strings
印刷・製本：モリモト印刷
Printed in Japan　　　ISBN978-4-86434-046-5
検印省略　ⓒ　2015
乱丁本・落丁本はお取り替えいたします。
本書より無断転載を禁ず。